BREEDING & TRAINING
VERSATILE HUNTING DOGS

FOR HUNTING &
HUNT TESTS

BREEDING & TRAINING
VERSATILE HUNTING DOGS

FOR HUNTING &
HUNT TESTS

BOB FARRIS

Table of Contents

Dedication

While still in my 20s, I found myself a single dad raising two children on my own. They were three and five years old, and at this time in my life I hardly knew how to operate a washing machine and dryer... let alone prepare a meal other than toasted cheese sandwiches or pancakes. Both kids, Brooke and Bryce, were learning to adapt to my cooking and makeshift household ways when LaFaye came into our world. We all called her Laffy as a nickname, but both children have only called her "Mom" since the day we returned home from our honeymoon. Now nearing our 40th anniversary and both my children with families of their own, I look back to find most of my successes and my children's successes stem from the guidance this woman has given over those past 40 years.

LaFaye hooked me in the beginning with her unselfish nature and wisdom. I can honestly say she is the most "street smart" person I have ever known, alongside my Dad. She raised my two children as though she was their biological mother and from day one to today. She always put them before her own needs and made most of the important family decisions along the way that would concern the two kids. From little league baseball and football with Bryce, to junior and high school rodeos with Brooke, she was their best fan and lead support person. With four grandchildren today, she can be found attending most of their activities.

When we met, she knew my passion for hunting dogs. I competed with three retrievers in AKC field trials around the Northwest, and hunted upland birds and waterfowl as often as possible. I have hunted four different species of wild sheep and nearly every other game animal in North America without ever hearing a question of despondency from LaFaye. She always encouraged these efforts, and rarely created family vacations that didn't focus on the kids.

She did have three requests when we married. I sincerely thank her for that wisdom still today. First, she wanted to get married on Valentine's Day. Second, she wanted a heart shaped diamond. And third, she didn't want to spend her anniversary night at our home. I'm sure she picked Feb. 14 hoping I would never forget our anniversary; I look at it as only needing to celebrate with one gift this way for two separate occasions. We have found ourselves in Kauai, Fiji, New Zealand, Florida, and most of the ski resorts in the Northwest on the night of Feb. 14.

If one is to dedicate the countless hours it takes to write a book as I have here, I felt that my readers should know a little about the person I am dedicating this work to. Anyone that has left our kennel facility with a puppy or met LaFaye wouldn't need to be given this introduction, as they are already aware of her dedication both toward me, her family, and also her puppies. She whelps and raises our puppies and always has a keen eye on those on our puppy reservation list just as she did 40 years ago with Brooke and Bryce when she became the mother of these two children.

This book would never have been written without the support and motivation given by LaFaye. Our Cedarwood Kennel and the Pudelpointers that have been raised here also would never have happened without the partnership I have had with LaFaye. I truly owe her for most all of my successes, to some degree, as without her support so much of my life's favorite parts most likely would never have come to be.

Team Farris (Bob and LaFaye) of Cedarwood Kennel.

Acknowledgement

By Dick Nachbar (Bob's friend and hunting partner)

Bob Farris is an avid outdoorsman whose passion for upland bird hunting and waterfowling has promoted his devotion over the past 35 years as a professional dog trainer in Idaho. He has also enjoyed a casual writing career during this period; his writings have been seen in *Pointing Dog Journal, Gun Dog Magazine, NAVHDA's Versatile Hunting Dog Magazine*, and *Sporting Classics*.

There are many experienced trainers that can breed quality dogs, train hunting dogs to the highest standards, and hunt their dogs to an extremely high level of professionalism, but very few can put their knowledge to print. This is where Bob differs from so many accomplished dog people, as he has a gift for writing also. This has been very evident over the years from his writings in various hunting dog magazines.

Encouragement from family, friends, and so many relationships made in the versatile dog world has created the interest for the publication of this book.

Bob has trained/handled 49 different versatile dogs successfully through NAVHDA's coveted Utility Test. He has also trained/handled more than 100 dogs in NAVHDA's Natural Ability test. His 20 plus years' experience as a NAVHDA senior judge has led to the experience and knowledge defined in his writings.

Before Pudelpointers and NAVHDA testing, Bob competed throughout the Northwest in AKC Retriever Field Trials with his Chesapeake Bay Retrievers while also using them for his winter waterfowling. English Setters were his original choice as an upland breed during these earlier years. Once converted to versatile dogs, he never went back to the specialty breeds he previously owned.

For the past 25 years, Bob and his wife LaFaye have owned and operated Cedarwood Kennels in Idaho, where they raise Pudelpointers. Bob also trains gundogs for outside clients.

Bob has involved his entire family in his kennel operation and Pudelpointers, from both his two children to his four grandchildren. Currently both grandsons own their own dogs and hunt waterfowl regularly on the family's "Swamp" property along the Boise River with their grandpa.

I first met Bob years ago when I joined a DU banquet committee that Bob was chairman. Seeing his four mounted sheep on the wall of his family room instantly inspired me to begin my own quest for a grand slam. Many years later and many conversations about sheep hunting with Bob have seen me accomplish this feat myself. Without that first meeting at Bob's home and the friendship that arose would probably have seen me only chasing mule deer or elk and the sheep inspiration would have never of come to be. So many talks in the duck blind and so many pheasant hunts on the islands of the Snake River have allowed me the opportunity to know him well enough to write this acknowledgement...

~*Dick Nachbar*

Dick Nachbar on an Oregon chukar hunt.

The First Step is Saying 'Thank You'

When initially asked to write and help create this book, I questioned the need. There were already countless articles on training dogs and just as many or more on breeding, raising and testing versatile dogs. I have in a wooden chest, every issue of The Versatile Hunting Dog Magazine, Gun Dog Magazine, and Pointing Dog Journal since their beginning. I realized, however, most don't have this resource available within their home and even if they did, finding that specific needed article would be nearly impossible. Also, those new members with their new hunting companion would never have a collection of magazines such as I've described. I don't feel that I am any more knowledgeable concerning training, breeding, testing... or hunted a versatile dog than the countless men and women representing themselves either as a hobbyist or professional. Most wouldn't find the time in their busy schedule to take on a feat this large. I've always enjoyed writing and have always had a sincere passion for hunting dogs so thus came the journey I have taken to attempt to give back what so many have passed forward to me over the years.

LaFaye with her pups and flowers at home in Boise.

Reflecting back over my career of training, handling, and judging versatile dogs, I have many people to acknowledge and thank. First and foremost is my family, especially my wife LaFaye, for allowing and encouraging me to pursue my hunting passion for all big game in North America, upland birds, and waterfowl across the United States and Canada. My extended sheep hunts during a period of our lives when raising children was a priority saw LaFaye at home taking care of Little League duties for our son while also pulling a horse trailer to rodeos to assist our daughter's barrel-racing fervor. I was able to take four different species of North American sheep during a period when my younger legs then accepted the challenge, but also a time in which my children required so much more chauffeuring, and she was always there. I have also traveled to Nova Scotia, Quebec, Florida, California, Arizona, Oregon, Washington and most states in between to judge hunt tests. These took me away from home for four to five days at a time and, while tending to our kennel chores, she never once complained.

Also a thank you to Bodo Winterhelt and John Kegal for following their vision and creating the versatile testing system that is used today by NAVHDA, VHDF, and several other organizations. For those who've never had the opportunity to meet Bodo, he is one of the most valued dog evaluators in all of North America. His charismatic personality has a magnetic way of winning one's heart. Bodo also brought the first Pudelpointers to North America from Germany. Again, I am truly indebted

Bob and Bodo Winterhelt in 2006 in Bandon, Oregon.

Bob judging with Chuck Johnson, Howard Zimmerman, and apprentice Kurt Merg in 2007.

to him as the bliss I have received from this breed has molded my life over the past 40 years. I purchased my first Pudelpointer in 1975 from John with help from Bodo. The harmony created with family, friends and customers over the years has been exceedingly rewarding.

We all learn most of our vocation from hands-on experiences or discussions and suggestions from others having the same zeal for the same passion as we have. Jim Reed owned a famous GSP (German Shorthaired Pointer) named "Ammertals Lancer D" back in the 1970s and Jim may have digested more hands-on dog knowledge than any person I've ever met. Winston Moore and John Lundy, who both championed Chesapeakes in AKC Field Trials, also tutored me in my beginner years of training gundogs. Most of what I recognize today as a top retriever (regardless of breed) comes from past experiences with these men.

Lastly, a heartfelt thank you to the greatest dog fraternity an enthusiast for sporting dogs can have, the NAVHDA judges. I was fortunate to meet and judge alongside so many experienced dog men and women while judging tests for some 25 years. We don't have space to thank all those I have judged with, but the core of my knowledge of versatile dogs primarily comes from this group.

Every dog trainer has a story about the life's journey that led them to this vocation. I feel that these journeys define the trainer and explain how the overall background and experience help support their training expertise and the various methods they use for their craft.

My strength has always leaned toward the retrieving aspect of dog training. An AKC retriever background has definitely influenced this, but loving waterfowling and never wanting to walk downhill to make a retrieve when chukar hunting has also influenced this distinguishing characteristic. During the 30 years that Cedarwood Kennel took in gundogs to train for others, I've estimated that as many as 600-800 dogs came through our facility. Most were Labs, Shorthairs, Brittanys, Setters and Pointers. The occasional Vizsla, Weimaraner, Griffon, Red Setter, and small Munsterlander also visited our kennel for training. Most were there for one to three months depending on the clients' needs and personal expectations. I learned something from every dog I worked with as most had some little idiosyncrasy that I had never previously experienced. And sometimes experimenting with a new training technique I had recently discovered from another trainer or read of in a Gun Dog Magazine or Pointing Dog Journal article became the answer.

I have extinguished the training flame that once consumed so much of my free time and plan to spend much of that time with my fly rods, golf clubs, and shotguns. Training my own personal dogs and continuing to raise several litters of pups each year gives LaFaye and I a good cause to get out of bed each morning. LaFaye does most all the routine chores at the kennel, addressing whelping and nurturing the litters up to the age to see them leave to their new homes. I now tend only to the older dogs and their necessary testing requirements. Some might say, "retirement is treating us both quite favorably."

Most of all I would like to thank all the wonderful dogs I have had the privilege to own and hunt behind.

Cedarwoods Dusty Rose.

Cedarwood Kennel's Beginning and History

Somewhere around 1970, I observed a beautiful English Setter cruising our neighborhood (as dogs were allowed to do then). The dog brought back a childhood memory of my father's dog Lindy as the Setter glided through our backyard and then on to the next. At that instant I fancied myself with such a beautiful dog to hunt behind. I had just graduated from Boise State University and taken a job at a local Boise hospital laboratory working as a Medical Technologist, and living in Boise had many upland bird hunting opportunities that I needed to start taking advantage of. And as I began pursuing this new adventure, I soon learned my new environment in Idaho was nearly "off the charts" during that period as far as upland bird hunting was concerned.

Bob Farris and his male Chesapeake duck hunting in 1985.

Pheasant, chukar, huns (grey partridge), and valley quail were plentiful with very liberal daily limits. A hunter was entitled to four pheasants, ten chukar, ten huns, and ten quail per day. In addition, there were also four species of grouse to pursue.

As soon as possible I purchased my first Setter and began training the pup in the spring of that year with the local Setter and Pointer enthusiasts of the area. There were spring field trials sponsored by a local club using the FDSB's (Field Dog Stud Book) format, and I soon found myself entering my youngster in the Derby Stakes at every trial. I had learned how to style up a dog on point and insist on standing birds until I had made the flush. What resulted from the spring field trials was a much more complete bird season the following fall. Also, when hunting with friends, I had a trained gundog whereas so many didn't, and that distinct advantage helped create the passion I developed in training hunting dogs.

Next, I discovered the excellent waterfowling opportunities offered in the local area. The Boise River, Payette River, and Snake River all had great numbers of ducks roosting on their water throughout the winter months. The season ran for more than 100 days with a seven bird daily limit. With three major rivers to hunt and a wildlife preserve that wintered more than one million mallards, I found another new hobby to pursue, especially during the winter months when upland bird hunting had closed.

This waterfowl addiction was quite new to me, but the instant love for this sport put me on a mission. I needed decoys, duck and goose calls, and a retriever. The decoys were easy, but learning to call ducks took quite some time. I had settled on a Labrador as a specialist for water retrieving and the search began. I hardly knew what a Chesapeake was at this time but when I watched several leap great distances into the water at a local AKC (American Kennel Club) field trial, I knew this was the breed for me and I passed on the Lab. Over the next eight years I would own four male Chesapeakes that had come from Dr. John Lundy's Aleutian line of dogs. As is the case with so many hunting dog enthusiasts, my first Chesapeake, Bob's Chocolate Kohi, was my best from this group.

I followed the same course as I'd done with my Setters and began training with Dr. Lundy and his friends as often as possible. Once the results began to show the fruits of these training efforts, I was off to the AKC Retriever field trials to compare

A young Bob Farris and the Chocolate Kohi after winning a 58-dog AKC Field Trial in 1975.

and evaluate my training skills, and especially my dog. At the time I had no idea how involved I would eventually become in this sport. The next three or four years found me entered in retriever trials routinely in six different states on the West Coast and Pacific Northwest. I most likely acquired a lot of my dog training knowledge during this timeframe, especially the retrieving skills. Visiting with the different professional trainers at these events always rewarded me with new ideas, methods, and retrieving drills to adopt into my current program.

It is an absolute joy to waterfowl with a finished nonslip retriever, capable of triple-mark retrieves and a blind retrieve on both land and water. The bonus for me, however, was the field trial competition. Showing up at a 50-dog AKC competition when all competitors were running black Labs and I had the only Chessy competing was "top dollar" for my ego at those few trials I won.

With a local reputation as an accomplished retriever trainer, I began receiving training offers from various doctors on the medical staff of the hospital where I was employed. I now had a young family and earning money as a trainer rather than spending my money field trialing made more sense and "Cedarwood Gun Dogs" came to be. I built extra kennel runs to house training dogs along with my own current hunting dogs (two English Setters and two Chesapeake Bay Retrievers).

I had started struggling with the whole field trial concept for some time and training other hunters' gundogs looked to have better personal rewards while also adding additional income for my family. While still staying friends with many of the retriever field trial associates, I headed out to hunt ducks one frigid December morning with four of these retriever friends only to find all four had left their Labs at home as the 27 degrees below zero weather forecast was too risky for them. Their dogs might learn to balk on a retrieve and this could carry over into competition trials.

My dogs were my hunting companions and I found that I really didn't have the same focus as so many of the others field trialing, and when I went hunting, so did my dog. It was a tough day for Kohi as he was a frozen icicle as soon as he left that frigid river following a retrieve. But he kept retrieving duck after duck for the five hunters that day. The river was flowing six inches of slush between the frozen edges extending some four to five feet from the bank. We could only put the decoys on the ice of the river's bank as they would not hold with the floating layer of slush floating on the river. I would watch Kohi's eyes as he blinked and, if he didn't open them quick enough, the water on his face would freeze so fast he couldn't open them! I would rub his face to free the ice so he could see to mark the next downed duck.

Setters and Chesapeakes: One would have to wonder how a versatile breed would eventually become my personal choice. As a hospital laboratory supervisor, I had been expected to create and submit a five-year business plan every year to the hospital's finance department. From this experience I began creating a five-year plan for my gun dog training business at my kennel. The thing I found from my data was that I personally had four dogs between the ages of six to ten years and to acquire new personal hunting stock in a retriever pup and also a Setter pup for my aging dogs would bring me to six total dogs of my own. Six of my 12 kennel runs would be occupied by my own personal hunting dogs. Simple math said that if a guy hunted with a versatile breed, his dog inventory would go from one to two dogs when the six to eight year-old replacement age comes into play. It made sense but could a versatile

Bob Farris with his two Chesapeakes in 1985.

breed do my waterfowling? How many negative 27-degree days would I ever see again, and would I even go again when conditions were that cold?

It was at about this time that a training customer showed up with a Pudelpointer at my kennel. He wanted me to hunt his dog on wild birds and he would pay my monthly training fee for this service. The young male Pudelpointer had been previously trained by Bodo Winterhelt and earned a NAVHDA Utility Prize II. I knew a little about NAVHDA at this time but my only experience with a versatile dog hunting was from friends' Wirehairs or Shorthairs. What a surprise I got when I took the client's Pudelpointer out for his first hunt on wild pheasants. This dog was everything my Setter was in the field. A good hard search. Strong intense point. But what he could do so effectively that my Setter was unable to do was track a crippled bird and retrieve it back to hand. Several trips jump-shooting ducks along the Snake River gave proof of his water retrieving skills. It was December and the young Pudelpointer had no hesitation in making 30 to 80-yard water retrieves on downed ducks.

I now had to re-program my five-year business plan as a Pudelpointer looked to be a good choice for my hunting needs and my entire family had fallen in love with the friendly/clownish personality of this breed. I took some vacation time and made arrangements to train with Bodo for a week to gain more knowledge of training versatile dog about this same time. Bodo was living and training dogs just south of Spokane, Washington then and had agreed to some tutoring. During this week of training, Bodo hooked me up with John Kegal in Ontario, Canada, and Jim Stevens in Alberta. From these two men I got my start with Pudelpointers.

A lot transpired during the next seven years as I added breeding Pudelpointers to my kennel business's 5-year plan and became a NAVHDA judge. In order to breed Pudelpointers, I needed to test my breeding stock in NAVHDA tests and becoming a judge helped make it possible to maintain a local chapter where I could test my dogs.

It also gave me the true understanding of the NAVHDA testing system and the merits received by breeders. I spent two years apprenticing to become a NAVHDA judge and was fortunate to work with the best judges in North America. I had previously judged many AKC retriever field trials during preceding years, where AKC events were an elimination competition with only one dog as the winner at the end of the day. In NAVHDA, all dogs are competing against a standard so that at the end of their day, every dog's work could possibly represent a perfect maximum score.

The NAVHDA format seemed to promote a unified cohesive relationship among the daily contestants, whereas in AKC events the personal individual competitors were inclined to be rooting against each other under their breath.

I believe I am quite a competitive person. However, I never looked back at AKC events once I became involved with NAVHDA. I did compete in Shoot-to-Retrieve Field Trials (NSTRA) for several years. I ran four different Cedarwood stud dogs during this period and retired each once they had taken a first place trophy from a 32-dog field. My purpose was primarily to see how my dogs compared in a head-to-head competition with the top pointing breeds. NSTRA dogs require fewer manners when on birds and the retrieves are not complete and are somewhat sloppy at times (when compared to NAVHDA events) so my adventure here was short lived. I enjoyed finished dogs too much and NSTRA competition seemed to take a finished dog back to their genetic beginning and erased a good deal of their obedience on birds and retrieving.

Since my introduction with Pudelpointers, NAVHDA testing and judging, and hunting exclusively with a versatile dog, there has been a most wonderful journey during this period of time. I still haven't determined where the final destination will take me or even what the finish line will be. I've been very fortunate to have owned several very special dogs that their presence will never leave my heart, but when the great ones pass, they are similar to a river; you cannot touch the same water twice because the flow that has passed will never pass by again.

Being able to share my dogs and my passion to hunt only good dogs with my family has also been a special bonus for me. Now with my grandsons each owning their own dogs and performing their own training, testing, and hunting may be the best bonus of all for me. Watching that smile coming forth on one of their faces when their dog has tracked that cripple mallard or rooster has that same special look as a spent dandelion blowing its petals in slow motion in a breeze, and there is a truth in the kids' eyes that says, "my pup has just earned their stripes!"

Bob Farris and a Crockett Setter preparing for an FDSB Field Trial in 1972.

Intense Vizsla standing in Montana. Photo courtesy Bridgett Nielsen.

The Versatile Hunting Dog Movement

Most sportsmen seeking a new hunting companion have previously owned a Lab or have had experiences hunting behind a Lab in the past. The medical issues and excessive shedding observed has prompted many to look to one of the versatile breeds for their next hunting companion. Also, wanting a family companion having a good "off switch" in the home has people searching for a better or different hunting companion that can match their Labrador's usefulness as a water retriever and a friendly house companion, but will add more stamina in the field while locating and pointing game birds rather than merely flushing birds, sometimes possibly out of gun range.

Many have had or seen self-hunting pointing dogs and now are seeking a good hunting companion that will hunt with them and not for themselves, as some of the specialty pointers bred purposely for horseback field trials offer. Most of the continental or versatile breeds are bred more purposely to hunt with you and exhibit a more cooperative field search where their performance is seen as a team searching for birds together rather than the owner searching continually for his far ranging self hunting dog.

The versatile breeds recognized by today's versatile dog community and are in most cases accepted for testing in hunt tests are (along with their abbreviated letters):

- BI   Bracco Italiano
- BA   Braque D'auvergne
- BB   Braque Du Bourbonnais
- BF   Braque Francais
- BS   Brittany
- CF   Cesky Fousek
- DP   Drentsche Patrijshond
- ES   English Setter
- FS   French Spaniel
- GL   German Longhaired Pointer
- GS   German Shorthaired Pointer
- GW   German Wirehaired Pointer
- GO   Gordon Setter

- IR   Irish Red & White Setter
- IS   Irish Setter
- LM   Large Munsterlander
- PS   Picardy Spaniel
- PT   Pointer
- PO   Portuguese Pointer
- PP   Pudelpointer
- SH   Slovakian Wirehaired Pointer
- SM   Small Munsterlander
- SP   Spinone
- ST   Stichelhaar
- VI   Vizsla
- WM   Weimaraner
- GR   Wirehaired Pointing Griffon
- WV   Wirehaired Vizsla

Many North American sportsmen and sportswomen look to one of these breeds as they don't want to give up winter waterfowling and are wanting an equal to their lab for this purpose, but also a dog that won't run out of stamina on extended upland hunts as their lab often does.

Labs and Golden Retrievers are known to be good with children in the home and are usually the waterfowling dog for that household. Many also have a pointer for upland game bird hunting which requires them to house two dogs for their hunting

Sheryle Tepp and her gang of Vizslas. Courtesy Sheryle Tepp.

purposes. As the years pass and it comes time to bring on a young replacement dog for the aging retriever and also aging pointer, this individual will now be have four dogs in his household. An aging retriever, an aging pointer, a young replacement retriever, and a young replacement pointer. Simple math demonstrates an easier path for the person owning a versatile breed, as when his versatile begins to age and he needs to introduce a replacement, he goes from one dog in his household to

Pudelpointer puppy posing for first photo.

only two dogs. Also, some of the field trial pointers are too busy in the home and not easily managed by one's wife or children as they don't have that necessary off-switch. Some of the versatile breeds come with so much affection that the family can manage these dogs easier as the affection helps create more obedience in a form of bid ability and a calmness, especially for the children's benefit.

Most versatile dogs are specifically bred by breeders attempting to pass on the values of a good versatile hunting companion's performance ideals by using NAVHDA test information, and making the batting average for getting a good dog much better than some of the specialty breeds that are from a backyard breeding with only the dog owner's evaluation of the two parents and four grandparents. Not that there aren't backyard bred versatile breeds, but the percentage of proven parents by field testing such as NAVHDA tests is much higher amongst the versatile breeds than the specialty breeds such as Labs or pointers.

Also, the pointing Lab has let most down that went down this road when looking for an all-around hunting dog for waterfowling and upland hunting that would point. Occasionally one finds a pointing Lab that demonstrates intense and staunch pointing instinct but the stamina required to hunt some of the game birds in North America like chukar, huns, or sharptail is lacking. Pointing Labs haven't been able to add the juice to their search and creating that extra desire needed to seal the deal for the experienced upland bird hunter. Also, their pointing instinct is quite often only seen at its best in the more submissive dogs, demonstrating a lower prey drive as they have a hesitation to pounce and attempt catching their game. I'm not attempting to beat up on the pointing Lab community, but only to clarify the distinct difference that they offer compared to one of the versatile breeds.

The versatile dog is the type of dog one wants in the foxhole with him when the conditions are at their worst: Frigid winter weather with ice floating in the river's

CLOCKWISE FROM UPPER LEFT: German Shorthair, photo courtesy Patti Carter; German Wirehair Pointer, photo courtesy Jim Pease; Braque du Bourbannais, photo courtesy Lonn Kuck; Vizsla, photo courtesy Bridgett Nielsen; Wirehaired Pointing Griffon, photo courtesy Steve Brodeur.

current to sultry fall afternoons with no shade during the hunt. While serving the interests of game conservation, the versatile dog aids the hunter by performing their best work before and after the shot, on land and in water. These are usually a foot-hunting dog which was developed for work under a variety of conditions in the field, forest, and water. Most of the versatile hunting dog breeds were developed in Europe during the 19th century due to hunting laws which required all game to be recovered after it was harvested. This change in hunting principles led to the need of a dog that could perform a variety of tasks. The European breeders took the most likeable traits from the best of the specialist breeds and combined them into what are known today as the versatile breeds. Today's versatile dogs, both in Europe and also North America, are expected to be intelligent, while demonstrating the necessary desire and also cooperation to complete most all of the required tasks asked of during upland hunting and also waterfowling. Searching, pointing, retrieving, and tracking wounded game is the expectations most have for their dogs that own one of the versatile breeds.

Cooperation and a trainable character are what helps make most versatile breeds a favorable home companion. Their intelligence and calm demeanor help create a favorable off switch when in the home when compared to their outdoor spirit. This off switch is also what makes them so compatible with children.

What's In A Name?

There is always a story behind the names of most kennels and the individual dogs they house. For me, Cedarwood Kennel was named after the street where we live. Bob Wehle named his famous English Pointer kennel by flipping his last name in reverse: Elhew Kennels.

Many of the female Pudelpointers I've kept over the years must have been names from the brothel I owned in dreams of a previous life. There was Cedarwood's Calendar Girl, Cedarwood's Knotty Girl, Cedarwood's Whiskered Playmate, Cedarwood's Pin Up Playmate and Cedarwood's Cover Girl. And the list goes on and on.

I have always purposely misspelled the names of all my own dogs for added personal character: Tukr, Cedr, Hazl, Jaspr, Danr, Razr, Tatr and so forth; and all have come and gone through the years.

Tukr (Cedarwoods First Offense) was named after my wildest high school friend: Butch Tucker. Butch's Dad, Harley Tucker, ran rodeo stock for most of the Northwest rodeos and Butch was exposed to and partially raised by too many cowboys in his youth. At 16 years old, Butch would sneak off to Reno for a good time while burning both ends of the night on these adventures. When I gave Tukr his name, I let him

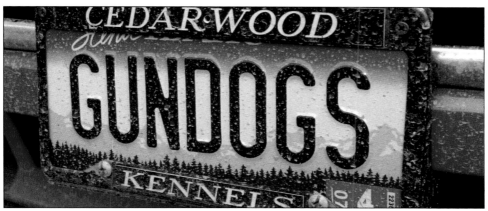

Bob Farris' personalized plates tell the complete story.

know he had quite a legend to live up to. He certainly did his best over his 14-plus years with me. In fact, he became the most coveted sire of pudelpointers in the breed's history. Even at 12, he still had that fiery look whether on point or chasing a wounded mallard.

Another of my stud dogs was Creightn (Cedarwood's Aces High), named after a childhood idol named Creighton Kooch, an outstanding Eastern Oregon athlete and a true gentleman. He raised Clydesdales and could be seen in most of the Northwest's parades throughout the 80s and 90s, just like the Budweiser horses seen worldwide. Again, my Creightn, like his namesake, turned out to be one of the nicest dogs I've had the privilege of working with.

So the next time you're chatting with a kennel or dog owner, put your curiosity to work and try to figure out where their kennel name or individual dog names originated. But a word to the wise: Don't try to figure out horse naming — Especially in thoroughbred racing circles.

Cedarwood Kennel's inside kennel runs.

A Breeder's Mission Statement

A breeding kennel should have a Mission Statement that is in print to ensure that they are always on the cutting edge of genetic studies, and that they set and meet their specific breeding goals. When in print, it is easily viewed and a reminder of where you are wishing to proceed to. A breeder's personal aspiration should be to personally hunt behind the best possible dogs they can acquire or produce. This is the passion that pushes the successful breeders to maintain the high standards in their program. Breeders representing any breed of sporting dog should always be capable of accepting constructive criticism from their peers and use the disparagement to field improvement. Acknowledging the successes of others is also necessary for a breeder wanting to cross over that horizon of success. Success comes when a breeder is capable of breeding with or purchasing breeding stock from one's strongest competitors in their marketplace.

Cedarwood Kennel with 12 indoor-outdoor Kennel runs.

Bob Farris entertaining a litter of pups.

With most kennels breeding versatile dogs, it has always been their profound aspiration to produce the absolute best along with the most versatile dog possible. This quest should not only be for the present, but also for the future for their chosen breed. Understanding genetics and attempting to avoid the many medical issues that plague our dogs is a must for all concerned with the future for their chosen breed. Many times monetary probabilities influence decisions that end up having a negative influence on a line within a breed. If this line continues to introduce recessive genetics representing medical problems, the entire breed may eventually suffer.

Breeders should strive to maintain the versatile hunting qualities that have secured their breed as one of the hunt test's top performing breeds. The NAVHDA test results are readily available online at www.navhda.org and any dog tested with the organization can easily be evaluated to obtain a performance picture of an individual dog, but also a performance picture of any kennel breeding one of the breeds of versatile dogs.

Again, my experiences are primarily with pudelpointers and NAVHDA testing, but I have enjoyed following friends and their kennel successes with other breeds of versatile dogs over the years. The NAVHDA website allows instant and accurate review of all test scores along with their monthly magazine publication. I am constantly analyzing the successes of my Cedarwood dogs that are tested. Both of the dogs that I have personally test, but also the dogs tested by clients that previously purchased a pup. The average natural ability score for Cedarwood Kennels over the years is 107 points. That is several hundred dogs making up this average. This average is a product of our Mission Statement and we continually analyze test scores while looking for possibly a better way. The average natural ability score of the breeding stock that has been used at Cedarwood Kennels is 110 points. This is the average of all the dogs ever used for breeding at our kennel and this average (mean) score is the common denominator for a 10-point average for our kennel overall.

During my working years as a Laboratory Supervisor, I had to submit a five year plan every January describing the new testing, new equipment, or additional staff that I was proposing. I have carried this knowledge forward into my kennel expectations. A much smaller budget required now as compared to a hospital's annual needs, but it does make me consider my expectations. When you raise pups and don't breed females after six years old it is necessary to keep track of the female inventory and their ages or you can easily end up with no breeding stock one spring. Having kennel goals and a three or five-year plan is what separates our top kennels from those merely raising pups for the monetary profits. This is where the discerning buyer needs to make good comparisons and judgment when seeking a new pup.

Most kennels producing versatile dogs that use hunt test testing as a standard reference for field and marsh expectations are committed to producing excellent personal gun dogs that can duplicate as a wonderful family companion. Mine are not mutually exclusive goals; all versatile dogs should have a calm, affectionate disposition within the home, and should display this same affectionate behavior toward everyone they encounter. However, these breeds should also have the ability to change gears when in the field or marsh to display the desire and prey drive necessary to earn them that pinnacle place among NAVHDA's versatile breeds.

A well-bred versatile hunting companion should be a sporting companion that a hunter never loses contact with in the field. The dog should adjust their range in the field to maintain visual contact with the handler as best possible. This cooperative search pattern finds the dog hunting for the gun, rather than the gunner hunting for the dog, as is often the case with some of our specialty breeds.

All of the versatiles are natural pointing dogs with a natural instinct to point, track and retrieve any and all game birds. Some of these breeds have an intense passion toward waterfowl. This intensity toward waterfowl, along with a breed's love of water, makes them a sound water dog in the months of December and January, rivaling that of the Labrador Retriever even when the waterfowling conditions get tough.

It should be the goal at all kennels producing one of the versatile breeds to provide sporting dogs that can hunt the upland game birds of North America equaling the prey drive of the specialist English Pointer, but in a cooperative and biddable manner; coupled with the ability to retrieve in icy water conditions nearly equal to the Labs, Goldens and Chessies. These dogs must also have the intelligence and cooperation required making them the best possible canine citizen in the home environment while living in a family environment.

Bird hunting should be the driving force behind all breeding programs. Versatile breeders should be found hunting grouse in September and early October. Ruffs, Blues, Sage, Sharptail, and Spruce are all native to North America and most regions have populations of one or more species. Most versatile dogs are excellent grouse dogs as their ability to shorten their range and maintain visual contact make them invaluable in the woods. October through December is the best time for pheasants, along with local waterfowl. There are different demands for today's pheasant hunter with many needing to travel and plan trips to find wild birds. December and January are the best months for Chukar, Hungarians, and Quail. Here the dogs need to range out significantly more and stand their birds from extreme distances. These are also the two months that see the northern waterfowl still inhabiting many areas. With all these hunting opportunities, I am disillusioned by how many that raise one of the versatile breeds that do not take advantage in these opportunities. Being a casual upland or waterfowl hunter makes it very difficult to understand the breeding necessities required to produce the type of gun dog most are seeking. Being a nonhunter makes the feat nearly impossible.

As a breeder it is imperative to know your client base. Often times a breeder's expectations are over the top for the clients they are attracting. Then the opposite can see the client with high expectations looking at a breeder with much lower standards for hunting. Awareness of the hunting requirements both for upland hunting and also waterfowling should see a focus on producing dogs that match well with the clients who are coming forth in search of that new hunting partner. Just because as a breeder you don't allow your dogs in the house doesn't mean you don't need to be concerned about how much nervous energy your breeding stock has if you are advertising good companionship with an off-switch when inside the home. If most of your clients are grouse-only hunters, you need breeding stock displaying a cooperative field search rather than an independent search where the dog is very comfortable searching being your view. Breeders in the West that primarily hunt Chukar, Huns, or Sharptail have range expectations that sometimes don't favor hunting in the grouse woods and this should be a consideration by both the breeder and the client before the deal is complete.

A breeder can put about anything in print on a website and advertise much beyond the truth. Those seeking a hunting companion should be taking their time in their investigation of possible kennels to purchase from. We are always receptive to visitors and I take favor with those that want to make sure they are dealing with honesty and that we are professional both in facilities, but also our breeding stock. I always bring four or more dogs into our home to demonstrate their off-switch and then go outside to demonstrate bird work and swimming. I think back over the years of some of the purchase mistakes I made by not doing enough research and evaluating. Today's social media and internet make it much easier to do efficient evaluating.

When looking for a breeder, of any of the versatile breeds, it is important to assess the options different breeders have for creating their litters. A breeder with just one female has huge limitations for selective breeding compared to the breeder with four or five different females. When it comes time to breed, the breeder with only one dog is always rolling the dice and hoping this solo female will have all the necessary attributes necessary to produce the high level of pups wanted by the hunting dog community. Many recessive traits don't show up in dogs until after the age of two years old and are passed on to the litter unexpectedly. If a breeder sees the quality in their litter to be less than expected it becomes much harder for the breeder to move forward while improving their pups' quality or the quality of their line. Usually this solo-owned female is bred over and over as that is the only possible breeding source available. It is rare to find someone that has expectations of becoming a breeder, discontinue with their female.

The breeder with multiple females can assess situations such as this and decide to spay the female and discontinue breeding any female that is not producing the quality expected. This breeder eventually finds the females in their breeding program that raise the bar of excellence for them and these are the ones they continue breeding.

One of the best females I have ever owned was a pup I kept for myself and named her Hemi. She earned a NAVHDA Natural Ability Prize I at four months old and a Utility Prize I at 15 months. This was my pride and joy. We bred her one time and had a truly wonderful litter out of her when she was two years old. The next winter she began showing signs of canine alopecia in her coat along her flank. But, the next winter the alopecia returned across both rib cages and on the top of her rump. One of the hardest things I ever did as a breeder was to spay Hemi and never be able to breed her again. Alopecia is not very well genetically understood and there are no markers to identify this in individual dogs at this time. It affects a variety of breeds such as Poodles, Pudelpointers, Griffons, German Wirehairs, and Airedales just to list a few; basically the breeds having a double coat. The dog loses flank hair when the days shorten in the fall and the hair returns again the next spring when the days lengthen. I was unwilling to gamble on whether Hemi carried alopecia as a dominant trait, as I

Bob and LaFaye Farris enjoying their retirement years raising their pups at Cedarwood Kennel.

could have destroyed 20 years of breeding with one single dog. Had I owned Hemi as my only dog and choosing to establish myself as a breeder, I probably would not have spayed her. Spaying her didn't change my agenda or cause me to start over, as I had five to ten other females to continue with. As I write this, Hemi is laying at my feet and her nighttime bed is next to mine so she has total inside privileges. She is ten years old now but still my go-to dog on a serious pheasant or duck hunt. I will never know if I made the correct decision to discontinue breeding her, but I will for sure know that by spaying her I don't have to worry about my line of dogs passing on alopecia to their pups for the new owners to deal with.

Mike Gowe with Cedarwoods Man O War (aka Boca). Boca earned a NAVHDA Versatile Champion title, an NSTRA Shoot to Retrieve Champion title, and a Hunting Retriever Champion title. Boca's pedigree has the motherlines of Cedarwoods Calendar Girl on both sides.

Breeding Better Versatile Dogs

All of today's different breeds of versatile dogs are a result of inbreeding. This is how the various breeds began. Inbreeding occurs through natural selection among a small isolated population or through the influence of man breeding selected animals to derive specific traits. Either way, inbreeding is responsible for setting enough of the dominant traits so that the resulting group breeds true to their individual type.

A dog's physical makeup, or what you visually see, is called the dog's phenotype. For each characteristic, a dog has a pair of genes, one inherited from the sire and the other from the dam. Each gene in the pair is called an allele. If both alleles in a pair are of the same type, the gene pair is homozygous. If the two alleles are different, the gene pair is heterozygous. While each dog can have a maximum of two different alleles at a gene pair, many different alleles are potentially available to be part of the gene pair.

The greater the number of alleles that are available at each gene pair (called genetic polymorphism), the greater the genetic diversity of the breed. A gene pair may consist of two dominant genes such as "AA," a dominant and a recessive gene such as "Aa," or two recessive genes such as "aa." A gene's alternate is called its allele. Only one member of a gene pair will be expressed in a dog's phenotype. Genes are dominant or recessive to its allele and never a combination or this would compromise results. This discussion is what primarily influences the color and coat.

A dog's genetic makeup is his genotype. Now, both members of the gene pair are expressed. When both of the gene pairs are the same, they are homozygous, such as "AA" or "aa." It is the heterozygous genotype such as "Aa" that is responsible for most of the questionable heredity misunderstandings. It is impossible for a dog with a recessive phenotype to carry a dominant gene in its genotype as the dominant gene is always expressed if present. If recessive genes are rare in a breeding, it will usually be masked by the dominant genes. This is why linebreeding concentrates the dominant genes of a specific ancestor or ancestors through their appearance multiple times on both sides of a pedigree. This spreading of desired ancestors is what helps to influence inherited genes from both parents to be identical and are called homozygous. If these genes are not similar, they are said to be heterozygous.

Gene pairs that create small gene pool breeds such as the case for most of the versatile breeds, must be homozygous for phenotypes and personality traits to be "true to breed." Hunting instinct, color, and size are influenced by variable gene pairs and by making use of them; a breeder can select the desirable characteristics and avoid most of the undesirable ones. Homozygosity greatly improves the chance that the pups can, in turn, pass on the desired traits of the specific ancestor to their own pups down the line. To accomplish his kennel's mission, the breeder must continue to select pups that display the desirable traits of the ancestors.

A common concern among many researching a new hunting companion is to have an avoidance of any breeding that was influenced by inbreeding. Through inbreeding, a rare recessive gene can be passed from a heterozygous ancestor from both parents, which creates a homozygous recessive pup. This is how undesirable traits are developed from inbreeding. Traits such as noise sensitive, people sensitive, or any of the various aggressions would be examples.

If a breeder is inclined to inbreed, the inbreeding coefficient (Wright's coefficient) should be established to keep an accurate count of the same-appearing dog on a ten-generation pedigree. A ten-generation pedigree would have 2,046 dogs listed that would be creating the calculation of the Coefficient of Inbreeding (COI). With a gene pool as small as most of the versatile breeds are, inbreeding should be avoided at all costs.

My breeding experiences are primarily with Pudelpointers and predominantly my Cedarwood Kennel. All of the versatile breeds of sporting dogs have the same influences as I'm discussing here, so the various versatile breeders' breeding insight is no different than what I have experienced over the years. My Cedarwood Kennel's

Cedarwoods Kennel's wall of memories inside the kennel facility.

line of Pudelpointers are the result of linebreeding back to an extremely successful litter of pups that Johnny Shulkey produced in 1983. The two male dogs appearing in the 4th and 5th generations of most of my pedigrees, Atom V. Shulkey and Adonis V. Shulkey, are two littermates from this famous breeding. They both can be found in the background of most all of my breeding stock today.

I wish I could take credit for the foresight of linebreeding my dogs from these two dogs, but it was actually the result of merely having these two stud dogs available with very little other choices for my breedings. The common denominator for my success always returns to these two dogs on my present pedigrees, however. I'm no different from many other breeders of sporting dogs that have looked back at the fruits of their achievements only to realize that mere accidental success is what their accomplishments are represented by.

What we have learned from our past breedings at Cedarwood is that a sound breeding primarily involves three generations, going back to the great grandparents, which involves 14 dogs; beyond that, the ancestors have little influence (especially when looking at an outbreeding). In a strong linebreeding with a COI of 20 percent or more one should probably be looking at pedigrees to the 6th generation where you are now looking at 126 dogs on a pedigree. In a perfect scenario we like to see the sire of a litter as the great-grandsire of the dam for a perfect linebreeding (a bitch can also be used for this model). Occasionally we need to nick our line with an outbreeding to give our line a "bump." Whenever we outcross our Cedarwood line to a top dog from a completely different family, we often get a heterosis bump, and often very exceptional dogs. This appears to be an outstanding way to combat the doctrine of retrogression, aka "drag of the breed."

For instance, when you breed two excellent dogs, the litter might produce a dog better than the parents, some dogs as good as the parents, and also some dogs that are lesser than the parents. Likewise, if you breed two lesser dogs, most of the litter should be better than the parents. In other words, the breed tends to move to the center of the bell-shape curve and this is how the purebreds keep a steady pace, with minimal improvement. To avoid this mediocrity, our breeding program keeps the positive bump from another family and then breeds back to our linebreeding to accelerate beyond the purebred's steady pace.

Many breeders, including Cedarwood Kennel, who are conscientiously linebreeding their dogs like to track the motherlines on their pedigrees. Motherlines refer to the whole of the bloodline of all the mothers on both sides of the pedigree. On our pedigrees, we like to see Adonis and Atom V. Shulkey's mother (Dulli VD Wilhelminger) appearing frequently on each side of the pedigree. Also, Cedarwood's Calendar Girl as often as possible on each side also. Bob Wehle of Elhew Kennels would have called these two females "blue hens:" females that a family of dogs could grow from. Some studies, in Germany, see the motherline success as coming from utilizing very important sex-linked genes present only in the DNA of the X-chromosomes of great-producing females. A male has 76 paired chromosomes plus an X and Y chromosome. The only place a male can inherit these important sex-linked genes is from his mother. When this male's son becomes a father, only his daughters get this valuable X chromosome, never his sons. When the resulting granddaughters become mothers, the art of breeding lies in selecting only the male offspring that inherited this valuable X chromosome. These great-grandsons will be able to pass this sex-linked gene on to their get.

This is all in theory, however, as there isn't sufficient supportive data to define the theory as reality. This process also brings forth the influence of the stamen female or Blue Hen, which is the genetic component that Cedarwood Kennel supports. A somewhat more simplified explanation is the belief that 60 to 80 percent of a pup's genetic influence has been derived from his mother. Using specific Blue Hens in a motherline concentrated pedigree is a much more traceable method of linebreeding, however. After all, if one is known to be a breeder, their first responsibility is to their mission or vision statement, which is in reality defined on their pedigrees and can be easily viewed for review.

This breeding language is what many of the past successful hunting dog breeders have felt to have led to their individual successes from their own chosen matings. It is hard to argue with the success of the Elhew Pointers, the Takoa Mountain English Setters, the Cascade or Sureshot German Wirehairs, or the Lancer D and Hustler lines of German Shorthairs in field trials. I have often wondered, however, how much of these breeding successes hedged from parlor room discussions when in actuality they were just mere luck and got a good "nick."

Genetic Diversity

Genetic diversity should be a concern to all dog breeders, and should especially be of trepidation for breeds with small populations or limited geographic disbursement. The apprehension is whether there is enough genetic variation within a breed's gene pool to maintain quality health. Breeders should be aware of their genetic diversity within their breed to help avoid breeding too close within a family or line. Limiting genetic diversity can also occur in large population breeds after a prolonged use of a line or family of dogs in a community and not extending breeding practices outside of that community for several decades.

If there is no breed diversity in a gene pair, but the particular homozygous gene that is present is not detrimental, there is no negative effect on breed health. The characteristics that make a breed reproduce true to its standard are, in fact, based on non-variable (that is, homozygous) gene pairs.

For most of the versatile breeds, their gene pools have expanded through breeding for many generations, resulting in a stable population of healthy dogs. The origins of the different breeds have a lot to do with genetic diversity. A breed established with a working phenotype tends to have diverse founder origins, and significant diversity. Even with substantial population bottlenecks, the breed can maintain considerable amounts of genetic diversity. Breeds established by inbreeding on a limited number of related founder individuals could have a reduced diversity.

There are two factors that must be considered when evaluating genetic diversity and health issues in a breed: The average level of inbreeding, and detrimental recessive genes. With a small population, there is a tendency to find higher average inbreeding coefficients (COI) due to the relatedness between dogs from common ancestors. There is, however, no specific level or percentage of inbreeding that causes impaired health.

The problems that inbreeding depression cause in purebred populations stem from the effects of deleterious recessive genes. If the founding population of a breed produces a high frequency of a deleterious recessive gene, then the breed will continue to see this disorder frequently. This can be observed as small litter sizes, increase in neonatal death, high frequency of genetic diseases, or various stages of impaired immunity. If these issues are being observed, then the breeder needs to seriously consider limited genetic diversity.

The issue of high average inbreeding coefficients is one that all breeds go through during their foundation. As the population increases and the average relatedness of dogs goes down (based on a fixed number of generations), the average inbreeding coefficient for the breed will go down. The effect of initially higher inbreeding coefficients in small population breeds will depend on the presence of deleterious recessive genes that will be expressed when homozygous.

Lord ze Strazistskych Lesu (aka Czar) is one of two male imports from the Czech Republic used for genetic diversity in the Cedarwood line of Pudelpointers.

Some breeders discourage linebreeding and promote outbreeding only in an attempt to protect genetic diversity in their breed in an effort to maintain a sound breed. It is not the type of matings utilized (linebreeding or outbreeding) that causes the loss of genes from a breed's gene pool. Rather, loss of genes occurring through the selection of breeding stock; the use and non-use of offspring. The concerning factor is if a breed starts limiting their focus to breeding stock from a limited number of lines, then a loss of genetic diversity will occur.

The process of maintaining healthy lines, with many breeders crossing between lines and breeding back as they see fit, maintains diversity in the gene pool. If some breeders outbreed, and some linebreed to certain dogs that they favor, while others linebreed to other dogs that they favor, then the breeds genetic diversity is maintained. It is the varied opinion of a group of breeders as to what constitutes the ideal dog, and their selection of breeding stock based on their opinions, is what maintains breed diversity.

The most important factor for diminished genetic diversity in dog breeds is the popular sire syndrome. The overuse of a popular sire beyond a reasonable contribution through frequent breedings significantly skews the gene pool in this direction, and reduces the diversity of the gene pool. Most all breeders of all the versatile breeds

Bill Athens' Czech Republic import Chajra Zestrazistskych Lesu has been a valued asset to North American Pudelpointers in genetic diversity. Photo courtesy Bill Athens.

have been guilty of this to some extent, and I am no exception. It was difficult not to breed Cedarwoods First Offense (aka Tukr) as his progeny always tested favorable in NAVHDA tests. And so he had many honeymoons and sired many pups over his eight year breeding career. Any genes that he possessed, whether positive or negative, will increase in frequency in the progeny. And from over breeding a sire, various breed related genetic diseases can occur.

Another menacing effect of the popular sire syndrome is the loss of genetic contribution being contributed from other unrelated males who are not used for breeding. There is a finite number of quality bitches bred each year. If one male is used in an inordinate amount of matings, there will be fewer females left for other quality males that should be contributing to the gene pool. The popular sire syndrome is a significant factor in both populous breeds and also breeds with diminutive or small populations. Knowing what I do now concerning this popular sire syndrome makes me question the validity of breeding Tukr to so many different females during his breeding career.

Avoiding the popular sire syndrome as much as possible and then using quality dogs from throughout the population will expand the breeds gene pool. Monitoring the breeds genetic health issues and also performing genetic testing for breed-related disorders will help manage genetic health issues as the gene pool for the breed expands. If breeders are making an effort to maintain a reasonable equal or close to equal numerical balance of sires and dams, they will help to avoid losing genetic contribution. The genetic health of a breed can be alternately exaggerated by continual inbreeding practices. Inbreeding should not be practiced with regularity in a breed, or within a line of that breed, without witnessing negative consequences.

The most commonly observed consequences are in longevity of life, unsuccessful reproduction, and an inactive immune system. These are all three negatively affected by inbreeding. One of the easiest ways to identify inbreeding on a pedigree is when the same sire or same dam's name appears in the same generation when looking at the 2nd, 3rd, or 4th generations. Also a father bred to daughter, or a mother by her son, or a cousin to an aunt or uncle. Before software such as BreedMate became available, this was how one could identify the difference in a linebreeding versus an inbreeding. People like Bob Wehle of Elhew Kennels used this procedure as their determining inbreeding map.

The COI of a ten generation pedigree (2,046 dogs) along with an observation for duplicating names in the 2nd, 3rd, and 4th generations, can help predict the degree of inbreeding or lack of inbreeding very accurately. Also, tracking a proposed breeding's unique number can also lend forecast to how well a breeder is staying within or outside his predetermined line. Software such as BreedMate, CompuPed, Breeders Assistant, and FSpeed will calculate the COI and reflect it as a percentage. When using a COI value to express the degree of inbreeding, as a rule of thumb, less than 10 percent would indicate an outbreeding, while 10-25 percent indicates a linebreeding, and greater than 25 percent indicates an inbreeding.

BREEDMATE EVALUATION

BreedMate software creates what displays as a pedigree for a proposed breeding (both sire and dam) or it can show a family tree of an individual dog for a breeder to easily view and make breeding determinations from. The significant information calculated from BreedMate is the COI, the COR, and the unique ancestor number.

The COI (Coefficient of Inbreeding) is a calculation from a 10-generation proposed breeding, where 2,046 dogs data is obtained to create this number. I personally feel that a COI less than 10 percent indicates to the breeder that they are looking at an outbreeding (2 fairly unrelated dogs). A COI between 10 and 25 percent represents a form of linebreeding which is primarily of a family of dogs (dogs from a line of dogs displaying individual dogs multiple times on the pedigree). A COI greater than 30 percent represents a very strong linebreeding that can hedge toward inbreeding based on where various dogs show as multiples on the pedigree.

It should be noted, however, that an inbreeding is basically when one individual dog appears multiple times in the 2nd, 3rd, or possibly 4th generation of a pedigree. Also a father bred to daughter, or a mother by her son, or a cousin to an aunt or uncle. An example to explain this best is that if two littermates were bred, the COI would be 50 percent and their sire and dam would both be present two times in the 3rd generation. Whereas, a COI of 25 percent that doesn't have any dog showing its name multiple times in the 2nd generation or multiple times in the 3rd generation would be a linebreeding and the high COI and this high COI was determined due to the dogs in these two generations being linebred themselves when they were created. Basically, they were from a strong family line.

The COR (Coefficient of Relationship) helps explain the value obtained in the proposed breeding's COI as one can determine which of the dogs on this proposed breeding are linebred and which were from outbreedings, especially in the first two generations of the pedigree. When I study the COR of my proposed breedings, I look to see the top performance dogs lending a higher percent than expected toward the DNA makeup of the pups... Both in hunting indices and also personality and confirmation, also. I'm looking for a stronger genetic path from these "stars" on the pedigree than from the "average performers."

In a complete outbreeding (a Lab to a Brittany), the COR of each parent should be 50 percent each (totaling 100 percent). The COR for the four grandparents should be 25 percent each also totaling 100 percent for that generation. The COR for the eight great grandparents should be 12.5 percent each again totaling 100 percent. And the COR of the 16 great-great grandparents should be 6.25 percent each for 100 percent.

Here is any easier way to see the diminishing percentages in an outcross breeding:

- **1st Generation:** Both parents contributing 50 percent of their DNA to the litter.
- **2nd Generation:** All four grandparents contributing 25 percent.
- **3rd Generation:** All eight great grandparents contributing 12.5 percent.
- **4th Generation:** All 16 great great grandparents contributing 6.12 percent.
- **5th Generation:** All 32 great great-great grandparents contributing 3.075 percent.

You can see that the genetic influence from the parents is eight times stronger coming from sire and dam than from the great-great grandparents. This means that most of the alleles creating the individual pups are primarily coming from the two parents and four grand parents. Out-crosses are always the safest breedings and usually work very well, but sometimes for only that first generation. The pups from this breeding are not as likely to produce as well as their own observed abilities and this is where "the drag of a breed" comes in; where the pups produced return to the performance medium of the breed. Doing only mere outbreedings over and over will find this effort returning to the center of that bell shaped curve and the average of the breed's performance characteristics. The statistics of a bell shaped curve express 68 percent of the population will fall within one standard deviation on each side of the medium and 95 percent within 2 standard deviations, while 99.7 percent will fall within three standard deviations.

Outbreedings tend to stay closest to the medium for the breed and within one standard deviation or 68 percent where most pups in the litter will be similar with little variation. Strong linebreedings show a larger variance in the pups in a litter spreading out to two standard deviations or 95 percent. The focus for a linebreeding should be selecting only pups for future breedings that are at the far right side of this bell shaped curve. This is where NAVHDA testing comes into play for the breeder. An example would be to select only dogs that have received 105 or greater in a natural ability test and only dogs that have received 180 or more points in a utility test for future breedings. One would expect to eventually see pups scoring greater than 105 consistently in their natural ability test and greater than 180 in utility tests after 3 generations of breeding to this standard; and avoiding "the drag of the breed" and returning to the medium of the breed or possibly to the left side of this bell shaped curve, which would be below average performers.

Linebreeding is the best effort to raise the bar for a breed, but only if one is honest about which dogs are influencing the genetic hunting instincts and personalities from a higher statistical effort. The alleles creating the genetic makeup of these pups need to come from dogs that they themselves show the desired indices one wishes to see come forth in their pups. Any average or below average performers on the first three generations of a proposed pedigree can influence the breeding leaving the breeder with pups not performing up to his expectations (especially if this below average performer came from a linebreeding themselves that had a high COI).

One should also look to see what the unique number of ancestors is on this ten generation pedigree. The pedigree has 2,046 locations for different dogs' names and the unique number is how many different dogs names fill these locations. If the unique number is calculated to be 500 it means that there were 500 different dogs on this pedigree so many of these dogs names showed up multiple times, anywhere from five to 50 times. This is where the real rubber meets the road with BreedMate; if a dog is on the ten generation pedigree 20 times and is a "star" (in your opinion) this is a realistic advantage to the quality of the litter. If a dog you do not favor is on the pedigree 20 times, however, you have a more likelihood of see unfavorable results in the litter. It is important to also look to see if this unique number is represented in the front of the pedigree or the rear to help determine where the strong genetic flow is

Wirehaired Pointing Griffon. Photo courtesy Joe Dobie.

coming from. One could assume that a unique number of 300 to 500 would represent a form of line-breeding and one of 1000 to be an outbreeding. This is somewhat hypothetical and most breeders using BreedMate have their own target values they wish to achieve.

It is fairly easy to understand why this unique number is so valuable to breeders using BreedMate, when you consider a stud dog from a breeding with a low unique number (linebred) will give much more of his genetic influence to a litter than a stud dog from a litter with a much higher unique number (outbred). The stud dog with the lower unique number will create pups more like he is, especially if the dam was from a litter with a much higher unique litter. Or a male with a high unique number (outbred) when bred to a female from a litter with a low unique number will produce pups more like their mother.

The first example is of the sire and dam that made Cedarwoods First Offense (aka Tukr). This breeding had a COI of 21% so Tukr was from a strong line-breeding of Cedarwood dogs. Tukr was used as a sire for my Cedarwood Kennel and also seven other Pudelpointer kennels during his breeding career. Eighty percent of his progeny that was tested in NAVHDA natural ability tests received a Prize I with an average or mean score of 107 points. Also, at one time there were 11 NAVHDA Versatile Champion Pudelpointers, and eight of them were out of Tukr. These statistics led me to believe his breeding prowess was partially due to his 21% COI and also from the

Pedigree of: CEDARWOODS FIRST OFFENSE NA 110 PZ I, UT 194

Date of Birth:
Colour & Markings:
COI (10 Gen): 20.9427%

Sex: M
Breed: 20.9427%
Reg No.:

PARENTS	GRANDPARENTS	GREAT GRANDPARENTS	GREAT GREAT GRANDPARENTS
SIRE: CEDARWOODS AMADEUS NA 112 PZ I, UT 190 PZ I COR=65.638% {1 - }	BIRCHWOOD'S FAVONIUS UT 188 PZ II, NA 112 PZ I COR=44.9131% {2 - 3}	ATOM V SHULKEY NA 110 PZ I, UT 202 PZ I COR=23.9621% {3 - 4}	DON V HUNFELDEN COR=14.858% {4 - 5, 4} DULLI VD WILHEINIGER COR=16.397% {4 - 5, 4}
		BIRCHWOOD'S CASSIE NA 96 EVAL, UT 193 PZ I COR=32.1412% {3, 4 - 4, 5, 5}	WINTERHELLE'S KNOCKOUT COR=21.6587% {4, 5, 5 - 5, 6, 6, 6, 6} KITTI V ERLENGRUND COR=14.2079% {4, 5 - 5, 6, 6}
	HAVERHILLS ALEETA NA 110 PZ I, UT 178 PZ II COR=46.3498% {2 - 3}	BIRCHWOOD'S DUNCAN NA 110 PZ 1, UT 202 PZ I COR=34.9914% {3 - 4, 4}	WINTERHELLE'S ENVOY COR=19.3541% {4 - 5, 5} BIRCHWOOD'S CASSIE COR=32.1412% {3, 4 - 4, 5, 5}
		WINTERHELLE'S GILLEY COR=24.1354% {3 - 4, 4}	WINTERHELLE'S FACT COR=14.1718% {4 - 5, 5} ANTA V HUBERTSWINKLE COR=11.3663% {4 - 5, 5}
DAM: CEDARWOODS IMAGE OF JAKE NA 112 PZ I, UT 201 PZ I COR=66.1669% {- 1}	CEDARWOODS BLAZE NA 112 PZ I, UT 188 PZ II COR=49.7067% {- 2}	BIRCHWOOD'S FAVONIUS UT 188 PZ II, NA 112 PZ I COR=44.9131% {2 - 3}	ATOM V SHULKEY COR=23.9621% {3 - 4} BIRCHWOOD'S CASSIE COR=32.1412% {3, 4 - 4, 5, 5}
		HAVERHILLS AXCELL NA 112 PZ I, UT 179 PZ III COR=35.753% {- 3}	BIRCHWOOD'S DUNCAN COR=34.9914% {3 - 4, 4} WINTERHELLE'S GILLEY COR=24.1354% {3 - 4, 4}
	CEDARWOODS CALENDAR GIRL NA 112 PZ I, UT 189 PZ II COR=45.0056% {- 2}	ADONIS V SHULKEY NA 108 PZ I COR=21.1605% {- 3}	DON V HUNFELDEN COR=14.858% {4 - 5, 4} DULLI VD WILHEINIGER COR=16.397% {4 - 5, 4}
		HAVERHILLS ALEETA NA 110 PZ I, UT 178 PZ II COR=46.3498% {2 - 3}	BIRCHWOOD'S DUNCAN COR=34.9914% {3 - 4, 4} WINTERHELLE'S GILLEY COR=24.1354% {3 - 4, 4}

I, the undersigned do hereby certify that the foregoing particulars are correct to the best of my knowledge and belief

SIGNED _____ DATE _____

number of Prize I Natural Ability performers on his pedigree (28 out of 30) through four generations. Basically, he was a pre-potent stud dog.

The second example is a breeding where Tukr is a grandfather, great-grandfather and also great-great-grandfather. His genetic influence on this litter of pups (COR) is 55% as a grandfather (instead of 25% as would be in outcrosses). Also, a COR of 55% as a great-grandfather (instead of 12.5% as in an outcross breeding) and also a COR of 55% as a great-great-grandfather (instead of 6.25% as is in outcrosses). He is on the pedigree in three generations and since his own breeding had a COI of 21 percent he is giving more genetic influence to the litter than both of the two parents. If Tukr hadn't been a star performer himself (just an average performer), this would have ended up creating negative results because his genetic influence would have a predisposed decline in the production of the pups.

Again, having a top performing dog multiple times on a pedigree is favorable but preferably not multiple times in the same generation (at least the 2nd, or 3rd) of that proposed pedigree. Also better results come from starting with this star performer as a grandparent rather than parent as many genetics skip a generation and then have his name also appear as a great-grandfather and great-great-grandfather.

The only way to support the value of hunting dogs for proposed breedings is through field evaluations such as NAVHDA tests and in Tukr's case, it is easy to recognize the common denominator for his breeding success, and why I linebred him and continue to today with his frozen semen.

Pedigree of: **SALLI BY JACK**

Date of Birth: Sex: F Breed: 19.2812%
Colour & Markings: Reg No.:
COI (10 Gen): 19.2812%

PARENTS	GRANDPARENTS	GREAT GRANDPARENTS	GREAT GREAT GRANDPARENTS
SIRE: Cedarwoods Jumping Jack NA 112 PZ 1, UT 201 PZ 1 COR=65.1891% {1 - }	CEDARWOODS FIRST OFFENSE NA 110 PZ I, UT 194 PZ II COR=54.8525% {2 - 4, 3}	CEDARWOODS AMADEUS NA 112 PZ I, UT 190 PZ I COR=37.6038% {3 - 5, 4}	BIRCHWOOD'S FAVONIUS COR=26.9584% {4, 5 - 6, 7, 5, 6, 5} HAVERHILLS ALEETA COR=31.2514% {4, 5, 4 - 6, 7, 5, 6, 5}
		CEDARWOODS IMAGE OF JAKE NA 112 PZ I, UT 201 PZ I COR=42.9987% {3 - 5, 4}	CEDARWOODS BLAZE COR=32.0182% {4 - 6, 5, 4} CEDARWOODS CALENDAR GIRL COR=38.5735%
	CEDARWOODS EASY PLAYGIRL COR=36.9193% {2 - }	PINERIDGE RUDY COR=12.317% {3 - }	EVAR Z OPCIZEN COR=7.46622% {4 - } ASTRA VALLOVA ZEM COR=5.72261% {4 - }
		CEDARWOODS CALENDAR GIRL NA 112 PZ I, UT 189 PZ II COR=38.5735% {4, 3 - 6, 5, 4}	ADONIS V SHULKEY COR=19.0412% {5, 4 - 7, 6, 5} HAVERHILLS ALEETA COR=31.2514% {4, 5, 4 - 6, 7, 5, 6, 5}
DAM: CEDARWOODS MUSTANG SALLI COR=65.0076% { - 1}	BRUEDERSTHAL'S AL COR=37.3897% { - 2}	KILLBUCKS HOGAN COR=40.8749% { - 3}	CEDARWOODS FIRST OFFENSE COR=54.8525% { - 4} GORA ZE STRAZISTE COR=11.2579% { - 4}
		KILLBUCKS JENNA MAGGIE NA 106 PZ II COR=14.6525% { - 3}	PINERIDGE FLICK COR=9.23557% { - 5, 4} HEIDI ZE STRAZISTSKYCH LESU COR=8.71606%
	CEDARWOOD'S ZABRINA COR=53.713% { - 2}	CEDARWOODS FIRST OFFENSE NA 110 PZ I, UT 194 PZ II COR=54.8525% {2 - 4, 3}	CEDARWOODS AMADEUS COR=37.6038% {3 - 5, 4} CEDARWOODS IMAGE OF JAKE COR=42.9987%
		CEDARWOODS NORTHERN STAR COR=39.1361% { - 3}	CEDARWOODS BLAZE COR=32.0182% {4 - 6, 5, 4} CEDARWOODS CALENDAR GIRL COR=38.5735%

I, the undersigned do hereby certify that the foregoing particulars are correct to the best of my knowledge and belief

SIGNED _____ DATE _____

The third example (BreedMate Example #3) is a BreedMate example where I was considering breeding two Versatile Champions and the marketing of a litter of pups from two VC's would surely have my phone ringing off the hook. Remembering the crossover rule from linebreeding to in-breeding as defined by the late Bob Wehle as seeing the same dog's name in the 2nd, 3rd, or 4th generations showed this as an inbreeding. Cedarwoods Amadeus and Cedarwoods Image of Jake both double up in the 3rd generation; and I passed on this breeding as it would have been defined as an inbreeding. This could have potentially created some great pups but the risks of introducing future medical issues into my line wasn't worth the risk. Under each dog's name lists where and how many times the dog is on the pedigree helping to make it easy to identify how many different times a dog appears on this ten generation pedigree.

Having a small gene pool as is the case with most of the versatile breeds helps, as one can accomplish data entry of all dogs within the breed into the BreedMate software, whereas with Labs this would be nearly impossible as there are just too many dogs in that breed to get them all entered into the database. A concerned Lab breeder could, however, do a five generation calculation as he would have only 60 entries to do where a ten generation pedigree has 2,046 dogs in its calculation to be added to the database. There would probably be fewer entries, however as many dogs on this five or ten generation pedigree would be present multiple times depending on the unique number or total number of different dogs being represented.

Pedigree of: *CEDARWOODS ORPHAN ANNIE BY MAN O WAR*

Date of Birth: Sex: Breed: 24.7028%
Colour & Markings: Reg No:
COI (10 Gen): 24.7028%

PARENTS	GRANDPARENTS	GREAT GRANDPARENTS	GREAT GREAT GRANDPARENTS
SIRE: VC CEDARWOODS MAN O WAR NA 112 PZ 1, UT 201 PZ 1 COR=70.2307% {1 - }	CEDARWOODS QUINCY DAN NA 112 PZ I, UT 177 PZ III COR=54.6802% {2 - }	CEDARWOODS BLAZE NA 112 PZ I, UT 188 PZ II COR=47.6733% {3. 4 - 4, 4}	BIRCHWOOD'S FAVONIUS COR=39.1374% {4, 4, 5 - 4, 5, 5} HAVERHILLS AXCELL COR=32.1135% {4, 5 - 5, 5}
		CEDARWOODS CALENDAR GIRL NA 112 PZ I, UT 189 PZ II COR=46.3506%	ATOM V SHULKEY COR=27.6804% {5, 4, 5, 6, 5 - 5, 6, 5, 6, 5} HAVERHILLS ALEETA COR=37.3334% {4, 4, 5 - 4, 5, 5}
	CEDARWOODS ZINFINDEL NA 110 PZ 1, UT 192 PZ I COR=57.8179% {2 - }	CEDARWOODS AMADEUS NA 112 PZ I, UT 190 PZ I COR=47.5276% {3 - 3}	BIRCHWOOD'S FAVONIUS COR=39.1374% {4, 4, 5 - 4, 5, 5} HAVERHILLS ALEETA COR=37.3334% {4, 4, 5 - 4, 5, 5}
		CEDARWOODS IMAGE OF JAKE NA 112 PZ I, UT 201 PZ I COR=54.6802% {3 - 3}	CEDARWOODS BLAZE COR=47.6733% {3. 4 - 4, 4} CEDARWOODS CALENDAR GIRL COR=46.3506%
DAM: VC CEDARWOODS ORPHAN ANNIE COR=68.5567% { - 1}	CEDARWOODS FIRST OFFENSE NA 110 PZ I, UT 194 PZ II COR=57.8179% { - 2}	CEDARWOODS AMADEUS NA 112 PZ I, UT 190 PZ I COR=47.5276% {3 - 3}	BIRCHWOOD'S FAVONIUS COR=39.1374% {4, 4, 5 - 4, 5, 5} HAVERHILLS ALEETA COR=37.3334% {4, 4, 5 - 4, 5, 5}
		CEDARWOODS IMAGE OF JAKE NA 112 PZ I, UT 201 PZ I COR=54.6802% {3 - 3}	CEDARWOODS BLAZE COR=47.6733% {3. 4 - 4, 4} CEDARWOODS CALENDAR GIRL COR=46.3506%
	KILLBUCKS FLORA COR=42.8454% { - 2}	ADI VOM MARIATHERESIA SCHLOSSL NA 100 PZ II COR=11.7821%	LOBO V GEWEBERWALD COR=6.78946% { - 4} FRANKA V D HORST COR=5.59683% { - 4}
		CEDARWOODS NEW ANGEL COR=49.7113% { - 3}	CEDARWOODS BLAZE COR=47.6733% {3. 4 - 4, 4} CEDARWOODS CALENDAR GIRL COR=46.3506%

I, the undersigned do hereby certify that the breeding particulars are correct to the best of my knowledge and belief

SIGNED _____ DATE _____

ENDPOINT EVALUATION

Along with BreedMate for my proposed breeding evaluations, I also use what is called Endpoint evaluating. Here I give an Endpoint to every dog on a three-generation pedigree for all my females and all my males. An Endpoint is an unfavorable trait or quality that you don't want to pass along to the litter. Examples would be soft coat, hardmouth, sensitive, independent, unsettled, skirts cover, avoids ice water, no furnishings, etc. Again, these are the qualities you don't want to see show up in any of the pups being passed on from their parents, grandparents, or great grandparents. Basically, you are trying to eliminate the recessive alleles that you don't want to see show up in a pup.

You cannot completely remove these undesirables, but you can certainly lessen the odds of them rearing their ugly face. It takes a gene from the sire's side and another from the dam's side of a pedigree to make an undesirable chromosome in most instances, so by pairing dogs for a breeding when an Endpoint on the sire's side is not present on the dam's side helps lessens the odds of passing a trait on that you wish to eliminate. You are always rolling the dice but a conscious effort certainly helps place the odds in your favor.

Endpoint requires two honest examinations: 1) You have to personally know each of the 14 dogs on a three generation proposed pedigree individually. 2) You have to be very subjective and honest about the individual dog's Endpoints for each of the pedigrees (both male and female). Again, the basis of Endpoint is that when you place the pedigree of the male and female's pedigrees on the table side-by-side, the identical Endpoint that may show on the male's pedigree will not show up on the female's pedigree. In other words, hardmouth or any other unfavorable trait cannot be present on both the sire and dams pedigree. Basically, we are trying to avoid passing on unfavorable traits and this has nothing to do with creating hunting prowess. Our hunt test testing is where we look for the hunting prowess.

Every dog has an Endpoint if you are being honest about your projected breedings. Tukr's Endpoint was "too sensitive" and I avoided breeding him to any female that had a dog with that endpoint in the first three generations of her pedigree. I looked for alpha females to breed him to and we often "hit it out of the park" when the nick was right. Everyone eventually gets to own that special dog that steals a part of their heart when passing and Tukr was that dog for me. He almost lived to see 15 and knowing what I had when he was four years old, I had him collected and his semen frozen. Now after his passing he is still producing and passing his genetics to very selective breedings. I have often wondered if the mistake was not freezing his father's semen as the best odds in recreating another Tukr would be more likely from breeding his father again to his mother than Tukr himself to another female. This is the presupposed "witchcraft" postulating that breeders eventually come to if you play within this breeding game long enough. When often asked, "Was Tukr the best I had ever owned?" My reply was always, "I have two children and neither were the best child I ever had; I love them both the same." And with my dogs, those that were allowed to live their entire lives in my home, each were valued as "my best!"

ENDPOINT EVALUATION FOR PROPOSED BREEDING

PARENTS	GRANDPARENT	GREAT-GRANDPARENTS
CEDARWOODS RERUN **ENDPOINT:** INDEPENDENT SEARCH	**CEDARWOODS EZ TOP** **ENDPOINT:** LACKS POINTING	**CEDARWOODS QUINCY DAN** **ENDPOINT:** LACKS WATER SEARCH
		CEDARWOODS ZINFINDEL **ENDPOINT:** TOO CLOSE FIELD SEARCH
	CEDARWOODS PINUP PLAYMATE **ENDPOINT:** ALOPECIA	**CEDARWOODS PRINCE FROM ZOEY** **ENDPOINT:** SHORT LEGGED
		DREAMWORKS HUSSY **ENDPOINT:** SOFT COAT
CEDARWOODS TOP ILLUSION **ENDPOINT:** LACKS COOPEERATION	**HIDDEN ACRES ATLAS** **ENDPOINT:** EXTREME AFFACTION	**BLACKHAWKS AUGUSTUS MCCRAY** **ENDPOINT:** BLACK COLOR
		OXBOWS BAILEY OF HIDDEN ACRES **ENDPOINT:** TOO SMALL
	CEDARWOODS BASIC INSTINCT **ENDPOINT:** UNSETTLED IN THE HOUSE	**CEDARWOODS FIRST OFFENSE** **ENDPOINT:** SHORT COAT
		CZECHMATES BOISE BROWN **ENDPOINT:** HARD MOUTH

SELECTING A STUD DOG

When someone owns a quality female from one of the versatile breeds, there often comes a time when raising a litter of pups comes into play. Sometimes the purpose is to personally acquire another hunting companion and selecting that new pup from your own dog has an added special meaning. Another purpose is the feeling that your dog's strengths and abilities would find value for the breed's gene pool and offer the same satisfaction to others that you have experienced in your dog. Unfortunately, a third purpose is often formulated from the monetary value you expect from a litter of pups, or raising a litter for the kids to experience has been the motivation where this approach has more negative results in the end than positive.

Whatever the purpose is, a stud dog needs to be found in most cases to proceed. Using BreedMate software and Endpoint determinations isn't always available to versatile breeders; especially not to the individual raising their first litter of pups. This is where the "witchcraft" of dog breeding comes into play for most novice enthusiasts wanting to breed their dog. There are some very proven breeding programs in North America representing the versatile breeds where the success has most likely been from a degree of experimentation in the beginning years with sound results seen from dogs with tremendous qualities and these are the dogs seen in the background of so many of today's pedigrees. Today's German Shorthairs with Shooting Starr, Sharp Shooter, Burkhart, Merrymeeting, Ducorbeau, Indian Brook, or Chippewa Kennel names on their pedigrees (and this just mentions a few) are from sound breeding expectations and from breeders primarily using hunt test testing results when formulating a proposed breeding. But before hunt test testing was available, one had to use what I term "witchcraft expectations" for evaluating dams and sires and most was more experimental in some fashion and based on personal biases. This is why the GSP breed of today is so much more advanced and more versatile than the dogs that were originally brought across the big pond in the 1960s from Germany. Much more information is available for today's evaluator to use effectively and leaving much of this "witchcraft" out of the formula.

I've enjoyed seeing some of the best versatile dogs of North America while judging hunt tests during a 20-plus year carrier as a judge. Judging in Nova Scotia and Quebec was a real eye opener for me as my expectations

Four puppies backing their mother, demonstrating the pointing and instinctive backing indeces we want to see passed on to an entire litter. Photo courtesy Calvin Harpe.

were not nearly as high as the quality of the dogs I witnessed there. The Ducorbeau GSP's in Quebec had the same top instinctive qualities of the Sharp Shooter dogs in Wisconsin I'd previously seen. Also, the Griffons from the Duchasseur Kennel in Quebec were even par with the Montana Griffs from Montana's Swift Creek Kennel. This experience has made me well aware of the testing commitment that has consumed so many breeders that were breeding versatile dogs. I've enjoyed watching many versatile kennels build impressive pedigrees over 25 years of judging and some true sincerity expressed for producing top versatile hunting companions.

My own personal breeding experiences are only with Pudelpointers. I've bred Pudelpointers and followed this breed now for more than 25 years and developed a special passion for this breed and a continued creation of sound performers. Thus, usually the same passion exists in most all breeding versatile dogs using hunt test results as a prime evaluator. The beginning years had many bumps for me as a breeder to maneuver over and I stumbled more times than I'd like to admit. Persistence and stubbornness eventually prevailed and I now breed and hunt with dogs far superior to my earlier expectations. This is the same evaluation I hear from many others breeding another breeds of versatile hunting dog. Most breeders eventually refine their personal dog inventory to a group of performers far superior to what they started with. I enjoy the conversations with breeders representing a different versatile breed than what I chose, as the crusade and path they took always seems to coincide with my own path.

While reminiscing the sound breedings by male Pudelpointers over the past 25 years, I am reminded of several male Pudelpointers that I feel have absolutely founded the current performance level of my Cedarwood dogs. These two males were Cedarwoods Amadeus and Cedarwoods Blaze. Both dogs were sired by Birchwoods Favonius, and each had a Haverhills mother, which was sired by Birchwoods Duncan. Both Duncan and Favonius were dogs a true versatile enthusiast would dream of owning. Both retrieved waterfowl from ice water in January and both had undeniable prey drive on upland hunts. In 1990, Bodo Winterhelt told me, "these are the finest two male Pudelpointers in existence today (Duncan & Favonius)." Having the pleasure of seeing them both perform in the testing arena and also on hunting excursions, I acquired a sense for the standard and expectations for this breed's male stud dogs.

VC, Intl Ch. Enzo Vom Ludwigstein, Mit. Photo courtesy Tom Swezey.

Let me describe each of these two males individually, and why I feel each contributed specifically in improving and advancing Pudelpointers as we see them today. First, Cedarwoods Amadeus; a 65-pound male having the hunting intelligence usually only seen in imported dogs, but also having that sincere prey drive asked for by the American sportsmen. Amadeus proved his value as a star performer when he earned both a NAVHDA Prize 1 in Natural Ability and also Utility in the same year while still of natural ability age. I competed in four NSTRA field trials with Amadeus and he placed in three of the four, taking a very convincing first place win with a seven-bird find in this run while braced with the previous year's NSTRA National Champion, Tricky Dickey. His most prominent seed can be seen today in Cedarwoods First Offense (aka Tukr), a past stud dog for many breeders and whose pups have raised the bar of excellence in NAVHDA testing. First Offense, like his father Amadeus, is a NSTRA field trial first place winner that was an explosive dog, both at the water and in the field, but also a perfect gentleman in the home where he resided his entire life.

The other male, Cedarwoods Blaze, was a stunning dog with that masculine phenotype every dog enthusiast would admire. He had the nose and pointing instinct seen in our English Pointers of today, but also all the retrieving and water skills expected of a top versatile gundog. Blaze has left his name on many of my Cedarwood pedigrees as five of Blaze's daughters, all hunt-test utility-prized, have added their names throughout my pedigrees observed today.

Both Amadeus and Blaze gave the Pudelpointer breed the desire level not accessible in the European imports. Until these two dogs, no one considered a Pudelpointer as competitors in NSTRA field trial competition. Not until Amadeus, had a Pudelpointer ever placed in NSTRA competition.

The North American sportsman expects to see much more ground coverage from their versatile dogs than that offered from dogs imported from Europe. This is the genetic imprinting that as breeders we should ask to see from our stud dogs, regardless of the chosen breed. Being able to produce pups that became equal to or superior to themselves is what I call "breeding up" and should always be the goal of all breeders.

From the statement, "this is the genetic imprinting we should ask to see from our stud dogs; being able to produce pups equal to or superior to themselves," comes the theme of this discussion. And the question always is, "Why is it so important that a breed's stud dogs need a higher standard of excellence than the female breeding dogs?" The answer is quite simple in its facilitated form. How else can we measure if a male is stamping the attributes of our expectations into his litters? We need a measuring bar and it can only be an expression of the stud dog's accomplishments so we can reflect a comparison to his "get" (sons) and their accomplishments need to be at least equal to or better than the sire's. A stud dog can be used for breeding from age two until age ten.

During those eight years he can produce five to ten litters per year or more. There is a possibility that this dog may sire 40 to 80 litters of pups in his lifetime if heavily used, or as many as 600 pups. If a male produced a hypothetical number of pups such as this and wasn't tested in utility, proving his values as a dog with enough "bottom" in him to take the rigorous demands of utility training, and didn't possess the necessary prey drive to earn a qualifying score in any of the hunt test's duck searches, he could possibly influence the performance level of a complete line of dogs to a lower expected standard than what the breed was currently experiencing. Especially in a breed with a small gene pool where the entire breeds standard performance evaluation could be affected.

Clyde and Marilyn Vetter and Billy. Photo courtesy Nancy Anisfield.

A female producing one litter per year from age two until age six could possibly produce 30 pups during that five-year breeding period which is a much smaller influencing number than that of a male. Sometimes to completely finish a female through utility testing sees the dog four years old before her first litter of pups and possibly five. A female five years old having her first litter usually struggles more to get pregnant and to have a decent size litter, whereas at two years old her ovulation produces more eggs to be fertilized and her uterus accepts these fertilized eggs much easier. It isn't that much different in humans as a woman that has never had children before she is 40 finds this task more difficult than if she were 20 or 30.

Don't be mistaken, however, I'm not suggesting female versatile dogs not be utility tested. I'm merely stating that the math doesn't always support every female earn a utility prize before being bred. Also the math clearly supports utility testing all males as their ability to influence an entire breed over an eight-year, very active breeding campaign, has little or no place for the average or below average male performers.

Let me give you something to consider when analyzing dogs, dog breeds, or dog breeders: First, when it comes to choosing a breed, pick from your heart, when choosing a breeding, look at the parents, grandparents and great grandparents' hunt test natural ability accomplishments. But when choosing a breeder, look at the hunt test utility scores of his breeding stock, as this is a direct reflection of the breeder's intentions. As previously discussed, we need to compare a stud dog's field abilities to his father's, and make sure the dog has equal to or better qualities than his father and grandfather, making sure the genetic line is not diminishing or breeding down. It isn't always possible to see a son, father, and grandfather line breed up, but if the bar of excellence is lowering, it will begin affecting the entire line.

Donate Thibault's VC Ducorbeau Hyros. Photo courtesy Donate Thibault.

Just as important is the need to qualify breeders themselves. It is the hunt test's performance or utility score that reflects the intentions of the individual breeders themselves. Any breeder readily willing to hang their hat solely on natural ability scores alone and unwilling to perform the work required to earn a utility prize for their breeding stock and personal hunting companions is breeding possibly more for monetary gains than for the pride of their kennel and dogs. There is definitely a lack of passion toward producing excellent hunting dogs when the primary goal points to the economics. In short, it is the hunt test scores that gives credence and displays the integrity of our breeders. We can go one step further and evaluate those that work toward and accomplish NAVHDA's coveted Versatile Champion title on their dogs. This in my humble opinion represents those willing to go that extra distance to own and hunt behind the absolute best. I truly admire some of the GSP pedigrees with three or four generations of only VC accomplished dogs representing this lineage.

When taking a further look at the male breeding incentives, it is easily understood why males can achieve higher standards, as their breeding window is much lengthier than their female counterpart, as previously discussed. Most females can only support an active breeding program from age two through six, whereas a male has three or four more years of active breeding available. An important consideration, however, is that if a female should only produce one litter per year, whereas a male may sire 20 or more litters per year. It is frequently claimed that breeding dogs on every heat or "back-to-back breeding" is bad for a bitch's long term health and well being.

However, the research in canine reproduction shows that breeding a dog each time it comes into heat can in fact be beneficial for its health. Scientists have shown that pseudo pregnancy (false pregnancy that can follow a heat cycle even when not bred) increases the risk of mammary cancers which are the second most common cancer in dogs after skin tumors. Personally, I could only breed a female once per year as the fall and winter months should be reserved for hunting and not tying up our hunting companions with a litter of pups.

Simple math tells me that a sire can show up five times more on a pedigrees than a female. Having that utility prize says that

Int Ch VC Sharp Shooters Man in Black MH (aka Cash). Photo courtesy Clyde Vetter.

this stud dog has the mental stability to take and receive the training required to pass this test and warranted of producing the kind of numbers just mentioned. There, also, is more ample time to let our males mature and then seek their utility title prior to breedings, as they do not experience the age limitations experienced by females.

As with so many animals, it is usually the males from most species that are "showcased" when setting an evaluation standard, especially when examined following competition. It is the Triple Crown in thoroughbred horse racing (Kentucky Derby, Belmont, and Preakness) that showcases these top horses each spring. Likewise, most AKC field trials whether for pointing breeds, flushers, or retrievers also display mostly only male performers as their most accomplished. There seems to be higher expectations for most all male breeding animals, so why would our versatile dogs be any different? All prominent breeders must have qualified breeding stock, as it requires titled dogs to earn respect from their peers. Any breeder/kennel not owning titled breeding stock is and always will receive tunnel vision of that of a puppy-mill. As we study or evaluate the successes for any breed of sporting dogs, it is the "showcasing" of their top titled dogs that separates the successful breeders from the mediocre players. It is no different with the versatile breeders and this is why the hunt test's performance or utility title plays such an important role in their breeding stock and kennel reputations.

At a much higher level of "showcasing" come the AKC Master Hunters, the NSTRA Champions, Hunting Retriever Champions, and the NAVHDA Invitation performers, especially those earning the coveted VC honors. These titles show the intent of a breeder and the pride held at their kennels. Many of the other less popular versatile breeds struggle constantly for favorable press supporting their breed and it is from this lack of commitment from their breeders willing to breed only dogs capable of achieving such credentials that hold back these breeds from complimentary expression. Most breeds of sporting dogs are no better than their breeder's expectations.

With further examination, versatile stud dogs should not be restricted to North American linebred superstars only. The Imports from Europe, even though not always possessing our level of desire, have a distinct place in our dogs formulated breeding program also. It is a must that these dogs have testing either in Europe or North America, however, supporting their ability to perform. Merely importing a dog and then breeding these animals just because they have been acquired from Europe should never be for breeding purposes as this is quite possibly the shallowest approach possible when attempting to advance a breed's prowess. Many imports don't possess the level of desire in their field search or water work as expected here in North America, but other accomplishments and indices such as tracking need to be recognized by those interested in their genetics; because usually the cranial expression of these dogs can offer an outcross breeding which finds the best from both the dam and sire in the litter.

Imports bred to North American versatile breeds give a very strong "nick" to a sound breeding program. A utility title or equivalent from Europe is necessary for breeding any import, male or female, as the desire necessary to earn this prize from the duck search shows the desire level necessary for sound breeding purposes. The import usually offers more solid nerves in the form of temperament than their North American counterpart whereas the North American bred dogs usually demonstrate stronger desire during water work and more intense pointing.

A concern that always requires some thought when selecting a stud dog is what is termed "the popular sire syndrome." What most don't realize is that breeding an individual male too many times during his lifetime has an adverse effect on that breed's gene pool and begins to decrease the genetic diversity. When there is an overuse of a single dog, after a time this dog's genetics tend to cause a drift in that dog's genetics influence. Since all genes come in pairs, one from the sire and one from the dam, the influence one sire may have on his breed over the years may end up as a negative effect.

Since a dog can have a maximum of two different genes in this pair there can end up being different genes that become potentially available making up this pair. Breed diversity is expanded when several genes are available for each pair. This gene pair is homozygous and doesn't have detrimental recessive genes so there is no negative impact on the breed. This is why all of the characteristics or indices that make a breed reproduce true to that breed standard are based on homozygous gene pairs having little variation.

USING HUNT TEST SCORES

After monitoring and evaluating the results of my kennel's hunt test scores over a 30-year period, I have come to the conclusion that the Aptitude or Natural Ability test offers the most beneficial data for a serious breeder. Now add the duck search score from the Utility Test, and you can formulate some valuable expectations. There is most likely quite a bit of conjecture involved when speculating progeny from mere field and water test scores, but history and past calculations seem to support this speculation.

What I like in natural ability testing is that we are merely judging the dog and its inherent genetic abilities as a hunting companion. The absolute key when looking at natural ability scores to forecast a breeding requires four generations of testing on both the sire and also the dam to claim validity. Here we are looking at 30 dogs on the sire's side and 30 dogs on the dam's. If all 60 of these dogs had a natural ability score of 105 points or more, it would be hard to find unfavorable pups from this proposed breeding. Here is where testing an entire litter of pups helps verify breedings where

both parents of the litter had a pedigree with four generations with all dogs on the pedigree having been tested and had earned greater than 105 points in their natural ability test. Breeders that have consistently tested their breeding stock for generations and created a standard score as a requirement needed prior to any and all breedings will always reap the benefits of a procedure such as this.

Some would disagree with this analogy, feeling that the NAVHDA Versatile Champions (VC) or AKC's Master Hunters or Field Champions are the ones that produce our best future candidates. I cannot disagree, but not all breeders can attend NAVHDA's Invitational as the annual test is merely too far to travel and the expense not within the budget. Creating a pedigree where 60 dogs represented would have a VC title would be extremely impressive, but again probably wouldn't fall within one's budget.

Past NAVHDA President Vic Connors.

Close examination would also probably show that all in the

Cedarwoods Pin Up Playmate (aka Hemi). NAVHDA NA Prize I at four months and UT Prize I at 26 months demonstrating the versatile dog breeds are becoming more refined.

background of these VC's and Utility performers to have top natural ability scores prior earning a VC or Utility title. It takes a huge amount of obedience to earn that Versatile Championship and a vast amount of training to succeed. Only dogs that are extremely trainable and also have a deep bottom in their training constitution can succeed. Training a dog for the Invitational is truly where the real rubber meets the road. There are continuous obedience expectations throughout the test and only dogs with great mental stability can maintain the purpose of the hunt while maintaining the needed field and water intensity in order to pass. All participants have each other's backs throughout the day of testing and applaud others performances. The participant companionship is quite the opposite of the field trial arena where competition pits all against each other.

Still others would only look at Utility scores when forecasting proposed litters of excellence. When one looks at a breeding that has parents and grandparents all owning a Utility title, I would have to admit that this is a much more impressive pedigree on paper than one sporting only Natural Ability scores. Every breeder ends up finding favor in a testing arena or even field trials as there are many venues offered for today's breeder. NAVHDA, AKC, NSTRA, and FDSB offer many avenues to take when on this course.

On a personal note, I have always felt the Invitational showcases trainers and the menu helps separate the casual trainer from the dedicated trainers wanting that special dog in the field and home to hunt with and live with. I only judged one Invitational during my judging days and what I witnessed over those five days were some tremendously focused trainers whose dedication was the common denominator to their success. It takes years to reach the level a trainer must become to earn a Versatile Champion title on their dog. Also, requiring only Utility Prize I performers to qualify sets the stage for the year's best versatile performers to earn participation. Many of the participants spend the summer training together in a group with others in their area that own a qualified dog, creating a person bond that carries on for years to come.

As an example of a successful breeding program using hunt test testing scores and BreedMate examples as their evaluating yardstick, one can review what the Alliance of Pudelpointer breeders in North America have accomplished over the past 15 years. NAPPA (North American Pudelpointer Alliance) has more than 30 breeders in North America that adhere to one simple standard for every breeder. Only female Pudelpointers earning 105 Natural Ability points or greater and only male Pudelpointers that have earned a Utility Prize are accepted for breeding.

After 15 years using this simple standard and the average Natural Ability score for more than 300 NAPPA bred pups tested is 107 points. When I began testing Pudelpointers in 1988, the average for the breed was 96 points demonstrating the success one can find from basically following that time-honored and proven axiom among animal breeders, "Breed the Best to the Best." Only here, a breeding standard has been the guardian to ensure honesty and forthright-ness. There are many kennels in North America producing pups from one of the other versatile breeds that have the same favorable results by using a similar testing standard of their own. Since I am most familiar with Pudelpointers, it is this breed that I continue to reference strictly from familiarity.

It wasn't until men like Bob Wehle of Elhew Kennel began not only titling their stud dogs, but also titling their dams prior to their breedings, that the consideration of the values needed from both sides of a breeding were accepted. Elhew Kennel began insisting that most all females bred at their English Pointer facilities needed a Championship title. "The Making of Snakefoot" written by Bob Wehle is an excellent read for anyone wanting more breeding foresight and also some of the pavement that has led to today's breeding practices of versatile dogs. Most everything we learn in life comes from the various roads we travel and those that we meet on our journey. Nearly everything I know and practice today regarding dog breeding has come from others along the path I have been on for the past 45 years.

READING A PEDIGREE

Being capable of evaluating pedigrees when seeking that new hunting companion is a science all in its own. We have all heard someone in a bragging sort of way state that their dog has a pedigree a mile long. This is true of any registered dog as basically the statement is founded only that there is a family tree supporting the ancestry of the dog. Being capable of assessing field accomplishments that are also represented on a dog's pedigree is the evaluation process that one should have concerns of when looking to make the best possible choice to acquire that new hunting prospect. There are many field accomplishments available to breeders to support the quality of

ARES vom Donaulenzenhof

PP 12517, DGStB 46856
dürrlaubfarben, sg/sg, HD 1, Stockmaß 63 cm
gew.: 24.04.1996

VJP: 52 und 70 Punkte
HZP: 180 Punkte
VGP: 318 Punkte, I. Preis, Tagfährte
Leistungsnachweise: HN sil

Bes. Volker Petruschke, Tel. 0 81 22 - 1 01 25
Roßmayrgasse 8, 85435 Erding

Eltern	Großeltern	Urgroßeltern	Ururgroßeltern	
	Aron vom Silberhagen	Don von der Rasselbande	PPS Basko v. Reinebg. Ld.	PP 7790
	PP 10764, DGStB 35082	PP 9602, DGStB 28564	PPS Dunja v. Centralhof	PP 7919
Timo von Tribergen	VJP HZP VGP			
	HN spl	PPS Imme vom Wittenmoor	Basko v. Pfeifersberg	PP 8623
PP 11463, DGStB 39803	HD 1	PP 10035, DGStB 30895	Amsel v. Schnettengrund	PP 9302
VJP HZP VGP Sw III Btr				
HN sil	Sally von Tribergen	Gido vom Burbrink	Hasso z Heylova laje	Cslp 411
braun sg/sg	PP 10683, DGStB 35041	PP 8597	Cilla vom Burbrink	PP 7266
HD 0	VJP HZP VGP			
	HN sil	Nanni von Tribergen	Bodo v. Reineberger Land	PP 7791
	HD 0	PP 9404	Jutta von Tribergen	PP 8766
	Cliff vom Neuhaus	PPS Kardinal v. Eulenberg	Castor vom Stevertal	PP 8413
	PP 10256, DGStB 31473	PP 9449, DGStB 28566	PPS Cora vom Eliefeld	PP 8668
Meggy von der Rhön	VJP HZP VGP			
	HN spl	Bärbel vom Neuhaus	Alf vom Haarforst	PP 7863
PP 11878, DGStB 44049	HD 0	PP 9870, DGStB 30572	Yvonne von der Wülzburg	PP 8940
VJP HZP VGP				
HN spl/sil	Hexe von der Rhön	Jago vom Wittenmoor	Don von der Rasselbande	PP 9602
braun sg/gen	PP 10891, DGStB 36247	PP 10262, DGStB 32262	Amsel v. Schnettengrund	PP 9302
HD 0	VJP HZP VGP			
	HN sil	Birke von der Rhön	Basko vom Pfeiffersberg	PP 8623
	HD 1	PP 9900, DGStB 29839	Nelli von Tribergen	PP 9406

NORTH AMERICAN VERSATILE HUNTING DOG ASSOCIATION – NAVHDA

PARENTS	GRANDPARENTS	GREAT GRANDPARENTS
		ATOM V SHULKEY
	BIRCHWOOD'S FAVONIUS	PSB 0475 NA 110 I UT 202 I
		BROWN-RW
	PP 0174	HD OFA DYSPLASTIC-LITE
CEDARWOODS AMADEUS		
	UT 188 II	BIRCHWOOD'S CASSIE
PP 0197	DARK BROWN-WR	PSB 0428 NA 96 EVAL UT 193 I
SIRE		LIVER-SW
NA 112 I UT 190 I	HD OFA PP-52G24M	HD OFA PP-139
DARK BROWN		BIRCHWOOD'S DUNCAN
	HAVERHILL'S ALEETA	PSB 0462 NA 110 I UT 202 I
HD OFA PP-96G25M EL2		DARK BROWN-WW
	PP 0177	HD OFA PP-24F24M
BREEDER:		
ROBERT FARRIS	UPT 154 III UT 178 II	WINTERHELLE'S GILLEY
	LIVER-WS	PSB 0522 NA 110 I UT 187 I
BOISE ID		BROWN-WW
	HD OFA PP-65G30F	HD OFA PP-28E35F
		BIRCHWOOD'S FAVONIUS
	CEDARWOODS BLAZE	PP 0174 UT 188 II
		DARK BROWN-WR
	PP 0209	HD OFA PP-52G24M
CEDARWOODS IMAGE OF JAKE		
	NA 112 I UT 182 II	HAVERHILL'S AXCELL
PP 0409	BROWN/WS DENSE	PP 0176 UT 179 III
DAM		BLONDE-8S
NA 112 I UT 201 I	HD OFA PP-109F34M	HD OFA PP-64G30F
BROWN		ADONIS V SHULKEY
	CEDARWOODS CALENDAR GIRL	10503 NA 108 I
HD PENNHIP RT.33 LT.38 14M		BROWN-RW
	PP 0271	HD OFA PP-80G107M
BREEDER:		
ROBERT FARRIS	NA 112 I UT 189 II	HAVERHILL'S ALEETA
	BROWN	PP 0177 UT 178 II
BOISE ID		LIVER-WS
	HD OFA PP-113E25F	HD OFA PP-65G30F

their breeding stock from field trials to field tests. The available NAVHDA test for the versatile dog community is the most widespread across North America and possibly the most user friendly for those wishing to evaluate a breeder's breeding stock or a breeding that they have done. AKC hunt tests also have the same favorable available information.

When monitoring and evaluating hunt test testing results, the natural ability test offers the most beneficial data for a serious breeder. Now if one adds the duck search score from any of the hunt tests performance or utility test you can formulate some valuable expectations. The duck search offers the best evaluation of a versatile dogs hunting desire or prey drive. Here the dog is primarily on its own searching a body of water or marsh of an acre or more for a released wing clipped duck.

The search is expected to last ten minutes without any commands or assistance from the handler. All of the natural ability results and the utility duck search results come primarily from instincts within the individual dogs and these instincts were passed on from the parents, grandparents, and great grandparents. There is most likely quite a bit of conjecture involved when speculating progeny from mere field and water test scores, but history and past calculations seem to support this postulation. Looking at the entire hunt test performance or utility score on a dog helps give the entire picture as the judged obedience in the field for steadiness and retrieving shot birds to hand along with obedience at the water and drag allows one to make sure the dog has enough "bottom" in their character to accept this strict obedience and still maintain the necessary level of desire to earn satisfactory results and a passing score.

In natural ability testing, the judges are merely judging the dog and its inherent genetic abilities as a hunting companion. The absolute key when looking at natural ability scores to forecast a proposed breeding requires four generations of testing on both the sire and also the dam's side of the pedigree to claim validity. You are looking at 30 dogs on the sire's side and 30 dogs on the dam's. If all 60 of these dogs had a natural ability score of 105 points or more, it would be hard to find unfavorable pups from this proposed breeding. Here is where testing an entire litter of pups helps verify breedings and where both parents of the litter had a pedigree with four generations and all dogs on the pedigree having been tested and had earned >105 points in their natural ability test. Breeders that have consistently tested their breeding stock for generations and created a standard score as a requirement needed prior to any and all breedings will always reap the benefits of a procedure such as this.

There is always what is called the "drag of the breed" which has a negative effect on purebred dogs. As generations of breeding within a breed there is a mathematical tendency for the progeny to slowly return to its origin or foundation as far as performance is concerned. This is why using test scores helps avoid this tendency. Simple math would tell us that if all 60 dogs on a proposed breeding had an average of 108 points in NAVHDA natural ability testing the average score expected of this litter of pups tested would possibly average 106. Now consider a proposed litter where the average of the 60 dogs on the pedigree was 95 points. The expectations due to the drag of the breed syndrome might be 90 points.

There will be dogs in both of these examples that will score higher than the average of the 60 dogs on the pedigree and these are the dogs that should be used to further that line to help avoid the drag of the breed. Eventually the scores may get to a peak where there is no room for improvement and averages cannot be improved or raised. If one considers the statistical bell shaped curve where the Standard Deviation (SD) is the measurement of the spread of the numbers in a set of data from its mean or average value, you can begin to see the variance that is seen in all litters of hunting dogs. This is said to be a measure of variability in the given set of data. This bell shaped curve is a symmetrical curve representing the normal distribution of the dogs from a line or even just a litter.

The term bell curve is used to describe the mathematical concept called normal distribution, sometimes referred to as Gaussian distribution. "Bell curve" refers to the shape that is created when a line is plotted using the data points for an item that meets the criteria of "normal distribution." The center contains the greatest number of a value and therefore would be the highest point on the arc of the line. This point is referred to as the mean, but in simple terms it is the highest number of occurrences of an element (statistical terms, the mode). The important things to note about a normal distribution is the curve is concentrated in the center and decreases on either side. This is significant in that the data has less of a tendency to produce unusually extreme values, called outliers, as compared to other distributions. Also the bell curve signifies that the data is symmetrical and thus we can create reasonable expectations as to the possibility that an outcome will lie within a range to the left or right of the center, once we can measure the amount of deviation contained in the data. These

German Shorthair decor. Photo courtesy Patti Carter.

are measured in terms of standard deviations. A bell curve graph depends on two factors, the mean and the standard deviation. The mean identifies the position of the center and the standard deviation determines the height and width of the bell. For example, a large standard deviation creates a bell that is short and wide while a small standard deviation creates a tall and narrow curve.

One standard deviation on each side of the mean (or average) will statistically represent 68 percent of the population; and two standard deviations will statistically represent 95 percent of the population; where three standard deviations will statistically represent 99.7 percent. This is often referred to as the "empirical rule" or the 68-95-99.7 rule. In the case of following versatile dog breeding successes, one would be very satisfied to see a mean natural ability score for a breeder of 108 points with a SD of 1 point. That would mean that 95 percent of this breeder's progeny had scored between 106 and 110 points following testing. If the breeder had a mean average of 90 points and had a SD of 10 points, 95 percent of the progeny would have scored between 70 and 110 points. To even begin to consider evaluations using mean and SD calculations for assessing breeders or kennel's successes one must have a minimum of 20 entries for any validity and 100 entries would be preferred.

The internet has many different examples for calculating the mean and SD that can be easily followed for performing these calculations. Several of the testing organizations allow for an open search of test results so obtaining information is readily available.

It goes back to that old saying in dog breeding: "Breed the best to the best." This is what hunt test results can help a breeder establish and also an individual seeking their new hunting companion with confidence from their chosen breeder. With some breeders merely having a dog pass a hunt test's puppy test is enough credibility to breed their dog with no consideration of the entire pedigree. It takes years to create a pedigree that can predict favorable results and if two dogs are mated with low scores and their ancestors had not been tested or also had unfavorable scores, the progeny expectations cannot be favorable.

There are many factors to consider in this evaluation process, however, when using hunt test testing results. Such as the experience of the individual that prepared the dogs for testing, quality of birds at the test, and how favorable the testing grounds were for scenting. These are just a few of the unknowns that will not be displayed on the pedigree or in test results. Also if a dog has been trained in a manner to mask unfavorable indices to avoid having them show up on a test result. An example would be to force-retrieve a dog to insure a maximum water score in natural ability on a dog that would not enter the water on its own. Also, completely steadying a young dog with low pointing instinct to get an approved or qualifying pointing score. Overtraining dogs prior to natural ability testing defeats the purpose of this evaluation and bestows no advantage to the breeder in the long run.

Learning how breedings vary from an outbreeding where both parents are unrelated to a linebreeding where both parents have similar family lines is also helpful when evaluating pedigrees. Breeding an import from Europe to a North

American bred dog is usually an outcross breeding. In an outbreeding the DNA contribution to the litter of pups would see each parent giving approximately a 50 percent COR (Coefficient of Relationship) to the litter, the four grandparents contributing approximately 25 percent COR each and the great grandparents contributing approximately 12.5 percent COR. Linebreedings produce dogs from breedings where the pedigree shows mostly a family of dogs from the 4th through 10th generations. Here many dogs' names are seen multiple times. An individual dog's name may appear six or eight times but only from the 4th generation back on the pedigree. In a linebreeding the individual dog's COI percentages can be much higher than that of an outbreeding, depending both on how many times individual dog's names are displayed on the pedigree and if that particular dog was a linebred or outbred dog itself. This is where the experienced breeder can help a client evaluate the expectations of a proposed breeding as they should personally know the individual dogs for at least three generations and hopefully five or six generations on the pedigree.

The third recognized form of breeding would be inbreeding. An easy way to understand inbreeding is "the mating of relatives." No matter how distant on the pedigree the two relatives are, there is some form of inbreeding, but when it occurs in the 4th generation and back, the breeding is usually referred to as a linebreeding of some degree. I find no favor in inbreeding as the possibility of bringing forth medical issues in a breed can be the unexpected result of inbreeding. All genes come in pairs, one from the mother and the other from the father. If both genes are the same type the pair is termed homozygous. However, if the pair are different, the pair is termed heterozygous. Most undesirable genes such as medical issues are recessive and are not seen in the dogs that are heterozygous having only one copy. The dominant genes are dominant and are expressed in all individual dogs within the breed. I look at the four grandparents' and the eight great grandparents' names on a pedigree and do not like seeing the same dog's name listed more than once in these two columns.

I'm not that much concerned after the 3rd and 4th generation, but the first 12 dogs' names need to all be different. Duplicating names in the 3rd and 4th generation raises the probability of recessive medical alleles pairing up creating a dominant trait in a pup's genotype that will not be seen or noticed until that pup is an adult and possibly bred several times. This is how various breeds of dogs have become carriers of undesirable medical conditions such as Von Willebrand's Disease, Addison's Disease, or impaired immune function. In breeding, there's good probability of creating that Kentucky Derby winner for a breeder merely looking for performance and one standout dog, but a serious breeder should be more concerned over the entire litter than in just one dog to be showcased for competition purposes only. Once these recessive medical genetics are accelerated in a breed from inbreeding practices and become dominant genetics for that breed, or line within a breed, it is nearly impossible to remove them; so why go there in the first place?!

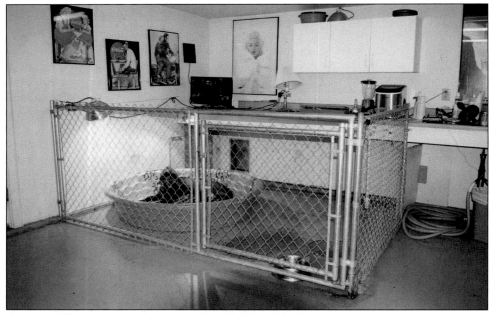

Cedarwood's separate whelping room from the kennel facilities.

Whelping and Raising Litters

As a casual thought, one usually sees nothing but joy and splendor when considering raising a litter of pups. The delight experienced by the entire family seem second only to Christmas morning. The reality can be as far from that elated Christmas morning as spending a weekend at an airport terminal while waiting for severe winter conditions to subside and once more allow air travel. If not equipped with favorable facilities and whelping knowledge, an overt wrinkle from Mother Nature can make the experience appear to be one similar to a seven-week long road trip with Linda Blair's character from The Excorcist.

The knowledge comes from years of experience and many litters whelped during those years. Having friends available that have experience at whelping pups and a veterinary clinic on-hand for consultation is a must for the beginner. The internet also has a wealth of information available but caution should always be a concern as not all information on the internet is factual. There are no checks and balances verifying validity of the information found here.

Facilities are key as improper facilities can cause and create problems never considered by the novice breeder. It is extremely necessary to be able to keep a germ-free environment for the pups and their mother to live during that eight to ten week period after birth. To maintain a germ free environment requires periodic sanitation procedures that are only available following cleansing with a light Clorox solution or a replacement of disposable bedding. The easiest procedure is when one has a designed whelping room that can be completely scrubbed down with a 5-percent Clorox solution periodically and especially between litters of different pups. Most all that plan to be scheduling litters for years to come should address their facility needs in the beginning as the payback while avoiding serious medical issues with a litter or even a single pup can be enormous. Bacterial or viral complications can consume the health of a litter of pups in a matter of several days and the outcome is always stressful to all and extremely time consuming.

We have gone to a small plastic kids swimming pools as a whelping box as they can be easily sterilized by a simple spraying of 5-percent Clorox solution, rinsed, and dried while avoiding bacterial growth. Wood whelping boxes cannot be completely sterilized as much of the pup's and mother's body fluids will eventually soak into

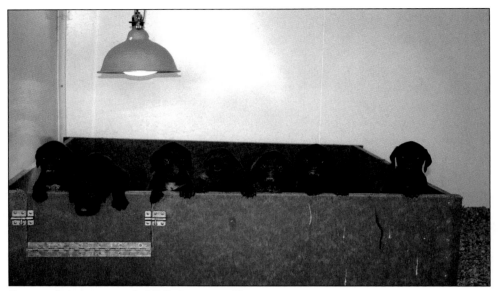

Pups ready to escape and visit their new world.

the wood making it very difficult to perform a deep cleansing. We have seen at times the need for a pig rail inside the pool and simple plastic duct material zip-tied to the inside serves this need quite well. As the pups begin to become mobile there becomes a need for thin indoor-outdoor carpet in the bottom of the pool to help give the pups traction to avoid swimmer's legs from only capable of motoring about by pulling solely with their front legs. Daily trips to an outside location such as the lawn or even in the house from two weeks old to four weeks old also helps avoid swimmer's legs and gets a good start on the socialization game. A small portable puppy pen that can be moved about in the lawn is a must as the pups become mobile.

We routinely rotate litters of six pups or more every four hours, half of the pups with the mother and the other half in the basket. Especially for the first three days to insure all pups are receiving colostrums from mom during those first few days. This also helps insure all the pups are getting their share of nutrition. They should all have nice full little tummies and should gain weight daily. Some weigh each pup daily and document weight, but as fast as they grow we can easily observe a pup that may be struggling with life outside their mother and are not gaining. When rotating it is important that the mother cannot get to the pups that are not with her as it can be disastrous if she attempts to relocate them back in with her. We keep them in a basket with a heating pad set on low with a towel between the pups and the heating pad. The 2:00am rotation seems to always fall on my watch, but considering LaFaye sits patiently to the completion of every litter whelped, I suppose this is only fair.

Once the litter is whelped, the work is nearly totally handed over to the mother until the pups are four weeks old. The first worming at two weeks old and clipping the front toenails are the only chores needed to be performed. Both these duties need repeated at four weeks. The mother will clean up after her litter and also clean the pups, but if the whelping pool begins to show the signs that she is unable to keep pace with her pups it will require a thorough cleaning to insure sanitary conditions.

LaFaye spends several hours every day before the pups eyes open sitting in the whelping pool and talking or singing to the

Whelping pool with pig rails for early puppy safety.

pups as she holds them on her lap. Since their eyes do not open until about two weeks old, the only way they can locate their mother to nurse is by smell. LaFaye maintains that by holding and cradling them before their eyes open that they learn that the smell of a human is also good just like their mother. Then once they open their eyes and visually identify a human from the human scent they are used to, they acquire an instant trust and fondness for human beings. I could never argue her logic as every pup when they hear her voice leaves whatever they are doing and darts over to her. This continues until the day each pup leaves to go to their new home. Most likely the time she spends daily playing and talking to the pups creates a major influence on this scenario and it's obvious that her voice rules with every pup at our facility. There is also a TV on in our whelping room that is on 24 hours every day. I've concluded that LaFaye is insisting that they watch Judge Judy daily in hopes they acquire a better cooperation level from her verdicts.

At four weeks old the pups and their mother are moved to one of our outside puppy pens. It is now time to begin feeding them a ground up mixture of puppy food and water. This needs to be quite runny for the first several feedings and each pup may require help figuring this new eating procedure out. The baby teeth are now beginning to break through the gums and soon they can be weaned from mom and be on solid puppy food. This is a busy week at our kennel as our goal is to have the pups completely weaned from their mother at five weeks old and on solid puppy kibble. As soon as pups begin digesting food other than mother's milk most mothers discontinue cleaning up after their pups. Our puppy pens are 25 feet square and have six inches of pea gravel as a base. There is an inside attached room for food, water, and a cedar chip-filled bed. The cedar chips have to be about the size of a silver dollar to insure the pups cannot swallow them or inhale cedar dust. This cedar chip blend can be sometimes hard to find and if not available several towels also do just fine.

Now that the pups are weaned from their mother and five weeks old the evaluation of each pup begins. A different colored puppy collar is put on each pup so that instant identification can easily be achieved. A clipboard with our puppy evaluation sheet is hung up in the puppy pen so identifiable traits can be documented. LaFaye does the personality identification of the pups and I document my observations on short field trips and their interest to birds. It's after the pups are six weeks old that I do most of my observations. Chasing cropped winged bobwhite quail several days in a row about the puppy pen is one rating and watching individual pups after they have come out of our swimming pool another. I take them about ten feet from the pools entry steps and let them swim back. I look for the pup that naturally swims like an otter and when they get out of the pool they merely shake and go play with their tail straight up in the air. One in ten pups will go off and sit down only to shiver and feel sorry for the terrible wet experience they just had. This is not the pup I would want to place with an avid waterfowler. The coats are also rated at this time along with a check for umbilical hernias and an evaluation of their bite. Most all of this evaluation process sees 80 percent of all our pups to be exactly the same between six and seven weeks. I'm primarily looking for that 20 percent (one in five) that displays too much horsepower or not enough at this young age. With all the effort we put into our pups it is still up to the new owner to put in their time also in developing a dog that they can be proud to own and hunt with.

Seven weeks seems to be the correct age for our pudelpointers to go to their new homes. Other breeds may require more time with their littermates to develop and are not capable of finding security on their own at seven weeks. These breeds may require eight or even ten weeks of age before separating from the litter. Leaving puppies together too long has the dangers of personality changes in some pups due to too harsh of play from an alpha aggressive pup. Much as the timid youngster in kindergarten tends to hide from the bully on the playground, a submissive pup will request no playtime from the other pups if there is an alpha pup continually dragging others about all day by an ear. Also, if pups are left together too long they become too attached to other dogs where they should be acquiring a connection with humans. The same difficulties humans have in raising twins are observed when dogs spend nearly all their time only with other dogs and don't interact enough with humans. Their focus is always primarily on their canine friends and not so much with humans. I have raised two littermates together twice and I hope I never do it again. The pups have to be completely separated from each other for them to begin to focus on anything other than their littermate.

Newborn pups nestled with mother. Mother Nature shows off her best tools at this stage of motherhood.

RAISING A VERSATILE PUPPY — 61

Raising a Versatile Puppy

It always seems to be a family's most celebrated summer when a new puppy is chosen to join their household. Very few realize the daily responsibilities necessary to develop that new hunting star of their dreams, however. We all know that socialization is key, but when done properly the task needs to go much further than just several trips to the city park. Most have good intentions for proper socialization, but as the family's busy summer schedule begins to reach its peak the pup's daily needs are overlooked. It goes back to that saying: "Time is like a river, as you cannot touch the water twice because the flow that has passed by will never flow by again." The same holds true for puppy development and socialization as we don't get a second chance once the pup is grown. Raising a pup in the backyard and expecting the pup to entertain themselves will never see the maximum potential reached. If an above average pup is sent to a home where the raising is poorly administered, the pup will grow up as a below average dog when compared to that breed. Contrary to this example is the below average pup that will grow into an above average dog following conscientious socialization and development.

Every time a puppy leaves our facility I remind the new owner of the genetic prowess that makes a great hunting companion. I explain that 50 percent of the final hunting dog comes from the genetics I put into the litter from the two parents of the pups. The second 50 percent comes from the genetics that the new owner's parents have given to them. There is usually a moment of bewilderment but it soon becomes apparent to them as to what I am presenting. They must do their due diligence in creating their anticipated performer.

Having a training schedule that can be looked at on a weekly basis helps remind one of the duties required in raising a pup. This isn't by any means meant to educate anyone on the specifics of dog training. The purpose here is to offer a schedule that is in a simple outline form as a reminder of some of the prime necessities required in raising a pup.

Training Schedule

The following is a week-to-week outline to help new puppy owners with some of the daily training chores in an age-related outline. I cannot stress enough that all the pups I observe at six months of age that impress me the most, are those that have had daily citizenship workouts with rules and expectations. You pay good money for any future hunting companion, so why not create a top notch dog that is a joy to live with and one you can take pride in when in the field? The first 20 weeks of a pup's life is an imprinting stage. During this period or stage the pup learns of all the good in their world and also what is bad. Thoughtful exposures are a must in order to help promote the best socialization.

8 to 10 weeks of age

1. This is the age that pups go through what is called the fear factor stage. Negative responses can create a lifelong imprint so be sure to create a positive outcome for every new experience at this age. Loud noises at feeding to call the pup to dinner. Start by clapping your hands and graduate to two pans. This is how we call our pups at feeding time. They come running when they hear several shots from my blank pistol, expecting to be greeted with food and a cheerful greeting from LaFaye. This way, at a very early age, they associate gunfire with something good for them to enjoy. They respond as a pack so it is important to initiate this routine with individual pups. Later we will make the same noise association with retrieving.

2. Five to ten retrieves daily with a soft toy down a hallway or in the backyard. The hallway guarantees the pup will return to you if all doors are closed. In the backyard it is necessary to throw the retrieving object to a location the pup is not accustomed to playing at which helps entice a return back to you. Always back away from the pup to ensure a good return; never stand stationary and calling the pup. The pup hasn't been taught a command to come yet and by standing stationary you are not luring to pup back to you. Make the return as much fun as their chase to the thrown object. Step out of sight so the pup has to come find you and make a big deal out of this return. Let the pup hold the toy for thirty seconds when they get to you as you praise their efforts. The retrieves must become farther and more difficult each day.

3. Two minutes chasing a wing or handkerchief on a fishing pole or broom handle helps create sight prey drive. The line from the end of the pole to the wing should be about the length of the pole. Don't let the pup catch the wing, raise it up and lower it slowly to entice pointing. This is sight pointing and not necessarily important to achieve as it is more of a parlor trick to show off your new dog to friends. Some pups have so much chase that they won't slow down long enough to sight point and that's okay. It's scent pointing that we eventually want to see, which comes later with age and this is what really counts.

LaFaye Farris working a pup on a wing at Oregon's beautiful Wallowa Lake.

4. Find activities such as Little League baseball games or merely neighborhood children to introduce your pup to. It is very important that puppies see and play with children. Dogs that were never exposed to children can grow up having a fear or dislike for them if they were never exposed. It is no different in humans; remembering the first time I saw a little person, it had me standing off and avoiding conversation or even a subtle greeting. The same can also be said for any kind of difference in humans. Take the pup to the grocery store, pet store, or hardware store and let him follow you up and down the aisles. Let strangers greet and visit with the pup. (Take a baggie or paper towel along in case they have an unplanned accident.)

5. Get the pup used to staying in a crate for several hours at a time. This may be where the pup will sleep each night in the home, also.

6. The flyswatter is a routine training aid at our house and often times found in my hip pocket for quick reprimands when in the house with a pup. Introduce the pup's nose to a flyswatter if he tries to join you on the couch or in your favorite chair. A sharp swat on his nose will discourage them and after several swats just showing the flyswatter has them backing off with good behavior your reward. Be consistent with your efforts as you should be with all training procedures. This can also be useful later on to get the pup to stop jumping up on you.

7. If your pup sleeps in the house in their crate, immediately after getting up in the morning carry the pup to the place you want him to potty each morning. If

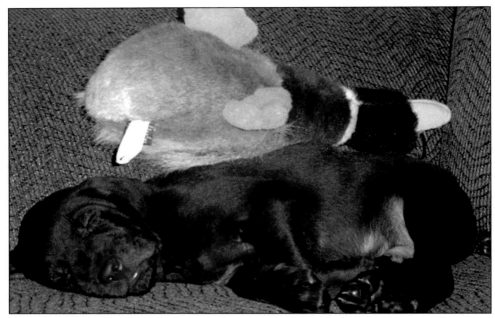

Worn out from play and napping with his favorite retrieving toy. Photo courtesy Jan Christen.

you allow a pup to walk out of their crate in the morning you are guaranteed to be cleaning up after them after about the third step, as he will form this habit for later years. This location will hopefully become a familiar restroom for the pup.

11 to 14 weeks of age

1. Continue the retrieving, but now introduce a frozen quail, chukar, or pigeon. A bird helps the pup get used to game and a frozen one prevents chewing. The retrieves can now be thrown into light cover so the pup's nose, rather than his eyes, is used to find the game. The pup can also be held with your left hand, bird thrown with your right hand, and the pup released once the bird hits the ground. Expect the pup to hunt short of the fall at first. Begin running away from the pup at the find to again create better returns. Never advance toward your pup on retrieves as your letting the pup know you are will to do some of their work. The bird can be refrozen after each day's training session and used daily.

2. Let the pup begin dragging a lead behind him on walks to get him used to a lead. He should also be tied up in a safe location for five minutes each day to help them gain respect for the lead. Ignore the crying, as it is no different than putting a two-year-old child down for a nap. It's just going to happen.

3. If weather permits, this is also the age to introduce the pup to water. Shallow water is the ticket and you need to wade out carrying the pup and let them swim back to shore with you. All pups vary as to their willingness to accept water. We are not entering the water from land; we're returning to land from water and this approach avoids habits like running up and down the shoreline looking for a bridge. Retrieving will come later but for now we are just introducing water as being as safe as land. Now instead of walking or running as they did on land the pup needs to swim.

4. If the pup respects the lead, walks should now be taken to introduce the pup to the sounds of traffic and other frightening noises and places that can only be expected when on a lead. This is also the age and time when the pup should have to cross streams and small bodies of water. With the lead, the pup should be expected to cross with you with very little hesitation. The lead helps the pup get started across each time. Don't call and ask the pup to come along, merely say nothing and slowly cross, letting the lead pull the pup along in the beginning. With time the pup will learn that hesitation and avoidance doesn't help as the lead always comes taunt and the must follow.

5. The "come" command should now be introduced. This is the only command necessary until the pup is five months old. Use the check cord and slight inward jerks, pulling the pup to you while saying "come" and kneel down giving a posture signal in addition. Do this drill in many different locations so the pup doesn't think one location is the only place expected to obey "come." Once you feel the pup understands the "come" command, let the pup drag the lead behind. Periodically grab the lead and insist that the pup comes to you on command. The lead helps serve as a reminder that obeying is always mandatory.

Retrieving frozen teal certainly lends confidence that the 6-week-old pup will enjoy retrieving birds later in life.

15 to 20 weeks of age

1. Teach the pup to stay in its own bed or on a rug in the house for periods over an hour. Get out the handy flyswatter and use the same love taps on their nose while saying "whoa." Don't give in to the pup's insistence to be with you. The dog bed or small rug gives the pup a boundary not to come off of. After the pup understands what you want, start leaving a chew toy in the bed and instruct him to go the bed with the command "bed" or "place." He will soon learn that this is a good place to go with a reward of a chew toy. When you release the pup from their bed, do so by tapping him on the head and saying "high-on." This procedure sets up future training which will be used later when working on steadiness on birds in the field. Also, your friends will appreciate your house dog's manners and this keeps leather shoes safe if the pup stays on their bed, as opposed to roaming freely about the house.

2. It's time to introduce the gun if no shyness has been observed from noise during the past processes. I like to start with a live, cropped-wing pigeon, but a dead bird will work. Go to a large field area and, as the pup searches away from you (at least 20 yards), make a loud banging noise as you did calling them to dinner, and when the pup looks back to the noise, throw the bird. Once the pup is onto this new game and anticipates retrieving a bird at the sound you have created, use the gun. It may take several sessions to thoroughly create the behavior you want to see. The first several gunshots should be with the pup twenty yards away and the muzzle blast in the opposite direction.

Bab Farris introducing a 7-week-old pup to the water.

Grandson Brett giving a 6-week-old pup swimming lessons.

3. It's also time to ask the pup to enter water for its retrieves. A shallow pond is used in the beginning, not swimming depths. I like to start with a live bird that is wing clipped. I take the pup into the water as previously done with a check cord. While the pup is in the shallow water with me I throw the live bird several yards in front of them on the water. The check cord is useful here to keep the pup from going to land with the bird as the check cord insists the retrieve is brought to me. These are retrieves from the water where the pup is not yet being asked to go from land into water for a retrieve. Once the pup is making successful retrieves it is time to ask for a retrieve from land into water. Pups that have a high retrieving desire take to water retrieving quite rapidly and can be weaned off bird retrieves quickly and on to dummy retrieves. Dogs with lower retrieving drive will require more birds and possibly some live duck chases to help create the necessary fun before moving to dummy retrieves.

4. This is also the age to introduce the pup to planted birds. Start with planted birds in the yard that can be seen from ten yards away. Bring the pup to the bird with the wind in his face. At first sight or scent, stop the pup from advancing; maybe give him a step or two to create more curiosity. Small jerks on the lead help set the picture that he isn't to advance. After a minute or two have a helper flight the bird. Go to the next several planted birds and do the same thing until

The parlor trick all pointing dog enthusiasts enjoy... pointing a wing.

a point is produced. Once the pup relates the scent to the sight of the planted bird, you're ready to plant birds in cover. The same approach is used with the same expectations using the check cord. The beginning scenario was sight pointing and not all pups will sight point, but they can be restrained and held off the bird with the check cord. the second scenario was sent pointing and for the most part this is what we are after.

5. Now that the pup is used to finding planted birds with his nose, we can begin letting hem search for short periods in different locations off the lead. No birds are necessary to create searching patterns but they are necessary to help create the searching purpose we expect to see in our dogs. I like to run all my pups on wild quail. I let the pups flush and chase and hope to eventually see some pointing. Young dogs need to flush their share of birds when young as it is the sound of the wings that helps ignite more purpose to their search. Use both open and wooded areas for these short searches. Occasionally stop behind a tree or sit down so the dog learns to keep an eye on you. If the pup demonstrates too much independence during his search, spend most of your time in the woods. If he is hunting too close, spend most of your time in very open terrain. Always make 90-degree direction changes to teach the pup to hunt to the front and keep an eye on you and where you are traveling.

5 MONTHS TO 1 YEAR

1. It's now time to begin some formal obedience. The field obedience training isn't necessary until the pup is demonstrating bold independence. "Whoa" should be the primary command taught at this age. "Whoa" and "come" are all a dog has to know to be a good citizen both at home and in the field. The pup should have a good understanding of what we want as he learned the command a month ago on his bed. Now we want him to both stay and stop, while maintaining a standing posture. We will apply this command during pointing to create staunchness on point. The dog should perform well when given this command and do so in many varying locations for periods up to two minutes.

2. "Heel" and "sit" can follow "whoa," but are not necessary unless you want your dog to perform these tasks when waterfowling. Some people require this while others don't.

Resting.

Winston Moore at 92, no longer gunning but still in the field every Friday.

The Aging Hunters and Their Dogs

As I've watched so many friends retire from an active career, there seems to be two very different retirement paths that people take. The first is to become more involved in the enjoyable delights they have not had time to enjoy to the fullest due to work restraints. The other finds that without a work schedule to keep them busy they have become lost for finding valued time spent.

Golfing, fishing, hunting, and gardening are just a few of the hobbies active retirees find to occupy their retirement years. Watching TV and surfing the internet seems to be the only enjoyment this second group finds to take up their time as they haven't acquired many interests outside of work.

Those that own a hunting dog seem to primarily focus much more on their canine friend following retirement. Both in the field and also in the home. This relationship usually finds a more sincere presence, especially in the home. The companionship found in their dog becomes a friendship that wasn't present during those working years. I have to wonder if there is a correlation between longevity of one's life and how occupied their retirement years are?

As what are termed one's "Golden Years" begins to encroach upon me, I am often reminded of my own senior friends that paved the way for me throughout the years both in training knowledge, but also as hunting companions in the field. Most of them, at some stage, left behind a personal hunting companion when they passed; as they found down deep in their own constitution the need to always have a dog at their side. Usually, there had been knowledge of the chosen friend or family member that would take the dog in when that time might arrive. These are the men and women that get much more enjoyment from their canine friends than merely when on hunting excursions. This enjoyment is taking place in the home and most places they venture to (within reason). Sharing breakfast and coffee in the morning and lying next to one's chair during the evening news can be the most satisfying times to relax with one's hunting companion regardless of one's age.

Then there are those that believe it isn't fair to own a hunting dog once they themselves can no longer trek after upland birds or no longer enjoy time in the duck blind. They will dismiss ownership and become comfortable spending their remaining years without a dog. It is this situation and retired hunter that I personally don't understand and in some sense feel regretful of or sorry for. It is very hard for me to get my arms around the idea that it is unfair to pass and leave one's hunting companion behind, thinking it is best to just not own one anymore as they are too old now for a dog. This is always the situation with unexpected deaths, so why not have enough foresight to have a simple exit plan to make sure your dog goes to a place where the appreciation and love will again be equaled.

I have had hunting friends that were my senior that fit in both of the mentioned scenarios. As I look back at each example, those always insisting on owning a hunting companion throughout their senior years had a much more devoted passion toward bird hunting or waterfowling, even before retirement. I'm sure just having that dog lying at his feet during the evening news gave a continued reminder of past trips to the field or marsh. Much the same reminder a mounted big game head hanging in the den resurrects numerous past hunting memories from time to time for those that have trophy heads displayed in their home. I am often told by inquirers seeking a possible pup that "this will be my last hunting dog." Then they will go on to explain that they are in their 60s or sometimes 70s. I want to ask them if the have cancer or some life-threatening medical condition as 12 to 14 years is a good life expectancy for most sporting dogs and if in good health they should, or could, outlive this new puppy. What they are, most likely, telling me is that they don't want to pass on themselves and leave behind a hunting dog. What I'm hearing, however, is that they are not a very passionate bird hunter or waterfowler themselves and owning and caring for a hunting companion isn't at the top of their senior citizen bucket list. I will most likely end up trying to find a more suitable client for that pup.

Winston Moore unloading his GSP "Buck" for a pheasant hunt.

During the 30-plus years that my kennel took in hunting dogs for training I was a Laboratory Supervisor at a local Boise, Idaho hospital. Most all the medical staff residing in Boise hunted upland birds or waterfowl as Idaho was one of the premier states for bird hunting; offering four species of grouse to hunt, three species of quail, along with chukar, huns, and pheasants. I had a captive audience in the doctor's lounge during morning coffee and many of the physicians were using my kennel services for gundog training. I maintained between five to 15 dogs in training throughout the spring and summer and over half of the clients were doctors practicing at the hospital where I worked. It was interesting how passionate the majority were about their hunting and the common denominator was the most dedicated of these clients will probably always have a hunting dog of their chosen breed at hand throughout their life.

One such client was Winston Moore, not a medical man, but a commercial real-estate developer. I trained six or eight different German Shorthairs for Winston over the years as he always had a brace of dogs to hunt behind; primarily pheasants. If one were to Google Winston Moore of Boise, Idaho you would find two very unique characteristics separating him from 99 percent of the residents of Idaho. First, would be his contribution to Boise as a commercial developer and how he has helped make Boise one of the most desirable communities to reside is much to Winston's credit. His personal vision is what has been most instrumental in the progressive change Boise has experienced. Second, you would find that he is one of the top salt water fly fishermen in the world. He has caught and released world record tarpon, permit, bonefish, and sailfish. Winston designed the teasing technique for sailfish fly-fishing using a last minute cast of a fly to make the hookup as the fish was teased within casting distance with a lure that was being trolled. He would make countless trips to Belize and fish from dawn to dusk day after day. But the obsession I observed in the man was his love for pheasant hunting. He hunted every Friday throughout October, November, and December. Usually alone with just his two dogs as his companionship. It didn't matter the limit, as once that was filled, the rest of the day was taken up just watching his dogs work on wild pheasants. This is the extreme passion rarely seen among bird hunters.

If one is ever fortunate enough to visit with Winston in his office this passion becomes quite obvious as the walls and hallways are decorated with pheasant artwork along with mounted roosters in glass cases and numerous pictures of his German Shorthairs. His office has been featured in The Wall Street Journal as one of the most unique offices in the U.S. I often take out-of-town NAVHDA judges by to meet Winston when time allows and the impression he leaves them with is always that of a sincere pheasant hunter whose enthusiastic approach to life itself reverberates its rewards with the presence of Winston's stature.

As is always the case, I received a prompt email from Winston after introducing both Tom Swezey and Phil Swain to Winston in his office. Both were in Boise judging a NAVHDA test and with extra afternoon time I had taken each by to meet Winston and see the shrine he had created for his past dogs in his office. That prompt email was just letting me know these two men measured up and were obviously dedicated to their judging efforts which came out loud and clear after he had met and visited with both. This is a man that ran Chesapeake Bay Retrievers in AKC field trials during the 60s earning an amateur field championship on his male Chesanoma Louis. Talking dog trials or tests is familiar ground for Winston.

I received the summons from Winston at the beginning years of Pheasants Forever and we started a local chapter here in Boise together. Twenty-five years later and Winston Moore is still the chapter's top contributors. As an individual contributor, I would guess he is probably one of the organizations leading contributors in the United States. Again, these birds are part of his passion and giving back would have to be what would make this man feel secure that there will hopefully be birds for generations of hunters to come.

Winston is currently 92 years old and when he was about age 85 he lost his wife Diane to cancer. The quiet house and lack of evening companionship soon found his German Shorthaired Pointer (GSP) Buck in the house to keep him company in the evenings. Next, he was taking Buck to the office every day and letting the dog enjoy constant companionship with his owner. There was a regained spark in Winston's life and it was openly apparent. Then, as is eventually always the case with 14-year-old dogs, I got the 6 a.m. phone call from Winston that Buck couldn't get to his feet. We shared the experience of saying "goodbye" to one of the best pheasant producers I'd ever seen, leaving Winston alone again and without a hunting and house companion.

I could definitely see my friend beginning to become lackluster and somewhat depressed during my visits following Buck's departure. Winston was about 88 years old at this time and I wanted to give him a puppy to possibly rejuvenate that passion I had always seen in the man. A puppy certainly wasn't the answer, as myself, at 22 years younger understood the demands of a new puppy. I now tell people that I would rather get into a bar fight than raise a puppy, so how could I expect Winston to take this on.

It was about that time that I watched a very nice GSP being trained at my training property by a local NAVHDA member. The owner had two GSP pups that were littermates and were about 6 months old. He also owned the pup's mother. I instantly became consumed with the notion that this male youngster just might be the answer to providing Winston once again with a companion both in the field, at home, and at the office. Especially once I learned that the dog was already completely housebroken. The young GSP fit Winston's needs like a new glove and he quickly named him Buddy. Shortly thereafter that sparkle returned to Winston's personality.

I gave additional field training to Buddy as every Friday was still to be a pheasant hunting day for Buddy and Winston (as it is still the case today). At 92, Winston follows Buddy in a Polaris Ranger and often times has his friend Travis shoot the pointed birds. Now walking most of the time with a cane for balance and insurance, riding and following his dog through the fields in his Ranger still allows the team to continue the Friday pheasant ritual.

At no point would Winston at 92 expect to outlive his 4-year-old dog Buddy; all of his past dogs have seen 14 years, so his expectations are to see Buddy alive for at least ten more years. Personally, I expect to see Winston still alive for 10 more years, but still the question was asked of me: "What will you do with Buddy if I pass before he does?"

I told him I had never owned a GSP, but it was most likely about time as I had trained several hundred for clients over the years and never had one I didn't like. After all, Buddy had now become one of the staunchest bird dogs on point I'd ever seen. I assured him that the dog would also be a house companion for the rest of his years most likely in my home. Winston reminds me of this obligation every now and then, demonstrating that sincere dedication he has and always has had toward his dogs of which he will never be without.

Some 20 years ago I lost my dad to a wood-cutting accident. He was 75 years old when the accident happened and the reality of this misfortune haunted me for years. I often leaned on Winston for advice when the correct answer wasn't obvious or easily recognized. I'm not sure that one ever finds a time in their life when some fatherly advice isn't needed and without Winston's knowledge I would often seek his support or approval when solutions weren't obvious to me. He has become that institute of knowledge and perception for my entire family.

My dad was a Marine pilot during World War II and flew a plane called a Corsair off Navy carriers over the China Sea. He was my rock up until the day he died and I didn't find closure for 18 years following his death. My dad had one cocktail each day when he came home from work and that was a swig off his bottle of Cutty Sark. One Memorial Day morning I left Boise at 4 a.m. with a new bottle of Cutty Sark and drove the four hours to Enterprise, Oregon to sit at my Dad's grave and share drink after drink with him while reminiscing all the great hunting and fishing memories I'd had with him. After several hours my wounds of his

Stan Farris on a cliff in Hell's Canyon.

death seemed healed and closure had been found. The only problem was that I was too drunk to attempt the four-hour drive back to Boise, so I drove out to the ranch he had owned to walk myself to sobriety. His ranch was 1,200 acres on the breaks of the Grande Rhonde River where we had hunted deer and chukar throughout my youth. I took many Boone and Crocket mule deer during my high school and college days on this ranch and always had that retired Marine to help retrieve them from Courtney Creek Canyon that surrounded the back side of the ranch. I left the half empty scotch bottle at his headstone and have never felt that hollow-empty feeling again that his death had given me.

Another friend to mention in this chapter would have to be Jim Reed. Jim owned a National Champion GSP named Ammertal's Lancer D. Shortly after meeting Jim, one of Lancer's sons, Ehlichers Abe, won the National All-Age Championship. As a new recruit in the hunting dog world I had mysteriously met and was hunting birds with Idaho's top field trial competitor. I have learned so many things about dogs from Jim that cannot be found in books or on DVDs as his knowledge and understanding is from personal experiences with many of his excellent GSPs. He would always remind me to keep my personal dogs active with their parlor tricks as that is what keeps a dog wanting to show off for you and not themselves. Jim had his dogs race on command to their individual kennels and retrieve their food dish before the evening feeding. This, among many of his other so called parlor tricks, keep his dogs wanting to perform in the field for him and not solely for themselves. As I think back through his theory I realize he was creating cooperation through obedience and the obedience was done in the backyard while not requiring harsh discipline in the field, since the dog had been programmed to work as a team from an early age.

Once when visiting at our kennel, LaFaye (my wife) took Jim out to see some young pups she was caring for. Jim spotted a pup that was off by himself and not accepted by the other pups in the litter. His quick evaluation was that the pup was probably more submissive in temperament than the rest of the litter and had learned to avoid the others and find security and safety from this behavior. "Much like the youngster on the playground," he commented. "Once bullied by the others at the teeter-totter while on recess, the kid has learned to play alone in a location where the rest of the kids didn't want to play," he continued. "Start putting several drops of honey or maple syrup on that pups back and the others will lick it off, boosting the little guys confidence," he instructed. You just don't find this knowledge or insight in books or on the internet!

Now in his 80s, Jim still hunts but has limited his hunts to mostly quail and always has several new tales to share with me when I drop by for one of our visits and a pull off his Jim Beam bottle. Our visits are always about the dogs, the expected hatch of spring upland birds, or Boise State football. He is one of Boise State's most dedicated football fans that is in the stands at every home game.

I've been blessed to have had Winston and Jim as friends for so many years and what they share and have previously shared with me is invaluable knowledge in this day and age. As I said, "you cannot find this knowledge in books, DVDs, or on the internet." This is the knowledge that our dog men of the 60s and 70s have to offer.

Enjoying Versatile Dogs Outside of Hunting

September through January consumes most bird hunting enthusiasts time with their dogs. This is only five months of the year and the other seven months are usually spent waiting for September to again come around to share time with one's dog outside of the home. There are fishing, camping, and hikes that often include the dog, but these adventures don't have the purpose connected that the bird season has given.

At our home each and every holiday, it is shared with our entire family. This is an expectation my wife LaFaye insists on. I have been able to reconstruct several of these holidays into a celebration that not only involves our entire family, but also includes our dogs.

These altered holiday traditions began one Thanksgiving years ago, as I couldn't see wasting one of the best waterfowl days of the year sitting at home watching pro football and stuffing myself with turkey and pumpkin pie. We had, what I call a "shanty," on my 40-acre duck hunting property (called "the Swamp") which bordered the Boise River. The shanty had a wood stove, kitchen table, and all of our secondhand furniture which was acquired over the years when we purchased new. This, to me, seemed like a perfect setting for our annual Thanksgiving dinner, and so the tradition began. We could begin hunting ducks at daylight and LaFaye could bring the Thanksgiving dinner down in the early afternoon.

This started with my son Bryce and son-in-law Rick both joining me for the hunt and daughter Brooke and daughter-in-law LeAnn joining LaFaye with all the food offerings. As the years have passed, two grandsons have joined our hunting party and two granddaughters have joined to help with cooking and food serving duties. After the Thanksgiving celebration is completed, we take several dogs on an hour or two pheasant/quail hunt to help digest all of LaFaye's food that we've consumed. This isn't the normal Thanksgiving celebration as seen across America, but our altered tradition is a day looked forward to by the entire family and most importantly is shared with our dogs.

Another holiday which has our own twist to the day is Easter. When our children were small we always hide boiled/colored eggs about our two-acre property claiming the Easter bunny had left them. Once we had grandchildren, LaFaye created a much

Easter always involved the kids using their dogs to locate the Easter eggs.

more unique Easter egg hunt on my 40-acre "Swamp" property. I had eight remote bird launchers which were used for training and a homing pigeon loft located on site at the "Swamp." The plan was to put a homer in each of the eight launchers and distribute them about the 40 acres. Instead of boiled Easter eggs, LaFaye wanted four plastic eggs laid on the ground surrounded the pigeon loaded launcher. Inside each plastic egg was a $5 bill. When you do the math for eight launchers, four eggs per launcher, and $5 in each egg the daily expense was $160. The only way to find the stash of Easter eggs is with a dog. Watching four youngsters race to keep up with Tukr and Zoey was quite a sight.

Tukr would take them through cattail sloughs and all the environmentally unfriendly locations that had given the property its given name, "the Swamp." As soon as one of the dogs went on point it was "game on" and a race to their find for all four kids. I'd launch the different homers as they were located and when LaFaye had seen six or seven return to the loft she would lay out some fresh dry clothes for each of the kids and begin setting out the dinner.

In the beginning years this had never been something I needed to budget for, but with today's Easters the ante is much higher. With four grandchildren ranging from ten to 17 the Easter bunny expectations are much higher. Now we put $20 dollar bills in those 32 plastic eggs. Now my Easter contribution has risen to $640. We now use kill pigeons instead of homers and the boys take turns attempting a kill at the flush. Each of my grandsons have their own dogs and we now use their dogs making it just a little more special. It's hard to complain about the rising costs for a Farris Easter celebration as at the end of the day, the enjoyment had by all is quite evident on everyone's face.

Halloween was Tukr's favorite holiday, as he thought it was one of our scheduled holidays. He acquired many different costumes over the years and LaFaye made sure he greeted every youngster that rang our doorbell. She even taught him to hold and carry the candy basket and present the goodies to the kids.

Facebook allows us to stay in touch with friends throughout the country and it is nearly instantaneous. Our friends Blaine and Patti Carter in Maine have similar family expectations as our family when it comes to complete family involvement. The one major difference is that they get much more winter snow in Maine than we do in Idaho and their snow stays on the ground much longer. All of their German Shorthairs are expected to pull their weight as sled dogs and the entire family gets involved travelling about behind a team of shorthairs. Another that is snowbound for much of the winter is Donate Thibault in Quebec. She also spends a great deal of time behind a sled being pulled by one of her GSPs. What a great way to enjoy the winter and a versatile dog.

I graduated from Boise State and purchased season football tickets during my first year following graduation. I trained several dogs for Boise State's assistant athletic director Ron Debelius and also Buss Connors the university's basketball coach. Ron ran German Shorthairs and Buss always ran a Brittany and my connection was as their dog trainer. We became friends and I spent many hunting days with one or both of these men hunting chukar. Both were exceptional athletes themselves; Ron had played both

Eli retrieving a kicking tee following a kickoff at a Boise State University football game.

Cecil, Bob and grandson Hunter preparing for a Boise State football game.

professional basketball and also professional baseball. These two friends were hard to beat on a serious chukar hunt as their athletic abilities always put them ahead of me. In both hiking and shooting. Years later, I was asked by Ron if I could train a dog to retrieve the kicking tee following kickoffs at the Boise State home football games. The athletic director, Gene Bleymaier, had always had creative visions for Boise State Athletics and this was an idea he wanted to pursue. After all, he had insisted on blue Astroturf for the football field and look at the attention that had created.

I trained three of my stud dogs to perform for this event. Cecil, Eli, and Duffy; but Duffy had to be permanently benched as his persistence to mark at every location where he retrieved didn't seem to look favorable; especially when the game was televised by ESPN. Eli (Cedarwoods Sharp Shooter) became the go-to dog at all the games, as his drive to get to the tee and get back to me saw him always at a dead run. I looked into his eyes before his first ever retrieve with Boise State taking on Oregon State and all of the lights in the house were definitely on and his stare looked like runway lights letting me know he was ready and pumped up to go. This was ESPN Game Day here at Boise State and the electricity felt on the sideline was hair raising and deafening. He did a complete flip as he grabbed for the tee and was back to me before the tackle was made by a Boise State defender. He had broken prior to a command to retrieve when I stepped out onto the field to watch for the tackle and see the referee call the play dead. From then on, I held his collar until it was clear to send him.

Again this became a family affair as I rotated taking one of my grandsons along at each game. Their job was to run out and retrieve the kicking tee if the opposing team ran the ball back past the 50-yard line making it too confusing and difficult for the dog as there would be 44 players both coming off and onto the field at the same time and the dog would be right in the middle of this confusion. I guess it was okay to let a child get run over by a college football player, but not a dog. Ironically, there never was a kickoff return past the 50-yard line in the two years that we were at the games. I did let my grandsons make at least one retrieve themselves per game so their time on the sideline wasn't a waste. It never was a waste, however, as the kids were there in awe throughout the games of the players they were mingling with. LaFaye attended every game with me and took care of the dog while she visited with cheerleaders and players on the sideline and I got to watch the game from the sideline which is definitely the best seat in the house. Team Farris had two very memorable football seasons with the dogs seeing plenty of action and spectator attention. In those two years, Boise State only lost one game and always seemed to score more than 50 points per game, so there were plenty of retrieving opportunities for the dogs. After two years I'm sure I could have run Eli for mayor of Boise and it would have been a sure win.

On Christmas eve we had a surprise visit from the Boise State coaching staff, presenting my two grandsons each with a white autographed football signed by all the players and coaches. Nineteen of these players went directly into the NFL after their senior year, so to six and eight year olds, this was better than an autograph from Brad Pitt or the like.

Boise State's "Blue Turf" and kickoff tee retrieving have both received significant exposure on ESPN over the years, and when Mario Andretti came to Boise for a

Eli and Mario Andretti having a meet & greet in Boise.

Firestone tire store's open house, he was asked if he wanted to tour Boise and see the university's blue turf. His reply was that "what I would really like to do is meet that dog I've seen on TV retrieving the kicking tee on your blue turf." I immediately received the summons to bring Eli to the tire store for an introduction.

All breeds of dogs are capable and many fill this companion role quite well within the home. The versatile breeds have been bred to be much more than merely a specialist for a single hunting purpose such as waterfowling or upland hunting. Most contentious breeders representing one of the versatile breeds focus on creating a dog that can waterfowl, upland hunt, and also be the family pet. Serving as a family member was not what hunting dogs were originally meant to be. Most lived outside in an enclosed kennel or were staked out next to their dog house with a water bucket and food pan nearby. Most versatile dogs of today live inside the home and are introduced as a family member. These are the dogs being produced by the most legitimate versatile breeders.

Mojo's 5th birthday is a family treat at the Kremers' home. Photo courtesy Dan Kremers.

Everyone Has Had a Best Dog

During most bird hunters' lifespans there were many unforgettable dogs that created the memories that are still rehearsed when a picture or the dog's name presents itself. These are always the special ones that just gave more than all the others. It may have been more affection, offered more prey drive during the hunt, or was just that dog that always out produced all others in the field. Choosing a best of past dogs is usually quite difficult and often seems unfair to the dogs not chosen and placed on this personalized pedestal.

The best hunting dog I have ever owned was a female named Cedarwoods Dusty Rose. Never have I seen a more determined or more skilled dog in the field. Dusty's diary has notes describing her pointing porcupines, deer, elk, bighorn rams, a bear, a fox, a pair of coyotes, a beaver, pheasants, and hundreds of coveys of chukar. I will always remember one opening day of pheasant season where I unloaded six NAVHDA utility prized dogs in a sugar beet field with myself, my son, daughter, son-in-law, and two friends from Portland, OR. When we returned to the truck when we had our 21 bird limit with all birds taken off point. My daughter Brooke gave Dusty her due diligence by proclaiming: "Not sure if you noticed Dad, but of our 21 birds Dusty pointed 18 of them." Dusty earned a NAVHDA Natural Ability and also Utility Prize I. She had her utility title at 11 months, demonstrating her value as a hunting dog at a very early age.

For me, "my best dog ever" has to be that dog whose passing put the most miles on my heart. The dog that I continue to miss every morning when I awake and look at his empty dog bed next to mine. I wear the pain of his absence is like a warm winter coat in the summer, always reminding me that he is no longer with me. That dog is Cedarwoods First Offense who went by Tukr. I have often told people that visited our kennel and met Tukr that they would remember this dog to their grave. His sincere affectionate personality was so forefront as he told every stranger how special they were to him.

Tukr swam laps in our pool every day with me and his 20 foot-plus water entry was breathtaking. He was an explosive water dog and also an explosive retriever. For me there will most likely never be a replacement for Tukr, at least not in my heart. He nearly lived to see 15 years and sired many of the standout Pudelpointers the breed has seen as he truly stamped greatness in most of his get as a pre-potent sire. He rode shotgun in my truck everywhere I went and went into most all establishments that I did (even casinos in Nevada). But with all this said, he was just my best friend.

LaFaye and I made a special gravesite at my "Swamp" property where Tukr and I had spent so much time together over the years. Hunting ducks and roosters there together has created some of my most cherished hunting memories. I am so grateful that I had the foresight to have Tukr collected when he was four years old. After his passing, I used his ten-year-old frozen semen to create a litter of which I kept two pups: Cedarwoods Frozen Image who I call "Ice" and Cedarwoods Frozen Centerfold who I call "Cuttr." There is a bench next to the gravesite and I spend time visiting with my old friend whenever I'm at the "Swamp" and often take the two pups along to visit with their Dad.

As I think through the many friends that I have known that were or are involved breeding, raising, trialing, testing, or just hunting their dogs, I am forced to wonder which of their many dogs would have been coined their best. It is very obvious with some as there was a standout performer from trialing or testing that put their name and kennel name on the map. The length of time one has a dog surely must play into this selection, however.

Cedarwood's First Offense (aka Tukr) at 8 weeks, sight pointing a pigeon.

Sometimes when we roll the dice on that new puppy selection the lifespan of the pup doesn't roll in our favor and this loss of years doesn't allow the unlucky dogs into our memory long enough to qualify as best dog ever. Helping a dog through their senior years is also a common denominator for that "best dog ever." There is a special bond that comes about as you begin to sacrifice so many expectations for that older dog that just cannot physically perform their duties as they had during their youth.

I think the dogs that become daily companions in addition to being the go-to top hunting dog are much more favored for earning this "best dog" posting. With me, a dog earns that spot in the front seat of my truck rather than the back by displaying a confident calmness and a sense of sincere appreciation for being allowed this position. It most likely is the reliable companion dog that is allowed extra privileges that worms their way the deepest into our hearts. I have to feel somewhat sorry for those that have never experienced this type of dog and are completely content housing their dog in a kennel while waiting for October to role around. There is so much personal joy to be received from our canine friends and when one has little or no interest in the friendship values a dog offers they are missing out on one of man's most treasured adventures.

Cedarwood's First Offense (aka Tukr) at 10 years old, still pounding the water.

It seems as though most all versatile dog owners regardless of chosen breed truly do cherish the relationship they have developed with their dogs. They see the rewards given daily from an animal that demonstrates a human acceptance as heartfelt and always seem willing to take that bullet for their owner and friend. Most owners should be thanking the Lord, every time they have him on the line, for such a wonderful companion to hunt behind and share their daily world with.

Versatile dogs are bred to be respectable companion dogs that usually have a wonderful off-switch when in the house and display a calmness offering honest human affection. With this said, it is probably the owners of the versatile breeds that lose the largest piece of their hearts when their canine friend passes.

At 12 years old, Tukr's kind eyes tell of his sincerity and kindness.

Personalizing the Memory of Your Dog

The special dogs we are fortunate to own in our lives are the ones we never want to forget. Pictures of these dogs, and occasionally a painting, will hang in the home as a reminder of the memories produced from adventures and experiences had when hunting or merely the companionship experienced in the home. Regardless of the foundation of these memories, there always seems to be a need for some sort of monument offering a tribute to evoke past accounts of this companion. Having only a gravesite of this friend is eventually forgotten and doesn't give complete closure as time passes.

Many veterinarian clinics now have access to a local crematorium and rather than burying a pet they can be cremated and stored in an urn within the home. My

Coopr posing with a decoy creating a memory that will live beyond the dog.
Photo courtesy Brian O'Keefe.

wife LaFaye has now had four different Shih Tzu's during our marriage that have been her day in and day out sidekicks, going everywhere she goes along with always being allowed sleeping quarters on our bed. Two are now deceased and in a small urn that rests on the headboard of our bed. She is confident that there is still room for two more in the urn when the time arrives as one of our current dogs is already ten years old, and the other nine.

I have taken hundreds and possibly thousands of pictures of my dogs on various hunting excursions but most don't represent the dog indicative of what that dog had truly meant to me beyond those hunts. Pictures seem to catch the moment but don't address the whole depiction of the individual dog photographed. Pictures also verify a time and place, but again, they don't describe the subject; which is your hunting dog, friend, and companion. My kennel facility has more than twenty 8 x 10 photos framed on the walls which are of mostly past dogs I have owned that are now deceased. I am often finding myself staring at these walls and reminiscing of an individual dog and the bliss that dog gave me from hunting, producing fine pups, to just providing an unconstrained friendship. Still, they are photographs of only a specific time and place with that dog.

Portrait pictures that have been setup with a specific backdrop seem to create much more meaningful memories than mere snapshots taken in the backyard or during hunting excursions. Especially that of a new pup where the expectations of delivery seemed to be endless. Creating a puppy picture with an established prop always seems to have more future meaning, especially after that pup has grown and has left you.

One very unique project I undertook several years ago to remember one very special dog, in my dog career, was to contract a painting that I felt only myself and this dog could find ourselves in. I supplied the artist with four different pictures. The first was a photo of the Bruneau Canyon near the Idaho/Nevada border where I loved to chukar hunt. This was a place on the canyon rim that had a vast picturesque view looking across to the opposite canyon wall. The other three pictures were of Cedarwoods First Offense (aka Tukr) who was usually on those chukar hunts in Bruneau country. One was his puppy picture at eight weeks old sight pointing a pigeon, another of him on point at four years old pointing during a training session, and the third was a picture when Tukr was 10, and only that of his head. The Bruneau backdrop was painted first with several chukar walking and several others taking flight. Next the three pictures of my dog added with the picture of Tukr's head larger than the other two. The likeness of the 10-year-old dog's head was nearly dead-on perfect.

I liked this concept so well that I recently contracted a local artist here in Boise to do a similar portrait of Tukr but with a waterfowling theme. Jenny Esplin is a local art teacher and winner of state duck stamp competition so I knew she understood the detailed importance of waterfowl paintings. The picture I submitted was of Tukr making one of his monster leaps out over the water during a duck shoot at my hunting

Metal cutout of Tukr by Idaho artist Chris Underwood.

property along the Boise River. This property is a special place that is dear to my heart which we named "the Swamp" for obvious reasons. In Tukr's 14 years with me I rarely left him at home when working or waterfowling at "the Swamp." What I didn't know, however, about Jenny, was how masterful she was at actual portrait painting until I saw some of the dog portraits she had done in the past. I'm not sure I have ever seen the professional detail that Jenny conquers with this level of distinction before.

I supplied Jenny with a backdrop picture of my waterfowl hunting property's main pond with Tukr making one of his colossal leaps out over the water with decoys in place and my favorite blind on the water's edge in the background. Jenny nailed the details of the picture in an oil painting and provided me with a near perfect illustration of how I remember hunting ducks over the years with this stellar retriever.

If you are seeking a portrait of your dog in either oil or pencil it would be worth your time to explore jenny's work. She can be reached for consignment painting at: jennyesplin@yahoo.com and her work is well worth the investment.

Another great memory concept was a gift I received from a friend, George Decosta. Knowing how I felt about Tukr and the probable memories this dog had given me over the years prompted George to have a metal cutout made from a picture of Tukr's head and shoulders. The result was a realistic metal portrait that the artistry and likeness to the original picture cannot be articulated and only appreciated when viewed.

RIGHT: Chukar hunting painting of Tukr showing his life stages with a favorite canyon he hunted so often as abackdrop. Art by Cheryl Temple. BELOW: Waterfowl oil painting of Tukr at my swamp property where he spent nearly 14 years retrieving waterfowl. Art by Jenny Esplin.

If there is a special dog in your past, I would strongly suggest creating a personalized memory that can be forever near you to retrieve the memories of the hunts and companionship that dog has given you. That special dog is usually the one that when they've licked your face, it was as indisputable as if they were kissing the eye of a hurricane, while showing their legitimate fondness for you and with all the planets overhead circling with admiration. This is the dog that deserves more than just a snapshot or photograph.

Preparing for Hunt Tests

In most all organized hunt tests in North America, dogs are judged to specific standards and do not compete for placements with other dogs. Hunt tests evaluate versatility in the hunting dog, as many hunters hunt a wide variety of game with one dog. Hunt tests are conducted annually in all parts of North America and are sponsored by a variety of organizations and most of these organizations have chapters throughout North America. AKC, JGHV, NAVHDA, and VHDF all offer testing programs to assist hunters and dog breeders evaluate natural ability traits and trainability for individual dogs in a public forum. There is usually a source of public records available of test results on individual dogs, litters, sires, dams, or selected kennels. Also, many of the versatile breed's breed clubs offer hunt test testing for the dogs of that breed, while many of the local hunting dog organization or clubs also offer a variety of opportunities for versatile dog owners to participate in their events.

Hunt tests offer several different levels of noncompetitive gundog testing. Natural Ability Tests (NA) or Aptitude Evaluation Tests (AE) evaluate inherent characteristics of abilities (instincts) for dogs up to usually no more than 1.5 to 2 years old. Utility Tests (UT) or Performance Evaluation (PE) measures a dog's usefulness in all phases of hunting as a completely finished gun dog. This level of testing serves breeders and individual versatile dog owners as one of the best definitive evaluator for owners wishing to test their dog's hunting skills at the highest level possible as a versatile hunting dog.

All of the organizations offering hunt tests separate dogs into various age groups for testing purposes and each has their own way of awarding competence in a pass or fail analysis. There is no competition amongst the performing dogs and no ranking system to separate dogs to determine a first place winner. AKC offers the largest variety of testing for hunting dogs, but for versatile breeds the Pointing Dog Hunt Tests see the majority of the participation. AKC awards a Junior Hunter title (JH) and also a Master Hunter title (MH). VHDF awards participants with a pass fail analysis in their Aptitude Test for dogs under 1.5 years old and also a pass fail evaluation for their Performance Test for finished dogs. In NAVHDA Testing, dogs are given a total score and also a Prize classification for their work in Natural Ability and also in Utility. A maximum or perfect score in Natural Ability is 112 points. A maximum or perfect

NAVHDA Invitational Entries. Photo courtesy Nancy Anisfield.

score in Utility is 204 points. Dogs also receive a Prize I, Prize II, or Prize III only if their scores qualify them. Dogs not qualifying receive No Prize.

Most of my personal experience has been primarily with NAVHDA testing. For this reason most of the hunt test training in this book will be slanted somewhat to this testing format. Regardless of AKC, VHDF, NAVHDA, or VGHV testing, all of the training necessary to pass the various evaluator's tests are very similar. A well trained dog should be very capable of entering any and all of these organizations mentioned and perform admirably.

When breaking down the junior dog's hunt tests, the testing expectations are usually in three major components: Field Search, Tracking, and Water, the preparation for each is uniquely different. Where and when this preparation begins depends on the individual dog's maturity and inherent abilities. One never trains a young dog for natural ability; the dog is prepared. Here is where the "rubber meets the road" for dog breeders. The last thing a responsible breeder would want to achieve is a test score where the dog's true natural ability and behavior has been masked by training. Examples include force retrieving a pup to get a favorable water score that could not have been achieved without force, or complete steadiness to flush and wing in order to receive a favorable pointing score.

AKC hunt tests for pointing dogs focus primarily on upland bird hunting and hasve no water work expectations. As a side note, I have judged several of our local GSP club's annual water competition and was amazed at the performance these dogs could achieve. The clubs primary focus was AKC hunt tests and AKC Field Trials, but the ability to perform at a desirable level for water work was also very solid in these dogs.

Preparation for natural ability can begin as early as eight weeks of age and as late as 12 months. Since the maximum age limit to test a pup is 16 months, there is plenty of time for the preparatory work. Seasonal weather conditions in different geographic locations plays a role in scheduling as does the age of a pup and available hunt test testing dates. A pup born in November will most likely be tested before its first birthday, whereas a pup born in March will most likely be tested after it has turned a year old. Being aware of the pup's birthdate and Chapter test dates should be part of the initial preparation and testing plan.

One would never wait until a pup turns a year old to begin the necessary preparation to develop an admirable hunting companion. This process begins the day the pup arrives at their new home. Socialization and creating a good citizen is key during the first several months. It is during this time period that an honest evaluation can assess the pros and cons of how biddable the new pup may be. GSP pups and Pudelpointer pups seem to have an earlier maturity and can be comfortably taken from their pack at seven or eight weeks of age. Some of the other versatile breeds such as a Spinone or Griffon often show this individual maturity several weeks later. After several days away from their puppy pack you should see a relationship extended to the new human family, replacing their puppy pack needs. All pups go through some sort of fear-factor stage at roughly 10 to 12 weeks old. Constant attention and fostering can make this stage unnoticeable.

The best advice I think I could offer someone with that new eight-week-old versatile pup is to play retrieving drills every day until the pup is four to 6 months old. Building a strong retrieving drive is much easier before the pup discovers birds and hunting. Begin by rolling a soft nerf ball down a hallway in the home with all doors in the hallway closed. The pup has no place to go once they latch onto their prize but to return to you. Never be in a hurry to take the ball away. As the game progresses, begin stepping out of sight and make encouraging squeaky sounds to help the pup find you. This can progress until you are in a different room of the house and the pup dashing back in an effort to find you.

Retrieving has three different inherent instincts. Most all of our versatile breeds have, and pass on, those traits. The first is to chase, second is to possess and parade, and the third is to share which returns the pup back to their owner. The sharing part is not seen as prevalent and that is where the "hide and seek" game comes into play. The pup needs to enjoy the return as much as the chase. One should never expect a young dog to return a retrieve to its owner who is merely standing in place begging the pup to return. Always be backing up or step behind an object such as a tree to encourage the same fun game in those beginning months once the retrieving has been taken outdoors. Eventually, with the dog's age and maturity, we will insist upon complete return retrieves through obedience, but for now we want to get as much as we can from the pup's inherent cooperation which was received from their line.

Pups at this young age need to witness complete socialization of places, people, sounds, and varying experiences. Because of the boldness of most versatile breeds there are usually little to no problems with socialization. A pup raised entirely in the backyard and only seeing adults for the first 4 to 6 months of their life may never have an equal chance toward normal behavior. What if you, as an adult human, had never seen a child before? Imagine how strange, and perhaps even frightening, that experience would be? It's the same for a dog who has never seen humans of different sizes, shapes, colors, voices, clothing, etc. For this reason, we need our pup to be introduced to and handled by as many people in as many variations as possible.

Socialization to noise is also necessary at this young age. Clapping and banging a spoon on a pan to call the youngster to dinner is always a good start. The experience of noise must be followed by something positive and rewarding. This is rarely an issue in today's versatile dogs, but when gun shyness or gun sensitivity rears its ugly head, it is a deal changer for the owner and their relationship with their dog. However, most noise sensitivities can usually be overcome. Many of our best hunting companions are fiercely afraid of thunder and fireworks. These are "startling" noises that have no meaning or understanding to a dog and are completely unrelated to a dog who is gun shy. A dog who is gun shy is aware of where the noise is coming from and completely shuts down in an effort to avoid the noise by hugging closely to the security of his owner or returning to a safe haven such as the house or vehicle.

I'm convinced that what we see as "super performance dogs" are made more by the owner/handler and the efforts and exposure the dog received from eight weeks to eight months. The genetics give our dogs the capability, and the individual raising the pup along with the exposure given, create what we like or don't like as the dogs mature to adulthood. If a below average potential pup is placed with an individual that is dedicated in raising this new youngster with the maximum amount of love, obedience, socialization, and exposure you will see an above average performer in the end. The end result of an above average potential pup if placed with an individual that merely raises this pup solely in the backyard with little love, obedience, socialization, and exposure this pup may grow up to be a below average field performer as an adult. The best analogy to this can be seen on a playground or classroom with grade school children. Those children whose parents' expectations were to raise a child that was a good citizen while having a broad range of exposure to life usually had the easiest time adjusting to the playground rules and seemed to enjoy this time the most.

During the hunt test's performance or utility test the dogs are evaluated on pointing, standing steady to wing, shot and fall then retrieving the shot game birds upon command. At times tracking a wounded game bird is also required. During the Utility water work, dogs are evaluated on steadiness, marking ability, locating, and retrieving game in typical duck hunting situations. Also a duck search where a live duck has been released without the dog's knowledge and the dog is evaluated on the thoroughness of their search. A 200 to 300 yard drag of a dead bird is used to test complete retrieving obedience when the dog is out of the handler's vision and control.

The dogs that pass a performance or utility testing, regardless of the prize received, are North America's premier hunting companions. These are the dogs that are expected to share all field duties with their owners at an obedience level that is a pleasure to experience. Their training foundation has been strict making it easy for these dogs to adapt to the various hunting expectations needed for their future. There are always ups and downs in the training necessary to get a dog to the Utility test's level of necessary performance required. I always took the stance that I wanted to make my training as difficult as necessary because if my dog was going to be a quitter, I wanted them to quit in training and not during a test. I learned quite early on in my dog training career that there is nothing that cleanses a stubborn dog's soul like a good old fashioned butt whooping, and success was usually soon to follow. Test day is the day of reckoning for handlers, so all of the harsh training needs to be completed a month or so prior to test day. Daily training success along with yard drills should be the last month's format while leaving all the harsh disciplined training in the past.

This publication is meant to help with training for any of the available hunt tests offered throughout North Amierca, and rewriting the information available on any of the different organization's websites would be pointless. VHDF offers the organizations testing expectations along with a calendar of events at www.vhdf.org. AKC hunt tests information is available at www.akc.org where they describe the Junior Hunter and Master Hunter expectations. A great resource for understanding the testing offered by NAVHDA can be found at www.navhda.org. Their Aims, Programs, and Test Rules is available as a PDF file and should be read by everyone expecting to participate in a NAVHDA event. Also, attending one of NAVHDA's Handler's Clinics holds top value for learning NAVHDA's testing system and expectations.

APTITUDE AND NATURAL ABILITY TESTING

THE FIELD SEARCH

During the field portion of this test, two random shots will be fired using blank ammunition to test each dog for noise sensitivity to gunfire. The dog will then be rated as "Not Gun Shy, Gun Sensitive" or "Gun Shy" as determined by the judging team. A gun sensitive dog is a one that abandons their search to be near their owner but recovers quickly and returns to the purpose of the search. A dog is considered to be gun shy if it leaves the search field or returns to the handler and then refuses to hunt and remains at the handler's side. Gun shy rated dogs do not qualify for a prize.

Game birds are previously planted in a search field that is usually about 40 acres in size. Three to five birds which are usually chukar are dizzied and planted at various locations. The search lasts for a minimum of 20 minutes. The dogs desire to search for the planted birds along with their cooperation are judged and scored from 1 to 4 with 4 being the highest. Each dog's use of nose is also judged during the 20-minute search and this score along with the desire score, the cooperation score, and number of birds located help determine the dogs overall search score.

The desire score is a direct reflection of the dogs purpose to search and find game birds. Lower scores are given to dogs that do not maintain a continued search and demonstrate an on-off pattern in their enthusiasm to maintain hunting. As a rule, the desire score and the search score find the same results on the judge's score card.

The cooperation score reflects the willingness to perform as a team player with their handler without needing verbal commands to fulfill these expectations. An easy way to look at cooperation is a dog showing instinctive

Apprentice Judge George Decosta preparing Courtney Kaufman for her field search alongside Senior Judge Larry Stone.

obedience without requiring commands in order to perform correctly. A lower cooperation score is given to the dog that demonstrated a self hunting pattern with little concerns as to their handler's chosen path during the search; requiring continual calling to maintain the partnership expected by the judging team. Also refusing to establish point on scented birds and flushing the birds themselves. As a rule, the pointing score and the cooperation score find similar results on the judge's score card.

The use of nose score evaluates the consistency observed of the dog's effort to locate game through scenting. When birds are located, the distance from the bird is also an indication of a dog's use of nose. the best indicator as to a dogs scenting abilities can be observed during the live pheasant track. The results are much more black and white for the judging team when the dog is tracking than when in the field search. The final use of nose score is usually influenced the most by the score given during the live bird track.

THE LIVE BIRD TRACK

A flightless pheasant or chukar is released in with the wind to the bird's back (downwind) or a cross-wind to the bird. The exact path the bird takes during its escape is observed and noted by the judging team. Once the bird is out of sight and has travelled a respectable distance the dog is called upon to track the bird from the scent left on the bird's path. At the discretion of the handler, the dog may or may not be shown the game bird before the bird is released. The dog is judged by how well and how far the dog can follow the same path the bird do. If the dog locates the bird and establishes a point, the point is credited on the dog's pointing score. Cooperation is also scored on the track and the best score given to the dog that remains in the tracking area and also if the bird is retrieved if caught. Desire is also judged on the track and the score given reflects the consistency that the dog demonstrated in maintaining the purpose of locating the bird. It is a thing of beauty to watch a master track performed as the purpose demonstrated is as intense as the eye of a hurricane at times.

Blaine Carter introducing tracking. Photo courtesy Patti Carter.

THE WATER RETRIEVE

In the water retrieve, the judging team is looking at the dog's desire and confidence to swim. Desire is also judged at the water retrieve and usually the water score and the desire score during this phase are the same. The dogs are expected to swim at least twice for a dummy thrown by the handler. A retrieve of the thrown dummy is not necessary and offers no additional score when retrieved. Dogs refusing to enter the water for a thrown dummy are given a second chance to perform with a dead bird replacing the dummy. Here the highest water score given is a 2 and the dog must go straight into the water to receive this score. Again, a cooperation score is awarded and a lower score is given to the dog that leaves the performance area or pretends to ignore the work by insisting on drinking.

OVERALL SCORING

The final search score is only determined from the observations during the 20-minute search. Ground coverage, the dog's observed purpose, and the dog's productivity help determine this score.

The final desire score is a calculation of the desire scores given in the search phase, the water phase, and also the tracking phase with the search and water phases carrying the most weight.

The final cooperation score is also calculated from the cooperation scores in the search, the track, and also the water phases with the search cooperation score carrying the most weight.

The final pointing score is a calculation of the pointing observed both in the search phase and also the track, with the search phase carrying the most weight.

The final tracking score is primarily determined from the judges' observations during the live bird track. However, if tracking is observed during the field search the dog is awarded credit for that performance.

The final water score is given only from the judging observations during the water phase of the test.

The final use of the nose score is a calculation from successful bird locations observed in the field search and also abilities witnessed in following the live bird track during the tracking phase. The score given during the field search carries the most weight when determining the final use of nose score.

There are seven scores given to each dog following the natural ability test: use of nose, search, pointing, water, track, desire, and cooperation. All seven of these scores reflects a different instinct acquired genetically from each dog's parents and their line.

Dogs tested in VHDF's aptitude test receive a score based on a 10-point system for each phase of their test and are awarded a final score with no prizing category awarded. In NAVHDA's natural ability test, 112 points is a maximum score and is based on a 4-point system. Their highest Prize awarded is a Prize I and dogs that don't qualify are given a No Prize. Many evaluate their dog's performance by the prize achieved, but I prefer to grade my dogs on the points they achieved. I look at

NAVHDA judging team preparing to read scores following a day of judging. Photo courtesy Nancy Anisfield.

a dog that has achieved 105 points or more as the superior performer. A dog can earn a Prize I with 99 points and for this reason I feel one needs to look at the score more than the prize when making future breeding evaluations. In my opinion, there isn't much difference in a dog scoring 105 points and a dog scoring 112 points, but there is a significant difference in a dog scoring 99 points. These higher scoring dog's performances shine quite a bit brighter and it is quite easily seen. There's a truth in these dog's eyes that always appears to say they are in control of their game and prefer to work as a team. AKC pass fail expectations see the dogs performing multiple times with a passing performance required each time before awarding their Junior Hunter title.

INTRODUCING BIRDS AND SEARCH

With a well-socialized pup that is somewhere between four to six months old, it's time to introduce the pup to birds in a very controlled environment, making sure only a positive experience with birds prevails. A frozen quail, chukar, or pigeon is thawed completely and now replaces the pup's favorite retrieving object for their simple retrieves. Picking up a dead bird is just the beginning of all the bird exposure the pup will see in its future, but patience must be practiced at this introduction as some pups are quite reserved to actually latch on and exhibit the parading we want to see. Most versatiles have strong prey drive toward gamebirds and picking up a dead bird and parading with it in its mouth comes quite naturally. If the pup hesitates in picking up dead bird, more teasing may be required before the toss. If the teasing proves unsuccessful, another dog may be necessary to create some competition and eventually the pup plays the copy-cat game of following the lead of the older dog.

I like to move forward at this point and introduce the pup to a live bird retrieve. A crop-winged pigeon or bobwhite would be my first choice. I feel it is important to make sure the young dogs don't have a fear for live birds as there is a small percentage that feel it is not natural to have something alive in their mouth. To maximize the prey drive we want to eventually see in the pup's field search, retrieving live birds helps instill this.

Once the young pup is showing confidence picking up and retrieving both dead birds and live birds, it's time to introduce live birds to be searched for in a field search. I like using pigeons for my initial introduction. The pigeons I use are homing pigeons so they can be used over and over but if one doesn't have a loft of homers, mere barn pigeons can be used. The difference is that they just fly away, not to be used again.

It is important to introduce pointing dogs to pigeons when they are young as during their training years, the amount of obedience expected for extended steadiness will require their seeing plenty of pigeons. At times the older dogs that have never been introduced to pigeons when young will look at these birds as a barnyard bird and have little interest, making training much more expensive as gamebirds will be the only birds one can use with these dogs.

My way of first introducing live birds is simply several fly-aways out in front of the young pup. The sound of birdwings taking flight has an electrifying effect on a hunting dog's prey drive so several flighted birds in front of the pup, with a chase allowed, should create the prey drive we desire.

Releasing a pigeon in front of a pup.

I do most of my training from an acre field adjacent to my kennel facility. I'm aware, however, that most need to travel to train, especially with birds. When training at my facility, I immediately pop the young student back into a kennel following every sound exercise. I don't allow any extended time of play afterwards where the lesson could be lost from the pup's memory. Sitting and waiting in a kennel also seems to help create the pup's desire to get back to what they had just experienced. When training at other locations I use the kennels on my truck to cool down dogs in the same way. This is one of the most important training tips I can share – to immediately isolate a training dog so the urge to repeat the positive scenario is fresh on their mind. Over the years I've watched while most folks do the opposite and allow their dog to play and goof off after a training session and a great deal of the learned lesson seems to dissipate into thin air as the young student finds playtime much more satisfying. If there is a trademark I have earned over the years as a trainer, it surely pertains to my consistent halt following a successful drill or training procedure and immediately resting my student in a kennel or crate. When in the field, I instantly secure a lead onto my dog and return to the truck at heel. I never allow them to hunt or run free back to the truck.

Now it's time for live birds on the ground to be found. I want this to be quick and easy and the pup should have been waiting in the kennel to return to chase flighted birds again. I double-lock the wings on three or four homing pigeons and lay them on the ground with their wings protruding into the air and visible to an approaching dog. It is always important to get down to a dog's vision level to make sure they are seeing what you want them to see. At this stage of bird introduction, the pup is on a 10 to 15 foot long check cord. As soon as the pup sees the protruding wings they will advance with curiosity to investigate this new sight. I help direct them with the aid of the check cord straight into the wind so they will be getting both sight and scent of the bird. At about four feet from the bird, I restrain the pup from advancing any further with the use of the check cord. Some pups will instinctively go on point and some will continue to lunge trying to catch the bird. I never say a word to the pup and unlock the bird's wings so it can fly back to the homer loft. If the pup is lunging too furiously in an attempt to catch the grounded bird, I often put a half-hitch around the pup's waist with the check cord to make the lunges more unpleasant. The waist half-hitch or gut-cinch is usually not tested by a dog as they would when restrained by only a collar. It isn't much difference in dogs than in horses – when you want a horse to pull a plow, place a harness around the horse's neck and ask him to pull. Put a bucking strap around that same horse's flank and he's ready for the rodeo arena. Much the same, dogs resent being secured around the flank and succumb to this restraint in a more submissive manner.

Following this three-bird wing-locked exercise, the pup goes immediately into a kennel to absorb the dog-to-bird experience. The pup had been restrained on all three birds at about four feet away with plenty of bird scent blowing in their face. All three birds had been released to fly away and the pup was not allowed to chase. Within about 15 to 30 minutes, we repeat the procedure.

The next day's session should have dizzied birds in the grass with a slight amount

Double locking the wings on a pigeon rendering them flightless.

of grass covering them so they are totally camouflaged from the pup's vision. The pup should remember the training location and eagerly begin searching with their eyes for exposed bird wings. Again, the pup is being restrained from possibly catching one of the birds with a short check cord. By bringing the pup downwind and with a crosswind pattern the pup will eventually scent one of the hidden birds and the same process as was done with the locked-wing birds should follow. Flight the birds by nudging with your foot and restrain the pup from chasing with the check cord. If no pointing, or at least stalking, takes place the second round of this procedure should have the pup restrained with a half-hitch around the pup's waist. Also, a dog collar can be placed around the pup's waist and the lead attached here rather than at the collar on the neck.

If the pup still is not showing instinctive pointing, it may be an age or maturity issue and it would be wise to back off. Allowing the pup to continue to lunge toward planted birds will become a habit that will be harder to break in the future. If you bench this dog for a week or two there often times seems to be some mysterious magic that helps direct their pointing instinct toward perfection. This was the same procedure my high school basketball coach had and it certainly did work well on me.

One must also remember that some dogs merely don't see or smell pigeons as a gamebird! Moving on to planted bobwhite quail or chukar would be the next step for this pup. We won't be hunting pigeons with this pup in the upcoming fall, but it will be more expensive to train using gamebirds only.

I must also add that training on wild birds is the ultimate experience for any hunting dog. The availability and time of year one wants to train make them unavailable for most circumstances. But, when possible, allowing young dogs to pursue wild birds is the best way to advance that youngster's prey drive to hunt and to primarily hunt with their nose.

Next to wild birds, I have found that homing pigeons launched from a remote launcher advances the young dog's prey drive quite rapidly. One wants to introduce the launcher first in a controlled environment as the sudden burst of the launcher when releasing birds can often startle the submissive young dogs which could possibly create blinking of the launchers later in the field work. I like to put a cropped wing pigeon in a launcher and place the launcher in plain sight in a familiar location to the dog and near my truck. I bring the dog in downwind on a short leash. I never let the pup get any closer than four feet of the launcher. When the pup smells or shows curiosity toward the visible launcher, I launch the cropped winged pigeon and allow the pup to retrieve the bird. I also let the pup take their time smelling the launcher and often give them multiple retrieves before ending this session. Now I feel confident that the sudden opening of the launcher and the noise it makes when opening will be a comfortable and familiar sound and experience for future field training. Now I can hide a launcher with a homing pigeon in the grass and check cord the pup up to the launcher and begin launching birds that can be chased following a well established point. Introducing pups to a launcher first by sight, followed by launching a live bird to retrieve is a much better way to get the pup off to the right start, as many young dogs pounce on the launcher as it explodes open in front of them and never see the homer flying away. This way they focus on the fleeing bird and avoid trying to retrieve the launcher.

Once I have a pup searching for planted birds while restrained with only a check cord it is time to free up the youngster and offer searches off-lead. Ten-minute

Staunching up a 12-week-old pup on a sight and scent point.

Releasing a pigeon and allowing the pup to chase.

searches are a good place to start and remember to leash up the pup as the search time ends and on the return back to the truck. I begin putting homers in launchers at this point. I keep a keen eye on the pup, determining whether the pup is searching with his eyes, his nose, or a combination of both. Young dogs begin searching exclusively with their eyes and it takes a great deal of work with some to convince them that their nose finds all the gold and their eyes just keep them from running into brush, trees, and other obstacles in their path.

To help stimulate more nosework, I often take a live chukar with me when planting my homing pigeons and launchers. I hold the bird by both feet and shake scent onto various low brush and foliage pockets. This gives added scented areas in my field and more locations for the pup to explore with his nose. In the beginning, I place the launcher behind small stands of brush. This helps accomplish two training positives: First of all, I want the pup to be far enough away from the launcher that when it opens it cannot hit the pup in the face and they have a good chance of actually seeing the bird as it is launched (at first all the pup sees is the launcher and misses seeing the bird catapulted into the air). Second, having the launcher hidden behind brush helps stop the pup and gets them on point.

When your pup is on point, you should instantly stop as they have, and enjoy their pointing instinct experience together. If a second dog backs its bracemates established point when hunting wild birds, it is honoring that find. As the handler and partner of your dog you should show the same cooperative honor. This helps settle and steady your dog. Contrary to this, if you always charge forward as soon as your

Donate Thibault GSP standing well off of a launcher. Photo courtesy Donate Thibault.

dog establishes a point, your dog will remain nervous, as your approach will create the unsteady picture we have all seen too often. When I do approach a dog on point, I always circle to one side or the other. I never approach to the rear of the dog as I want them to be totally aware of my approach from the corner of their eye.

The one thing I never do when preparing a pup for natural ability is to dizzy or plant a chukar as will be done during the dog's test. All it takes is one caught chukar when training and that curse can be hard to break.

I also avoid allowing my dogs to point every homer in a launcher that they locate. I try to launch a good many of the bird the exact moment that I see the pup scent the launcher. Allowing dogs to point every planted bird certainly is a warm-and-fuzzy training feeling but in all actuality what we are teaching is that the bird will allow the dog to advance until the dog can actually see the bird. If allowed, dogs will creep and relocate until they are confident of the bird's exact location and often times discontinue scent pointing only to road-in on their birds until they can sight point them. This certainly is not what we are training toward.

I can honestly say that, of the last 20 dogs I have personally trained and handled in their NAVHDA Natural Ability test, none have pointed a planted chukar without check cord reinforcement. The IQ of today's dogs is much higher than one would expect from a mere canine, but the learning curve toward bad habits is just as quick as to our proposed training ideals.

CREATING A COOPERATIVE SEARCH

The judging team is evaluating each dog's desire (pre-drive), their use of nose, and cooperation (bidability). If the desire score is lowered it means the dog did not display the necessary purpose toward finding birds that the judging team expected. Also, of the birds found, it required the judging team to lead the dog to a close downwind location of the bird. From here the pup is expected to show improved purpose and find birds on its own. A lower use of nose score usually indicates the dog had difficulty in locating planted birds, even when helped to downwind locations. A lower cooperation score in the field search is created by a dog displaying self-hunting and not hunting with its handler and/or has taken out birds found with no indication of pointing.

When a dog is allowed to run wild in a self-hunting manner, the dog usually doesn't make the necessary effort when the pointing opportunities present themselves.

All of my young dogs have been taught to come with a verbal command and then reinforced with an E-collar. I use an E-collar that has a pager mode which vibrates as a cellphone would. When on 20-minute searches during training sessions, I continually change directions and apply E-collar vibration as I change my course. My direction changes are usually either 90 or 180 degree variations. It doesn't take much of this and the dog learns to keep an eye on me and that instant direction behavior avoids the E-collar's vibration. I feel that the obedience I am asking for from the dog is given back to me in a more cooperative search. A more cooperative search usually means we will see better partnership during bird finds which means better pointing. The only way to create more cooperation in a dog is to apply more obedience. These two have similarities but when simply stated, cooperation is a dog doing things correctly without being asked, whereas obedience requires a command.

Every dog seems to have their own search range where the wheels begin to fall off that cooperation balance we wish to see. It is important to be aware of different dog's cooperation range as once a dog sprints outside this range a quite different dog often emerges. For the sake of positive repetition, it is important to keep a dog within their cooperation range during training sessions. When a dog points a bird and remains

Make sure dogs are allowed to sightpoint a launcher and witness birds launched to avoid a launcher springing open and frightening your dog.

on point for the handler to flush repeatedly during multiple training sessions, the more likely this will become a preferred habit in the dog's mind.

I believe today's versatile dogs are performing at higher levels because our breeders are looking much more at cooperative dogs to breed and these dogs perform to please their owner/handler more than themselves. Cooperative dogs enjoy hearing your happy voice and are quick to learn what they need to do to hear this happy voice.

I have heard some at various hunt tests complain that the advanced test is all about obedience and not enough request for performance in the dogs. Personally, I feel the success there is from well-bred dogs that display considerable cooperation making these performers quick studies and their obedience much more solid and reliable.

Steadiness training on table.
Photo courtesy Nancy Anisfield.

Being capable of molding a dog's performance without strict discipline in the form of obedience will always find a dog much more willing to please and perform for their owner. And this is the cooperative versatile dog. I also hear complaints that the Field Trial performers are wild self-searching dogs that are useless as hunting companions. Again, I feel that if there is enough cooperative nature in the dog they will learn to compete and also hunt with the gun when asked and will know the difference. I always think back to Jim Reed's GSP Ammertals Lancer D who was a National Champion Field trial performer and also an exceptional hunting dog throughout the Fall. Also, Field Champion Tekoa Mountain Sunrise, an English Setter that was a horseback field trial performer but during winter chukar hunts I went on with his handler Richie Robertson, Sunrise was a very cooperative dog to follow on foot. Again, he knew his expected range when competing and again when hunting.

INCREASING DESIRE IN THE SEARCH

It is very difficult to add desire to a dog's character. Each individual dog is born with their own behavior indices and desire is just one of these many indices. Sometimes a jumpstart is necessary to get some youngsters performing at a level where improvement can be seen on a daily basis.

If a pup is too young and too immature for the desire to search and find birds to present itself, the handler just has to have the patience to wait. There are several things that can, however, be done to instill more desire (predrive) in young dogs.

The easiest method is to plant crop-winged birds that cannot fly very far and that the dog can catch. Make sure these birds are visible as the ramifications of this can be a dog that no longer points scented birds. I prefer to put these crop-winged birds in a launcher and merely launch the birds when the dog gets into the vicinity of the bird. Here the confidence that birds will be present whenever taken to the field helps develop desire as nothing promotes desire like getting live birds into a dog's mouth.

GSP showing intense desire while standing a planted bird. Photo courtesy Donate Thibault.

Beginning to shoot planted birds that are pointed can also be of benefit. This is for the dog that understands the need to search in order to locate birds, but is too lackluster in their efforts. Getting birds into a dog's mouth regardless of the method seems to improve desire and give a dog more purpose toward the hunt.

My last tip is to turn several chukar loose prior to a search hoping to create some inherent tracking opportunities. I see this often when running pups on wild quail. Adult quail run through sagebrush flats like roadrunners and they truly stimulate young dogs' search desire. Obviously putting a dog on wild birds is the most effective method of improving desire, but this option doesn't always present itself due to nesting seasons and one's distance involved to reach wild bird habitat.

INTRODUCING THE GUN

Hopefully the pup's socialization process has continued with different and increasing noise added to his daily life followed by positive reinforcements. It is now time to introduce the gun and its sound to the pup in the field. I have a routine that I have used for years and I never alter or shortcut this procedure.

It is imperative that the pup understands that the best possible reward is going to follow immediately following this noise. In this case it will be a live bird to retrieve. There is a two-fold benefit for the pup after introducing this method. First and foremost, the understanding that the noise signals a possible retrieve and the pup should be looking in the direction of the noise for a falling bird to retrieve. The second benefit is that the pup learns that noise coming from a gun will not harm them.

I never gamble when introducing the gun to a pup and always begin with a day or two beginning my drill without involving gunshots. I take the pup to a familiar field with three or four pigeons in a shoulder-strap bird bag. When the pup is busy searching away from me, I holler "Hey! Hey! Hey!" as loud as possible. When the pup looks back to me, I throw a pigeon off to the side that has had all flight feathers either removed or clipped from one wing. This renders the bird flightless, but it can still fly 50 yards or so before coming to the ground. The pup will chase down the bird and if you are lucky, he will bring it to you. Remember, you are introducing your pup to the noise of a gun and if the retrieve is not complete or even favorable, you shouldn't make anything of this and be prepared to deal with this at a later date. Running away from your pup once they have chased down the bird often encourages a favorable retrieve just as was done when the pup was younger and beginning to enjoy retrieving that Nerf toy.

Some pups insist on chewing a live bird until it is lifeless. Again, this can be addressed later in the training schedule, but for now you want to avoid any discipline for chewing on birds. Merely go to the pup and take the bird away.

After three or four cropped-wing pigeons have been thrown for the pup to retrieve, it is time to leash up and immediately return the pup to the kennel where they will, hopefully, be building desire to return to this exercise as soon as possible. The key to this first step to gun introduction is the handler yelling "Hey! Hey! Hey!" just before throwing each of the birds to be retrieved.

On the second day you will add the noise of a gun to the retrieving drill. I use a blank pistol in the beginning and often wrap a towel around my hand and the gun to muffle the first several shots.

I make sure I am back in the same familiar field as on the previous day. The difference for the second day of gun introduction training is that now I blank the gun first and as soon as the pup turns to identify the new noise, I holler "Hey! Hey! Hey!" and throw a cropped-wing bird off to the side for a retrieve.

The "Hey! Hey! Hey!" is my ace-in-the-hole to help the pup realize the sound of the gun is a quick precursor to the retrieving drill they have previously learned and enjoy. Having some insurance in the event that the pup's response to the noise from the gun is submissive is well worth the time taken over a several-day gun introduction process. The value of this procedure will also be seen later in the description of hunting in heavy cover and instilling the need to track rather than search for downed birds.

As time goes on I add louder noise until I am using a shotgun. You know when

Introducing the noise of a shotgun with the dog well out in front and on a serious chase.

you have created the correct training message when your pup is leaping in the air or attempting to stand on his hind legs hoping to create better vision to see something falling. While this may be the best possible way to introduce the noise from guns in a positive manner that makes total sense to the pup, it can have a shortcoming when running the pup in a natural ability test. During the first several minutes of most puppy hunt tests, two blank shots are fired to test each dog for gun sensitivity and gun-shy behavior. Since our noise-prepared pup expects to get a retrieve following gun noise, they have been cued into the retrieving mode and could easily attempt to retrieve their first located bird instead of establishing a point. For this reason, I routinely call my pup to me as soon as the two shots have been fired and take a moment to offer my pup some water to drink, attempting to get their brain out of "retrieving mode."

In the event that anything negative happens in this gun-introduction period, one should discontinue the noise of the gun and spend many consecutive days performing only the retrieving drill with "Hey! Hey! Hey!" signaling retrieves.

Dogs with severe noise sensitivities will quickly learn that the dreaded noise comes only from a gun and will begin displaying a gun-shy behavior as soon as they see or even smell a shotgun. One way to desensitize the dog to guns is to place a shotgun on the floor next to the dog's bed in the home. For obvious safety reasons, care must be taken when employing this method. Guns must always be unloaded and never left out in the presence of children.

INTRODUCING TRACKING

In most hunt test testing for finished dogs, the "deal breaker" in their tests is usually from the dreaded duck search. In a hunt test for aptitude or natural ability test, it's the live pheasant track that disappoints more handlers than most of the other components combined.

Most of the other components in natural ability test allow for multiple chances for success, whereas, in the tracking portion there is rarely given another opportunity to demonstrate a better performance. There are variables, also, that can affect one dog's performance much differently than other dogs at the same test. Examples would be a pheasant making several direction changes in its escape route where most run in a straight line, a fast running bird not making occasional hesitations (which leaves additional scent), and a bird choosing to run only where the grass or cover is minimal. Also the daily air temperature can alter scenting conditions as the day warms up from early morning to afternoon where the birds body scent begins to equal that of the of the ground along with the moisture content of grasses and existing cover can vary the tracing variables that handlers and their dogs are continually dealing with.

After one becomes conscious of the many varying conditions and factors affecting tracking, and only having one chance to demonstrate the best possible performance, it seems as though being blindfolded and throwing a dart at the wall may have a better chance at seeing repeatable accuracy than that of today's tracking expectations. The good news is that most well bred versatile dogs can easily handle all of these varying circumstances and the variables mentioned previously and do so much easier than most can imagine. Most versatile dogs can handle and perform to a much higher degree when tracking than most would expect and it isn't like rolling the dice when taking your turn as to which pheasant you drew and which location you have been allotted to run your track on.

After handling more than 100 dogs in NAVHDA Natural Ability tests and judging more than 1,000, I came to the realization many years ago that the biggest mystery and unknown factor of this test is always what each dog will do on its pheasant track. There is no way to foresee how cooperatively the pheasant may run and every dog gives a performance all its own.

One conclusion I drew was that most handlers had taught their dog to chase rather than track. Once a young dog gets the notion that there has been a bird running from a feather pile, their first instinct is to attempt to catch this invisible quarry by chasing. When one releases a live pheasant to scamper to cover and follows this by releasing a dog to find the bird, what is actually being taught is to chase down the bird rather than tracking. This is where many fall into the trap of testing their dog rather than preparing and teaching the best way to recover the bird is by tracking.

To the casual eye, tracking and searching look to be quite similar, especially at the fast pace we see in today's dogs. However, the truth of the matter is that there is quite a difference as far as what the dog is actually doing. Basically, during a defined search, the dog randomly looks for a bird while running a pattern that the dog feels increases the odds of a find. The nose is key to a dog's search but the purpose is to find scent that will hopefully identify a hidden bird. During a track, the dog is following a scent trail and there is no random pattern expressed here. The scent trail is on the ground from a runaway bird and the dog may track with a low head or may track with a high head. It is very hard to distinguish the difference in a dog tracking and a dog searching if the dog tracks with a high head. Knowing the path of the running bird helps solidify what is actually happening.

In order to track effectively, a dog needs to be able to concentrate and maintain focus on the task at hand. For this reason, very young dogs and very high-powered dogs are handicapped when asked to track. A very cooperative dog with a keen nose is usually the best candidate for a successful track. They have learned what you want them to accomplish and eventually find themselves performing just as much for their owner or handler as they perform for themselves.

When I train tracking, I like to begin with a five or six-month-old pup. I initiate with a simple drag of a dead bird. I pluck some feathers from the bird (usually a chukar) and do my initial drag into the wind and only about 50 yards. When I bring the pup to the feather pile I give the same command that was used to avoid gun-shyness in my introduction to the

Bob Farris returning from a successful pheasant track.

Return to the owner following a successful NA track. Photo courtesy Nancy Anisfield.

gun drills. I fluff up the feathers in front of the dog's nose and very quietly say "Hey, hey, hey." This helps ignite the pup somewhat, but most importantly, it tells the dog to retrieve. Most versatile dogs breeze through this initial drill, but if they struggle I might drag a wet water-soaked duck by the feet to add a much stronger scent line. Dragging the bird by the feet is pulling against the lay of the duck's feathers and leaves considerably more scent. Whenever I drag a duck for a pup I still leave a dead chukar for the reward and retrieve.

Remember to trot away from your pup once the bird is being retrieved to help ensure a complete and speedy retrieve.

I will continue doing dead-bird drags for a pup for several days, making sure some have multiple direction changes or curves built in and the distance between 100 and 200 yards. Varying wind directions should also be used so the pup is comfortable in both upwind and downwind tracks.

It doesn't take long for the pup to see a feather pile, have it fluffed up in their face, and then it's "Game On!" for the youngster. Adding a soft "Hey, hey, hey" adds just that much more excitement to this process.

Now comes the difficult part of tracking training. We have to now convince our student that tracking a live bird can also be done exactly the same way. When we were pulling that dead bird, our pup was most likely following the scent left by the person pulling the drag. It will be roughly 100 times harder to track a single bird than it was the human pulling the dead bird.

There are many ways to create a track with a live bird, but the most important thing to be aware of is that there can be no human scent in the field with the bird's scent. If there is human scent, the dog will stay focused on this and will struggle to get off this scent. I like to pull the bird across the tracking field with a spinning rod equipped with 50-pound test line. I also prefer to use live chukar for all of my tracking drills. I feel that a chukar is harder to track than a pheasant which helps create a more difficult task for the dog and when it comes time to track a rooster pheasant in the dog's Natural Ability test, it will be easier for the dog to stay focused on the job. Many handlers continue to confuse the difference in performing a drag and performing a track. During a drag the dog is trailing the scent of the person that pulled the drag bird. During a track the dog is following the scent line of a live bird. A dog performing a drag should be expected to retrieve a dead bird, whereas during a track the dog is expected to point a live bird.

I place some feathers on the ground as I did before when pulling dead-bird drags. Next, the chukar is attached to a harness at the end of the spinning rod's line. I only pull 50-yard tracks across short green grass. To avoid having my scent in the field near the track I walk in a large arc making sure I create this arc on the downwind side of where my track is going to be. As I walk I'm releasing line from the reel on the spinning rod. Once the arc has taken me to a point directly across from the bird, I begin reeling the bird across the field to my location some 50 yards away. At the very end of my track I drag the chukar about ten feet into the wind and set the spinning rod on the ground to anchor the chukar down. Now I have to return to get the dog and I use the same arc on my return path.

The dog is on a short 10- to 15-foot check cord. The check cord is secured at the dog's collar and a half-hitch wrapped about the dog's waist creating a belly-cinch.

Exposing young natural ability dog to feathers left to pheasant track.

I never let a dog perform a track in training without being on a check cord that is attached to me at the other end. The first time any natural ability-prepared dog should perform a track on a live bird and not be confined by a check cord is on test day. Never allow a pup to perform a track in training off lead. The reason is that once they feel the independence to perform a track off lead, the young pups develop a sense that by merely searching they can find the bird quicker and easier. You now have a dog very unwilling to stay focused and concentrate on a track to the end.

I follow the pup as it tracks and every time the pup strays off the track, I jerk them back onto the scent with the check cord. Having a half-hitch around the waist helps slow the pup down and when jerked back to the scent it creates a "silent" form of discipline letting the student know they are not performing adequately.

When the dog gets to the end of the track they will lose it for a brief moment. When they realize the scent has shifted directly into the wind, the pup should scent the bird itself. Here I make sure I get a strong point out of the dog just as was accomplished when introducing to birds for the first time.

I like to give a pup three or four tracks every day and no other training during this period. I am also keying the dog's nose to chukar which will be helpful during the pup's field search and I am also demanding steadiness on a planted chukar by handling the pup on a check cord using a half-hitch. This is invaluable for pointing during future field searches.

My pups see 20 to 30 short tracks on a chukar as most of my preparation during the final two weeks before their Natural Ability test. Never off-lead and a point on the chukar at the end of every track.

When I take a pup to the judging team after they have released my pheasant, the pup is walked to the pheasant feather pile with a 10-foot check cord and a half-hitch around their waist. This lets the pup know we are going to do a track just as they have done many times in training. I very quietly take the lead entirely off the pup without them knowing they are free from my control.

I show them the feathers and fluff them up with my right hand while holding their collar with my left. I avoid any releases that can distract the pup from the task. I just give a soft "Hey, hey, hey" and walk three or four steps and release the dog.

By always having my pups point the chukar in training, it becomes an expectation for my dogs and I see over 50% of them point the pheasant on their track during a test. When a dog points its pheasant at the end of its track, the dog is awarded this point and it will be averaged in with the dog's pointing score from the field search.

I have found that by running short 50-yard tracks in training, my pups stay better focused on their tracking job during their Natural Ability test as they feel the bird is close in and long casts to search won't be beneficial.

I cannot emphasize enough that when most versatile dogs are released during training to track off-lead, they will learn to search rather than track for birds.

WATER RETRIEVING

When I was first introduced to hunt test testing, it was commonly thought that the water portion of the puppy tests were an indication of the individual dog's "love of water." After 30 years enjoying this testing menu, I personally feel the water portion is more of a retrieving indicator and using water as a retrieving field just "ups the ante" and separates the men from the boys, so to speak. If anything, I feel the results suggest a dog's fear or dislike of water more than their love of water.

One must remember this test was created in the 1960s shortly after the movement to bring imports to North America from Europe. At this time, the dogs tested needed a retrieving test to look for the stronger instinctive retrievers and using water allowed this separation to be much more valid and visible.

With the vast majority of dogs entered in Natural Ability tests today, the water portion is quite meaningless, especially in the eyes of the versatile breeders. It gives the judging team a chance to evaluate the individual dog's coat when wet and also get an accurate mouth evaluation, but as far as determining which dogs possess the most "love of water," I would have to disagree and say they are primarily looking at "love to retrieve." Most likely, the evaluation of the water portion of the puppy test is coming from my retriever background and many will hang onto the notion that the retrieving is what is being used to display the pup's love of water. If this is truly all the judging team is looking for, throwing a rock and making a splash would be a better way to evaluate a dog's water enthusiasm.

The interesting point to be made when considering what this part of the test really defines in a dog's inherent skills is that most all preparation and training focuses on retrieving. We start our pup at eight weeks old retrieving down a hallway in the home and advance to throwing training dummies as far as our arm will allow across a field by the time a pup is six months old. Eventually one goes to water and repeats the same retrieving expectations here.

If the water portion of the beginning hunt test isn't a definition of a dog's inherent retrieving desire, I would have to agree that it might possibly be an indicator of the dog's fear of water as opposed to their love of water. Possibly the dogs that struggle the most at the water test don't perform well because they lack confidence when in water and their performance is due to their fear associated with swimming. Dogs that have a strong desire to retrieve, however, will most likely overcome their fear of water to retrieve when something is thrown into water.

It is at this point in the test that I personally abandon the data for breeding purposes. I believe the Utility test gives me a better resource in their duck search when I'm looking at a dog's possible aversion to water. During the duck search there is nothing thrown to entice a chase into the water. It is for the most part a blind retrieve and the dog is asked to enter the water entirely on their own.

The preparation and training for the water portion of hunt tests Aptitude or Natural Ability test is, however, the most enjoyable for most handlers. If one were to rate all individual natural ability performers on a scale of one to ten on their desire to chase and retrieve, we would quite possibly find that those rating seven to ten were nearly instant swimmers when their favorite retrieving toy was tossed into water. It is

Enthusiastic return to handler during NAVHDA Natural Ability water portion of test. Photo courtesy Courtney Kaufman.

the dogs scoring one to six that require a sound introduction to water with a specific program in mind.

Water exposure should take place at a young age, shortly after the pup has matured past its inherent fear-factor stage of life which is usually between 10-12 weeks. I like to compare the initial water introduction as close to that normally done with small children. No one would consider throwing a child's toy into swimming water and expect to see favorable results. Children are usually introduced to water with a parent carrying and holding the child, offering security with no emotional stress. It would be hard for me to believe that Michael Phelps merely jumped into water over his head at his first introduction. So why would anyone expect anything more from a pup's first exposure? For this reason, young pups should be carried out a short distance into water and learn to swim by swimming back to shore. The more enjoyable playtime in water a pup has with its owner, the more confident the pup will be in the future when asked to retrieve from water.

We need to always consider the fact that the water portion of the Natural Ability test usually always follows the field search and the tracking portion where the dog has been encountering gamebirds. Now at the water site we are asking our dogs to retrieve something made from canvas or plastic. After having birds all morning at the test, it doesn't surprise me that some dogs just refuse to enter water to retrieve anything other than a bird. Again, the dogs having strong retrieving desire don't seem to get swallowed up with failure when expected to make a water retrieve with something other than a bird.

I like to begin all water retrieving with young pups in reverse of the expected final outcome. I have the pup in the water with me and give small retrieves back toward shore. Once I see a confident swimming chase, it is time to reverse the procedure and ask for a retrieve from land into water. I have waders on and am always prepared to assist the pup at this point. If there is any hesitation, I lead the pup into the water and we both go to the retrieving object together. This is usually a bird in the beginning and I graduate to a dummy with a bird wing zip tied onto it and eventually to just a dummy.

One of my preferred training drills once a pup will reliably retrieve from water is to begin asking them to go to a splash. Here I toss a rock into the water and, as soon as the dog focuses on the splash, I toss the retrieving dummy just beyond the splash. It doesn't take many of these drills for the competitive dog to begin to enter the water and swim to the splash. At this point I toss the retrieving dummy over the dog's head for them to retrieve. My goal here is to have a dog that will swim to a splash which is often necessary in hunting to get a dog quickly across a river or pond to locate a downed bird they haven't seen go down.

For the pup that just plain doesn't like retrieving dummies and isn't reliable making water retrieves, you need to use a bird to get the pup swimming for a water retrieve. Use either a live bird or dead one, depending on the dog's aversion. Once the dog will swim to a splash, expecting a bird to splash in front of them, you can switch to a soft canvas dummy with birdwings zip-tied to the dummy. You can usually wean the pup back to using just the canvas dummy.

I learned years ago when training gundogs for clients that a dog that was hesitant to retrieve a bird on the ground would usually be much more eager to retrieve from water once they swam to the object. Maybe they figure they had done all that work to swim to the bird, they might as well retrieve it so it wasn't a wasted swim!

With dogs that initially struggle at water retrieving, the trick is usually getting them into the water. We have had an in-ground swimming pool in our backyard for more than 35 years and watching people enter the water is very similar to the approach used by dogs entering a pond or river. When people begin wading into our pool at the entry steps, they instantly halt once the depth of the water reaches their belly. Now they do one of two things before advancing – they quickly dunk themselves into the water up to their neck, or they lunge forward. Regardless, they quickly get wet as they don't like the water just slowly advancing up their body. If they get out of the pool and re-enter, they are willing to wade until the water is up to their neck because their body is still wet. Another similar phenomenon I see happens when someone wades from the shallow end of the pool toward the deep end. As soon as they realize that the next step they take will have them in water over their head, they stop and actually take a step or two back. The same scenarios are seen in our dogs in the beginning stages of waterwork. Until thoroughly wet, they either hesitate or lunge on water retrieves. They also hesitate or halt when the depth of the water reaches their stomach. This often causes them to give up and retreat, but the attentive handler will quickly advance into the water himself and help the dog finish the retrieve. Eventually, and hopefully, the pup will realize that backing out on retrieves is not an option and this subtle form of obedience will create a cooperative response from the dog to retrieve.

TOP: Sending a dog for water retrieve in NA Test. BOTTOM LEFT: Dog returning with retrieved dummy in NA water test. BOTTOM RIGHT: Dog delivering dummy in NA water test.

There should never be any begging of the dog to make retrieves at the water. A dog unwilling to do this work should never be allowed to run up and down the bank looking for a bridge to the retrieving object. When allowed, this behavior soon becomes a habit and one hard to break. Always be prepared for the worst at the water when training water retrieves and have a game plan to halt any unwarranted behavior. Always be prepared to just cease all training and immediately put the pup up for the day. Even possibly several days!

HUNT TEST'S PERFORMANCE AND UTILITY TRAINING

When one advances from hunt test's Aptitude and Natural Ability test to the Performance or Utility test, your "dog training 101" is not going to provide you with enough knowledge and expertise. It takes a good dog to pass this Utility test, but it takes a better trainer. The training can take anywhere from three months to three years depending on the dedication and time availability. During this phase, a good number of birds are required; both chukar and ducks creating more expense than seen during Natural Ability training. Most everything involved in the Utility test involves training and for every hidden negative trait a dog may have, it is okay to train to mask these traits. This test and the training for it are an attempt to mold and create the most desirable hunting partner you can own. Utility-prized hunting dogs have a reliability in the field and at the duck blind that no other titled dog has.

I sat in a duck blind one cold December morning years ago on Idaho's Snake River with two AKC Field Champion retrievers present. I had a 178 Prize II Utility female Pudelpointer along that day and when the decoys were being picked up at the end of the hunt, it was very obvious that the true workhorse of that day's hunt was not going to be either of the two AKC FC retrievers. Understanding how to track a cripple and keeping the necessary persistence on diving cripples was the primary difference. But what set the dogs apart the most was the ability of my dog to sit some 20 yards downriver by herself on a burlap bag, somewhat camouflaged behind a

NAVHDA judging team. Photo courtesy Nancy Anisfield.

simple makeshift brush blind. She understood not to break on any birds until one was shot and splashed down onto the flowing river. Being stationed downriver gave her an immediate advantage on most retrieves as the river's current was bringing her the birds. While my dog wasn't a superior dog to the others, she was, in this case, a better-trained hunting dog and it was the Utility training that gave her that edge.

On another hunt at about this same time, I hunted chukar in Oregon with the handler of a Field Champion English Setter. This dog had been to the FDSB Nationals several different years and was considered to be one of America's #1 performing Setters in American Field Trials. I took my two NAVHDA Utility-prized females for the hunt and returned to the vehicle with a cozy limit of eight chukars after about three hours of hunting. To my surprise, the Setter had plenty of finds but most birds had walked off before anyone could make the trek to get to the dog. Few birds had been shot over the Setter since the dog didn't retrieve that well and any long-distance downhill kills meant the handler would be required to make these retrieves. Again, I didn't have better dogs than the Setter, but I had better-trained dogs for hunting because of their Utility test training.

If one of your dreams is to someday own an excellent hunting dog which has been trained to be a true "partner" on your hunts, I would strongly suggest signing up to train your dog through and complete one of the performance level tests of one of the available hunt testing organizations.

The hunt tests usually have multiple separate components: Field search, water search, water obedience, and drag. As important as the training is, understanding the judging may be just as important. One should realize from the beginning that about 80% of the judge's scorecard revolves around retrieving. If your dog is not well schooled and reliable in retrieving, it will be hard to near an admirable score. Oftentimes, attending a NAVHDA Handler's Clinic is well worth the time prior to training and handling a dog in a Utility test. Here a NAVHDA senior judge and designated clinic leader put on a two-day clinic explaining the judging of the test.

Before you can begin training for an advanced hunt test, your dog should be completely through a force-retrieve course. With so much of the test's focus related to retrieving, this is a must for the majority of dogs. I personally have never force-retrieved a dog in my life. I did, however, trade training with other trainers or paid other trainers to do the force-retrieving for me. As soon as the dog would pick up a dummy off the ground, I would take over and finish the training so I could begin practicing the retrieving drills the local retriever trainers were using. It is nearly magical how a dog begins to relate toward their owner following force-retrieve training. There is a true partnership that the dog develops and an honest, sincere attitude seen from this dog.

Most people immediately want to begin steadying their dog in the field as they begin Utility training. This is actually the last part of the test I train for. The test itself has a way of see-sawing back and forth between asking for a very obedient dog to asking the dog to show complete independence. The duck search and drag components both ask for the dog to work independently from the handler. The field and water obedience

Clyde Vetter showing what a steady dog looks like in the Utility Field Search. Notice his confidence in his dog. Photo courtesy Nancy Anisfield.

components both ask for a cooperative dog displaying complete obedience. This is the beauty of the test. When John Kegal and Bodo Winterhelt created the Utility test in the 1960's, they wanted to reward the dog with high performance desire in the search, but also wanted to reward the same dog for demonstrating complete obedience and cooperation when asked.

I always begin Utility training with the duck search and drag. Here I'm asking for as much independence as possible and if I had started with field obedience or water obedience I may not be able to get as much out of the dog in terms of independence since the dog may have lost their hunting edge following so much obedience training. The obedience has a dog looking to the handler for direction and this is not what we want to see from a top duck search performance. A good duck search performance needs to see the dog independently penetrating cover and expanding its search for approximately ten minutes while never looking to the handler for direction or assistance.

The water obedience portion of the test follows duck search training in my order of Utility training as this helps set the stage for the field steadiness. Steady by blind, remaining by blind, and finally steady for the retrieve of the shot bird gives the dog a sound pathway toward steadiness, which will be the prime goal in field search portion of the test.

At the end of any of the hunt test testing days, the scores of each of the individual dogs are read before the participants and all that attended that days test. The senior judge usually takes this honor and the suspense of these results puts every handler on the edge of their chair. There are times when you feel as though your dog has drug your heart through the test grounds dirt all day long and there are also times when you feel as though you just hit it out of the park. However, your day ends up, it is for sure a day of reckoning for you and your dog.

Duck Search Training

If you were to ask ten successful trainers to describe their training program for Utility duck search, you would most likely receive ten different scenarios. I don't believe there is any set program that warrants better results than others. I'm pretty sure, however, that those with success would all agree that it takes ducks...lots of ducks.

I want to begin where the dog understands I am giving a command, not asking, to find the duck. By the time most dogs reach Utility training, they have retrieved hundreds of plastic dummies off water and they could visibly see every one of them before entering the water. This is one of the obstacles to be overcome and a redirection of water retrieving needs to be initiated. I begin with basic retrieving drills that are an extension from force-retrieve training. If done correctly, your dog will now retrieve a plastic dummy from the ground 10 to 20 feet in front of you on command (usually "fetch"). The dog needs to return to you and sit holding the dummy until taken. If the dog has been E-collar trained during the force-retrieve, you will get much more mileage from your dog throughout all of the Utility training, but especially for duck search training. Once the dog will successfully retrieve one dummy and return without dropping it, it is time to place two dummies side-by-side and ask for them to be retrieved one at a time. Here the E-collar may be needed to remind the dog on the second retrieve. I continue this drill until the dog will retrieve five dummies from a pile and do so at several different locations.

The desire wanting to be observed in the Utility Duck Search.

Once you have a dog that will retrieve five plastic dummies from a pile at a 50-yard distance, it's now time to move to the water. A small area of water is required as you will be sending your dog to the same pile of five dummies except this time across water, beginning at a 10 to 20 yard distance. Here is where you will see an honest evaluation of how well you completed the force retrieve. You will possibly see a dog dropping the dummy to shake as he leaves the water on the returns. You will definitely see a dog that will act as though they have no idea where that third, fourth or fifth dummy actually is (even though they can easily see it.) Once you get passed this stage you will begin seeing favorable results and a dog that seems to trust you and actually wants to please.

From here on during the training, you will get to see if your dog has the built-in fury to search a water source or marsh. Not all dogs have it in them to do Prize I duck-search work, but most all versatile dogs can earn a qualifying score, and that is what should matter.

Here is where I differ from most trainers as I move on now to a bird-launcher and a cropped-wing pigeon to be launched out into the water on the other side of a pond. My launchers have a built-in duck call that can be requested at the remote. Once set up I have my student at my side on the opposite side of the 50-yard pond. I ask for the duck call and when the dog focuses on the noise, I launch the bird. As soon as the bird splashes in the water, I send the dog. As I repeat this drill at different locations of the pond I quit sending the dog at the splash and take them for a short walk only to come back and send them then. Before every send I verbally offer confidence to the dog with a "dead bird" encouragement. I eventually get to where I can return the dog

Frank Schmidt preparing to send his dog for his duck search.

to my vehicle and, after a cup of coffee, will return the dog to the site and send it for a search and eventually a retrieve. There is always a live cropped winged pigeon in the third launcher and when I have pulled the dog to its vicinity, I launch the bird for a retrieve. What I'm teaching the dog is to perform elapsed-time memory retrieves combined with a search. This isn't a duck search at this point, but at any time if I get a refusal from the dog to perform, I can reinforce my intentions with the E-collar and the dog totally realizes why the retrieving obedience is being reinforced and the only way to avoid the E-collar discipline is to do the work. Any stimulation must be very light as you want to advance with the dog enjoying every new phase of the training.

Since I have three launchers that each have a built-in duck call, I oftentimes hang several in an overhanging tree and use the noise from the launcher to draw the dog to different locations of the pond. Having the launcher out of reach of the dog is mandatory as if they find the launcher and there is no bird present you have counterproductive training in play. This training program works quite well and certainly helps promote the idea of expansion about the marsh by following the noise of the duck calls from the launchers. However, one must be careful not to overdo this tactic as we are teaching our dog to hunt with his ears and not its nose. In the beginning we were trying to overcome the need of the dog to hunt with their eyes and only as far as we could throw a dummy. Our focus up to this point of our training has been to encourage or dog to search water just as they do land and always find success through expansion. Having launchers with a built in duck call is not a requirement to train for duck search and it only assists me in my personal approach in training. Not having launchers merely means one may use a helper or other means to entice a dog

A successful Utility Duck Search. Photo courtesy Rolf Ryberg.

Duck search in flooded timber. Photo courtesy Courtney Kaufman.

to search the other side of a marsh. The importance is that a dog is taught that the duck is always on the opposite side of the marsh and the dog should not be searching the same side of the marsh that they have been sent from. This is where the force retrieve drills help instill this discernment. The duck is always somewhere on the opposite shoreline.

When I look back at my past retriever training days, the duck search is somewhat like a blind water retrieve that retriever trainers train for. They first teach a land blind retrieve and move forward to a water blind. The key ingredient in retriever training is that the dog becomes confident there is a bird to be retrieved in the direction they have been sent. The basic difference is that the retriever trainer will use hand signals to direct their dogs and the hunt test duck search trainer will expect their dog to search without help from the handler. Both require confidence there is a bird present on the opposite side of the marsh.

It is now time to ask our student to start searching with his nose. Here I pull a drag with a clipped-wing duck on the opposite side of the pond, leaving a fresh scent line for the dog to follow. When the dog gets to the end of the drag I have a helper toss a clipped-wing duck out of the brush in front of the dog. If I do not have a helper along, I put the duck in a pheasant launcher directed toward the water. Once the dog begins chasing the flightless duck the real duck search education begins. I am a believer too that these duck chases on crippled-acting birds is what "ups the ante" from the dog's perspective and the serious work now begins.

From this point on I merely show up at a good duck search pond and throw a clipped-wing duck out onto the water and the dog and I watch it swim off to cover. I don't send the dog however. I load the dog and may go for breakfast at some local café or may just go for a drive. When I return and take the dog to the place where I had previously thrown the bird, I am again asking the dog to perform an elapsed-time memory retrieve. If there is any hesitation to cross and enter the cover to search, I have my E-collar and the past experience doing retrieving drills across water as my enforcer. Also, you can always use a second duck with a helper or just perform the sequence again and send the dog as soon as the duck swims out of sight.

Duck-search training is primarily an attempt to instill as much confidence as you can in your dog that a duck really is out there and, by continuing to expand to new locations and penetrate cover, the greatest result will happen – a duck chase!

Several things to be aware of that can affect your score: If you have to resend your dog because they quit, it will drop your score one point. If you are at a non-qualifying score, a resend is a must and often a well-thrown rock will give more favorable results than just a verbal resend. The splash of the rock is much more convincing to the dog. Also, if your dog should happen to break and begin the search before you have given a release command, it is best to just let him go as his breaking will only affect their obedience score and not their duck-search score. The duck-search score is nearly all desire.

In training, it is imperative to teach your dog that the search is not over just because you found and retrieved the duck. You will be asked to resend your dog if the search time was too short in the judge's opinion. If your dog thinks their job is finished and won't resend demonstrating a positive search attitude, your score will be lowered. In your training, having a second duck in place every time your dog returns successfully will teach your dog to resend with the same confidence as was seen on the first duck. I have a helper slip a second duck straight across from where I originally sent the dog in the beginning when the dog has caught the first duck and is returning. I want the resend to be much easier and quicker. For this reason, duct tape has been used on the second duck so it cannot use its feet or wings to escape.

When training for duck searches, every trainer needs to avoid merely "testing" your dog as will be done on test day. You should stay focused on creating more confidence in your dog's mind that there really is a crippled duck somewhere. This means moving about the pond or marsh with your dog in the beginning sessions just as you did when teaching your dog to search a field. Never merely stand in place as the dog will continually want to check back to make sure you are still there. Some trainers move about with their dogs in a canoe or kayak to help create confident expansion. Eventually your dog will realize how this new game is to be played and you can begin remaining in place.

During the actual hunt test, the duck search is started with the handler firing a blank shot out over the water to create the illusion that a crippled duck has been dropped without the dog witnessing it. I never fire this shot in training until I am totally satisfied I have maximized the dog's ability to search. The shot is eliminated for two reasons. First is that my initial training uses the command "fetch" to start the search and I want the dog to search because I told him to retrieve and the shot in the beginning would mask the command. Second is that the shot is my "ace in the hole" to help stimulate a stronger search if I need it for a particular dog. For the dog that needs a desire boost, I fire a live round across the pond giving the dog a splash to go to. Shooting live rounds on water can, however, be dangerous as the pellets will ricochet about off the water and you must be very aware of the backdrop and surroundings when using this technique.

If your dog has been asked by the judges during a test to resend following a successful retrieve, you will not be allowed to fire a shot on the resend. So having your dog familiar with beginning a water search with just a verbal command will also help on resends.

The duck search is the most difficult component of the Performance or Utility Test for a high percentage of dogs tested. They must earn at least a 2 (which is considered 25-50% of the expected job) in order to be awarded a prize. Many other components of the Utility Test only require a 1 (0-25% of the expected work) in order to prize. It is for this reason, once I begin duck-search training with a dog, I only train for water and marsh searching until the dog's training is complete. Mixing in field work or water obedience during duck-search training tends to reestablish a dependence in the dog in taking directions from the handler.

The one component I will add to water-search training is an occasional field drag once the dog begins demonstrating a willingness to search independently. Field drags have the same necessary independent search need as the water searches with tracking used to locate the quarry.

Again, what you have read in this chapter is not the only way to train for the Utility duck search. Nearly every trainer in North America has their own rendition of the perfect technique. Probably no different than the cars we choose to drive or the breed of dog we choose to hunt behind, our duck search training is our own created version. I have always liked Marlboro Red cars or trucks and Pudelpointers with nearly every vehicle I've owned being red. Clyde Vetter, owner of Sharp Shooter Kennels, on the other hand, has always preferred yellow vehicles and GSPs. I guess we both want to be noticed and these differences are also what makes a good horse race.

FIELD DRAGS

What looks to be the easiest and most fun component of any of the hunt tests would certainly be the drag. It is also the component that can cause a "no prize" quicker than any of the other parts of the test. If your dog cannot locate or will not retrieve the drag bird, the dog will receive a zero and there will be a no prize regardless of the rest of the day's work. In the beginning, the test was initiated to help identify the defiant dog who lacked cooperation. During the early years of testing, roughly one in 20 dogs (5%) would fail this part of the test by refusing to retrieve the bird, burying the bird, or mutilating the bird after tracking and locating it. It is important that the bird is dragged far enough and left at a location that is completely out of view of the handler and, in turn, the dog is aware that the handler cannot witness any misguided acts upon the bird. A dead duck is used for the drag as it lends a greater possibility of abuse from the dog than would a gamebird.

The judge who pulls the drag remains with the bird but hidden from the dog. This judge will witness if any misconduct occurs when the dog finds the bird. Also, a prolonged pickup will be noted and can lower the final drag score.

As I think back and remember all of the drags I have handled dogs to in actual tests (not training) there are two dogs' performances that stand out in my mind. Neither had ever shown a flaw in training, but both showed their true colors on test day. They both picked up the bird as trained, but both set it down as soon as I came into their view on the return. After they picked the bird back up, they tried to take it to the spectator gallery and not to me. This required a strong "COME" command to get the delivery back to me and with this came a lower score. As I think back about this one in 20 stat and the performances of these two dogs, there were several similarities justifying predictions from those early years of testing. Both were males with persistent headstrong personalities that required harsher training requirements to convince them my way needed to be their way. Also, one had growled at me early on during obedience training. I can vividly remember never allowing young children around this dog as I had a conscious mistrust for him. This male was used for breeding and I honestly must admit that pups from his litter showed the lack of cooperation that we just cannot accept as breeders.

Frank Schmidt leaving a small feather sample before dragging the dead duck 200 to 300 yards and leaving it out of sight of this starting point.

Still today, however, the drag is the one component of the hunt tests that is hardest on my nerves. Again, if the dog returns without the bird, you fail the entire test. Here is where I feel the force retrieved dogs acquires a better understanding of the drag expectations. The dog's cooperation usually gets the job done quite satisfactorily, but the obedience from force retrieve helps insure perfection. Especially at the delivery to the handler. The duck must be delivered to hand to receive the maximum score.

In the beginning, the training should be short drags at about 50 yards. Be willing to walk out with the dog the first few times if necessary. Leaving a small amount of feathers at the beginning is what gives the dog the signal that they need to follow scent rather than search and a consistent command such as "dead bird fetch" to send them on their way. Make sure your dog is willing and enjoys retrieving a dead duck before ever starting drag training and leaving a duck to be retrieved. A chukar or pheasant can also be used in the beginning but a dead duck will be used in the Utility test so make sure your dog will handle a duck prior to test day.

During training for the drag there is nothing I focus more on than making sure my dogs know there is a judge hiding and watching their pickup. This is a mandatory piece of my training as I have seen too many dogs leave their bird because they saw someone was hiding and there might be trouble if they were caught stealing his bird. I make sure my dogs have gone to drags and a total stranger is standing near the bird. In training the individual that pulls the drag stands in plain sight in the beginning.

If the dog displays any reluctance to pick up the bird to retrieve it, I have my assistant pick the bird up and give it a short toss back in the direction the dog had come from. Just as the bird is tossed, an encouraging "hey, hey, hey" is also used to let the dog know it is okay to retrieve and then a "fetch" command. Again, I want my dogs to feel that that judge hiding in the brush will become the enforcer if needed to get them to pick up that bird. This needs to be very thought through training as discipline by a stranger when the dog is out of your sight can be a dangerous adventure and poor results and responses from the dog can become a nightmare and habit hard to overcome.

When training alone, as I often do, I like to pull drags in a horseshoe pattern so that all I have to do is walk about 20 yards in the direction of the placed bird so I can observe the pickup without the dogs awareness of my presence. I can then quickly demand a pickup with a sharp "fetch" command if necessary. It always amazes me how the dogs that are not aware of my presence will return on the path back to me which is the 200-yard path they took getting to the bird rather than the twenty yards directly over to me. With the dogs taking this long path back I'm assured that they didnt know I was able to observe their pickup.

I always put one and usually two bends in the drag. The bends give the dog completely different scenting from crosswind to downwind to possibly upwind. These bends help create more concentration on the dog's part to get to the bird.

When pulling a drag, one must understand that the dog is usually tracking the person that pulled the drag and not necessarily the bird being pulled along the ground. Dogs that track with a good amount of speed will oftentimes run past the drag bird and not see it, ending up at the feet of the person that pulled it. This especially

TOP LEFT: Frank Schmidt dragging the dead duck. TOP RIGHT: Frank sending his dog on the fresh scent. BOTTOM: Dog is proudly returning with the dead duck.

happens on crosswind tracks where the dog is running several yards downwind of the actual track. In this scenario, the assistant needs to help the dog backtrack to the bird's location. It is important that if the dog finds the individual that pulled the drag before finding the bird that they also know that their bird is nearby and not to run off randomly searching.

My dogs have always been encouraged to bring things to me since puppyhood by my running away from them. This I have routinely done in training exercises. I have found myself turning my back on a returning dog in a test to ask the judge standing behind me a question just before the dog arrives back if things begin to look as though the dog may quit early.

There is no need for a fancy delivery from the dog to the handler. The same amount of points are awarded when a handler snags the bird from his dog as it passes by the handler as the dog that heels up automatically and calmly sits holding the bird until taken. A dropped bird will cost regardless of the retrieving technique so during training expect the dog to deliver properly and be in no hurry to snatch the bird. In the test you can surprise the dog by instantly taking the bird.

I always require my dogs to carry their bird while walking at heel back to my vehicle during training rather than taking the bird from them once they return to me. This helps diminish that quick delivery expectation most dogs develop as they anticipate letting go of their prey once they get to their handler. I do the same in duck search training when the dog returns with their duck and also in field search training with the last bird retrieved. This really shows its rewards when waterfowling as my expectations are to bring every duck retrieved into the blind and patiently wait for me to take their retrieve.

WALKING AT HEEL

What should be the easiest part of the Utility test is quite often the spoiler from a Prize I. Usually because the handler doesn't understand what the expectations are of the test and also the increased difficulty when asking a dog to walk quietly and at your side toward water with visible decoys to be seen on the approach.

Seeing water and also seeing decoys in this water tells the dog there are going to be ducks involved and this often ramps up a dog to a level the handler has never witnessed.

Missing gates by the dog in the established slalom course or having the lead

What many feel is the easiest part of a UT test, walking at a heel, often becomes a nightmare. Photo courtesy Nancy Anisfield.

tighten to where it restrains the dog will cost points. A good sharp "heel" command in the beginning is the only command one can give and, to help create more anticipation for the dog, the handler must carry a shotgun.

I have never understood how someone could spend so much time training for any of the hunt tests and make a shallow attempt at the walking-at-heel component. Once my dogs understand my expectations to walk at heel, there is a sense of bonding harmony that usually surfaces. This command, used in the duck blind on waterfowl hunts and also when jump shooting ducks, creates the partnership I expect from my dogs.

In the beginning training process I use a three-foot long broom handle with a snap attached to one end. I anchor the broomstick across my waist with a hand on each side of my belly. As I walk and turn, the anchored broom handle keeps the dog in perfect placement. When I stop, the dog stops. The dog can never pull ahead nor lag behind as the rigidity of the broom handle keeps them in place.

Many exercises in the dog yard with other dogs at play and with trips about the neighborhood provide enough distraction to get the dog in trouble for not paying attention and a sharp "HEEL" and quick discipline eventually lets the dog know the seriousness of heeling. Every time I place the dog back in correct placement with the broomstick, I give a strong verbal "Heel". At every point that the dog reacts favorably I reward them with a soft "gooood."

Eventually one needs to take the dog off the broomstick and either move on with a soft lead or go totally without a lead. For sure, every dog finds this to be a great opportunity to challenge your commitment to this new command and exercise they have just learned. Some serious discipline and reinforcement usually produces the required adjustment quite rapidly. My discipline often comes from a fly swatter I keep in my hip pocket. Being a mere fly swatter means nothing to a dog until they have been switched with it, then they look at all fly-swatters as the "whooping stick from Hell!"

I have even stacked live birds out in my exercise yard to create the strongest distraction possible to test where my training is at for walking at heel. I always win in the end and the best part of this training will show on fall and winter hunts along with their Utility test.

As I train while walking through a slalom course I continually stop and expect the dog to halt instantly. Also, when I slow up the dog must slow up. Distractions along the way and especially at the end help to overcome anxiety issues all dogs have in the beginning training exercises.

Just remember to not take the walking at heel for granted in the Utility test. Countless dogs every year find a Prize I dropping to a Prize II or even a Prize III because the dog didn't know the perfect serious expectations of this test. Every miscue can be a point deduction.

REMAINING AT THE BLIND

The handler is asked to leave his dog in a standing, sitting, or laying down position at a duck blind at the edge of the water. The handler goes out of sight of the dog and fires two shots about 10 seconds apart while the judging team remains watching the dog. The dog is expected to stay in place and not following the handler or advancing to the handler or into the water once the shots are fired. This is strictly an obedience test, but extremely useful if you enjoy waterfowling from a duck blind.

When training for this component, I like to walk away and fire two blank shots from my starter pistol. I then walk back toward the dog but slip off in the opposite direction and blank two more shots. I perform this sequence sometimes as many as five times or until my gun is empty. Here I am again training beyond the test expectations.

If I have a helper present when training for the remainder at the blind, I always have the helper perform any discipline needed if the dog decides to follow me or advance when I have fired a shot out of the dog's sight. I want my dogs to feel as though one from the judging team would step in and give the discipline in the event the dog should decide to move during the actual test.

Whining during the handler's absence is a deduction if the judging team feels it would take success away from a hunt. Some submissive dogs will have a problem with this part of the test and will whine when staying put by themselves seems to be too much for them. I have performed additional training exercises in the home to help

Patiently awaiting her owner's return.

extend confidence, but must admit with little favor. The dogs that insist on whining just usually have to take their deduction for it as this seems to be part of their makeup. The only success I have heard of was to put a bark collar on the dog during training, but my guess is that on test day the whining will return.

It is important to me that my training yields a dog that understands that leaving their post is a serious infraction as this will be continually used during the next winter's waterfowling. I like to place my dogs off to a side when decoying waterfowl and they are expected to stay on their pad until a duck is shot to retrieve. That training all begins here at the remaining by blind training.

Years ago I did quite a bit of field goose hunting. The goose decoys we used were G&H 747 shells and they were large enough that a dog could lay under one. My 70-pound male Tukr had been taught to hide under one during hunts and to stay put unless we shot. He eventually began trying to get under his shell by himself if geese were approaching and we were caught drinking coffee during what we thought was a lull in the day's hunt. He usually scooted the shell across the plowed field until it tipped over but he knew his place when the action was coming in after several hunts. We would oftentimes forget which shell he was under and would have to call him to wake him up as he came to enjoy his place as one of the team.

STEADY AT BLIND AND DUCK RETRIEVE

Here again, what is being judged is obedience. The dog has to remain through a series of shots and after the fourth shot is sent to make a 50 to 80 yard water retrieve. The test itself isn't that hard, but just as in the drag, if the dog does not deliver the duck to you a zero is awarded and the dog cannot earn a prize for the entire test.

Things that can go wrong include that the dog doesn't see the bird thrown and has no idea where to swim to find this unmarked bird; or, in looking for a shoreline retrieve, either while going out to the bird or on the way back, the dog gets lost and never completes the test.

LEFT: Remaining by blind and firing a blank. RIGHT: The proper way to send a nonslip retriever for a water retrieve. Photo courtesy Nancy Anisfield.

The distraction gunner used in this component of the test is just that. His two shots are to divert the dog's attention from the obvious location a bird should splash down. Positioning your dog to face the location the duck will be thrown is important and, if possible, you should stand as close to your dog and be facing that same direction. It is always wise to have a rock in your pocket as insurance in the event your dog completely misses the throw of the duck.

Knowing the wind direction before throwing a rock can also help complete a retrieve gone bad. Dogs can usually smell a duck 10 to 20 feet downwind of a floating bird so your throw and splash need to be downwind if possible.

One of my pet peeves in water retrieving is a dog running the bank to either make a retrieve or to bring back a retrieve. This unquestionably remains a negative for me from my past retriever days. I always enjoy seeing arrow-straight retrieves, both out and back, and bank-running looks like sissy work to me. In most hunt tests, a dog is not penalized for running the bank, but this is usually what results in a dog

Steady by blind. Photo courtesy Nancy Anisfield.

incapable of completing their water retrieve, so it is best to train for good straight out and back retrieves.

I set up simple bank-running drills and have my helper on the bank holding a broom to assist in getting the dog into the water on the way out or keeping them in the water on the way back using diagonal bank retrieves. That broom looks like a great big fly-swatter to the dog and several swats into the water usually gets the point across, and the out to the mark while taking the angle into the water and swim all the way back leaving the water directly in front of me. This is just a simple drill that I like to do with all my dogs to help take the bank running cheating away from them and discourage looking for a bridge all the time to avoid getting wet and having to swim.

Dogs are expected to be a nonslip retriever in the water retrieves of the Utility test. The basic steadiness requirements apply here just as they do for field work or duck search work. Throwing dummies in the beginning and advancing to shooting live birds out over the water in front of the dog that is on a "whoa" command are the usual training methods. The dog can either be standing or sitting, but sitting is the position that usually finds the steadier dogs. Making a dog honor another dog retrieving is the soundest way to insure you have a nonslip retriever at the water, however. Training beyond the expectations of the test should always be applied to your training and expecting your dog to honor other dog's retrieves is another way of training beyond the test expectations.

If your dog should happen to break as the bird hits the water it is usually best to let them go and not insist on them stopping when in the actual Utility test. Your dog has already broken and the infraction noted by the judging team and so it is usually best to take your deduction and not attempt stopping your dog and risking them taking their eyes off the marked bird and end up failing for not locating the bird at all. During training never allow them to break and give the dog every opportunity to do so, as again, mistakes give the best overall training foundation if corrected and the discipline understood.

Teaching the Dog 'Whoa'

"Whoa" is likely the most universal and widely-accepted command used among pointing dog trainers. To the casual retriever trainer, the command merely means "stay." But to the enthusiasts who train pointing dogs the command means both "stop" and "stay."

There are many ways to teach the command and it seems as though every trainer has their own version. The version that I use advances from the simple verbal "whoa" command to the vibration of the E-collar and finally to my whistle. I use this three-fold method as I find that when hunting wild birds, I get the best results and have the best advantage for success. The vibration is silent and doesn't alert resting birds to our approach and the whistle has much more authority than a verbal "whoa." Not always having a whistle or E-collar present requires the use of a verbal "whoa." Also, the verbal "whoa" around the home seems to find continual use.

I begin with a simple 20-inch dog collar that I put around the dog's waist. Then a ¼-inch cord that is 18 inches long with a snap on each end is attached to both the collar around the dog's waist and also the collar around the dog's neck. Basically I have a cord attached to each collar and lying parallel to the dog's back.

I begin by teaching "whoa" as a "stay" command. I lift the dog slightly off the ground just an inch or two by lifting up on each collar. I then slowly lower the dog and just barely give them their foot to the ground. The dog tends to stretch downward to regain their footing and, in doing so, tend to freeze up their body in a rigid posture. At any point that I sense the dog wants to free themselves from this posture, I give slight, uncomfortable small jerks up on both collars simultaneously and a sharp verbal "whoa." In short order, the dog learns to stand still to avoid those jerks upward on the collars at every point that they move. To release the dog, I give two soft strokes along the dog's right side with the palm of my right hand followed by a tap on the back of the head. This exercise needs repeating 30 times at 30 different locations in the dog

TOP LEFT: Teaching whoa using a simple gut cinch. TOP RIGHT: Attaching a short checkcord to the gut cinch and applying pressure. BOTTOM: Standing in front of the dog and applying whoa pressure.

yard to help create a lasting habit. I was once told that it takes 30 repeated practice sessions before it becomes a habit in a dog's world. I have never heard this since, but the number 30 seems to be a good choice as it has worked well for me.

The next step is to teach the dog that "whoa" also means "stay even if I have walked away." Here I slip a 10-foot check cord to the cord running from the two collars. There is a snap that allows the check cord to slide along that 18-inch cord. Now I can lift straight up and begin walking in front and behind the dog but still give small upward jerks to reprimand the dog for moving. Walking in a circle around the dog will entice the dog to move and face you and the discipline for movement is the use of the two collars attached together and primarily the flank collar. As with most all training the dog learns the most following mistakes, so creating mistakes will usually advance the dog's training quicker and is more enhanced.

This is quickly advanced to where I can walk away, sometimes back to the kennel facility or house, leaving the dog in place. Again, failure to stay in place is disciplined by use of the two collars, but primarily the flank collar.

Now we are ready to begin teaching stop also as a "whoa" command. There are going to be times when stopping the dog when creeping or "cat walking" in on planted birds will be necessary. This is especially helpful when hunting wild birds and you sense your dog may be tracking a running bird but could be getting too close and a flush may result. Most importantly, however, is that this may save your dog's life if something across the street or highway seems too inviting not to pursue or chase. If you can avoid BF Goodrich throughout your dog's life, you will also be avoiding a lot of family emotions, and with this you are "winning."

As was done to teach "whoa" as "stay," we are going to go through the same sequence, except this time the dog will be walking at heel. At first you stop with your dog as you command "whoa" and lift on the harness. From this you can advance to a hesitation and then only you keep moving. It isn't long before you can command "whoa" when at a fast trot and you can continue on as your dog stops and stays in place until you return and give a head tap to release.

"Whoa" is going to be a command you will use throughout Utility training and testing. Also when hunting upland birds, waterfowling, and around the house. Your dog will forever test your authority of this command and you will need to stay steadfast supporting the rules; "whoa" means stop or stay until released by a head tap.

When hunting I try to be as quiet as possible, avoiding verbal commands in the field. For this reason I start my "whoa" training again from the beginning using the vibration on the E-collar instead of my voice. Re-teaching "whoa" with the E-collar goes quite rapidly and within a day or so the dog understands what I want.

In the past I have taught "whoa" to a long tweet on my whistle as I have found that, once taught, dogs respond much better to a whistle than verbal commands. I merely go back through my original sequences of "whoa" training using my whistle and a long continuous tweet until the dog stops instead of the vibration from the E-collar or a verbal "whoa." The whistle has provided more favorable steadiness results during a utility field search than relying on my voice when it becomes necessary to halt a bad performance on a planted bird.

It is important to find ways to use the "whoa" command with a playful approach and find ways to cheerfully congratulate your dog for obeying. If this command is considered to be the "command from Hell" to your dog, the results will produce a sour dog and part of their performance may suffer due to this attitude.

As I said in the opening paragraph of this chapter, there are countless ways to teach this command and everyone feels they have the best "whoa" training basics. It isn't so much how you get there, but that you do get there.

This will be the command that during your dog's lifespan will be used the most and will assist your dog in giving you the most favorable and memorable hunting results over their lifetime. Always remember, we don't own the special dogs that touch the inner soul of our lives, these are the dogs that we have the honorary status of caring for and that care includes their safety.

FIELD STEADINESS

Field steadiness training is where most novice trainers begin their utility training and instantly begin planting birds and attempting to steady their dog to flush, wing, shot and fall on a planted bird. This is by far the hardest route to take as the habit of exploding at the flush of an upland bird from previous hunting experiences or training exposures distorts most dog's memory at the instant of a flush.

I prefer to hold off and make this component my final exercise after all the water obedience and duck search training is complete. The dog's I have run in Utility testing have all gone through the routine force-retrieve training before any other training started for this test. There is a new relationship between the handler and

Patiently waiting with dog on point helps ease the anticipation of the flush and a possible retrieve.

a dog completing force retrieve training with a new level of cooperation from the student following completion. Since 80 percent of the judges score card in a utility test revolves around retrieving of some sort, it is absolutely necessary to have the retrieving performance as good as one could expect from a given dog. Once achieved the dog's performance habits will reflect the value of this training. I have only handled one dog in a Utility test that had not had force-retrieve training. I did, however train this dog to hold and carry and never put anything down on their own but there wasn't the cooperation and eye-to-eye focus coming from this dog as all that completed the entire force retrieve training. Much like the respect a marine private has for his drill sargent following basic training we find that same respect given to the handler following force-retrieve training. These dogs will now always give a very focused eye to eye stare to their handler as if to say "I'm ready for work, now what do you want me to do?"

The entire Utility training process needs to make sense to your dog and they should have a very clear picture as to your expectations of them during all successions of steadiness training. You will be attempting to corral up the enthusiasm your dog has acquired from hunting seasons and natural ability testing as their past several years have been to run and gun with all bird encounters handled their way. The dog's hunting passion and past year or two chasing birds once they have flushed has become an instant habit that instantly drives the dog back to this chasing habit that previous hunting, training, or testing has instilled in them. An easy analogy representing this is that our dogs have learned one sport in hunting and from early training that is very similar to a child that has learned to play soccer. Then at age two or three we ask the dog to discontinue chasing birds and this is much like asking the child that is an accomplished soccer player to instantly be proficient at basketball.

For this reason I prefer to break all the sequences down (flush, wing, shot and fall) into individual phases that can be taught by field drills. I also begin these lessons in reverse order of how they will take place in a Utility test. The absolute last thing I allow the dog to do is to establish a point on a planted bird until they completely understand this new game I'm introducing them to. Again, just as teaching our proficient soccer player to play basketball, we need to teach the youngster how to dribble and pass a basketball before we expect to see 3-point shooting. I must also add that I perform, or another dog performs, all retrieving until steadiness training is complete. If the dog is anticipating retrieves they continually attempt to cheat their training and break on their own. If they expect to always have to wait and watch their trainer or another dog make their retrieves, the steadiness expectations will be much more understood, as the retrieving anticipation will not be interfering with the learning process. In the steadiness sequences we need to be teaching our dogs how to find the "end zone" and where all the out of bounds sidelines are at. Our end zone is completed steadiness and our out of bounds is merely breaking during any phase of the steadiness sequences.

I begin by walking the dog at heel out into a training field. I give the "whoa" command and walk some ten feet out in front of the standing dog. I then pull a dead bird from my bird bag and throw the bird away from the dog so that I am between the dog and the bird in case I need to interfere with a possible break. I then retrieve the bird myself. I continue this until the dog looks to be going to sleep from lack of retrieving anticipation. We then move to other locations and perform the same drill over and over. Eventually the dog is completely comfortable to honor me retrieving and begins

Shooting flushed bird.

expecting this with every thrown bird. There will hopefully be times when the dog breaks to retrieve the bird and I intervene before the dog gets its mouth on the bird. Remember, the best learning circumstances come from mistakes performed by our pupil and corrected instantly by the handler/trainer.

Next comes a live cropped-wing bird from my bird bag and we repeat the exercise where I put the dog on a "whoa" command, walk about ten feet to the front of the dog, toss the bird, and I make the retrieve. I continue to walk about the training field, "whoa" the dog, toss the bird, and make the retrieve myself. Again, mistakes from the dog with instant correction for the handler is a good indication our correction is teaching the dog the proper behavior for this new game we are teaching and our expectations for this new game.

Next comes a shot prior to throwing the bird. At this point, I know the dog is well aware of the rules of this new game we have started to play. We have previously used our "whoa" command at the water obedience training but the dog's anticipation level is much less when facing water to break into compared to breaking in the field as they have been permitted to do for several years and especially to retrieve a bird. At times I train dogs to "whoa" in the field while searching at the sound of a shot. The theory here is that at every shot throughout a Utility test the report of a shot is telling the dog to whoa and remain stationary until released in some fashion by the handler. This is reserved primarily for the very hard to steady dog that continually insists on breaking whenever they feel they can get away with it.

It is now time to put a complete sequence together. Let the dog find a planted bird, go on point, and remain steady through a shot and the bird falling. I will be retrieving the bird again for this sequence. I like to attach the "whoa" training harness to the dog as a reminder. The dog can search easily with the extra collar on its waist and I can apply instant "whoa" discipline if needed.

When the dog establishes point on the planted bird I walk to the dog, take hold of its collar, walk the dog in a small circle and put the dog on a verbal "whoa" as was done at the first stage of "whoa" training. The reason for this is to remove all habits of breaking at a flush and put the dog into a trained "whoa" rather than allowing an instinctive point while letting them stand by their bird like a coiled up spring ready to explode. Physically taking the dog from their instinctive point by walking them in a small circle and putting them in a standing stance with a whoa command

Gunners shooting flushed bird. Photo courtesy George Decosta.

reminds the dog of the past steadiness training sequences that they have been taught and again helps the dog to understand our expectations.

This seems like a lot of steps and a very lengthy process as one reads through the outlined steps. Once you have absorbed the theory, the steps should make sense and one can easily progress through this in several days. Be sure to apply each step at various different locations as we want to make sure the dog doesn't merely believe this new procedure only applies at one given location.

At this point I like to shift gears somewhat and move to "stop-to-flush" training. Here we are teaching the dog to stop and "whoa" at the unexpected flush of a bird. This is the only part of steadiness training where I use an E-collar to enforce the rules. Stop-to-flush training is a two-fold process using homing pigeons or barn pigeons. To begin, I take the dog into a training field and let the dog search. There are no birds planted at this point. As the dog crosses in front of me during the search, I flight a pigeon for them to chase. As soon as the chase begins, I press a continuous stimulation on the E-collar set at a mid-low level. When the dog ceases its chase, I let up on the button. I then "whoa" the dog with a strong verbal command. I often flight another bird while the dog is parked on the "whoa" command. I continue the process and with each bird I turn the E-collar up. Eventually the dog will "whoa" itself at the sight of a bird in the air and, by doing so, will avoid all E-collar stimulation. This education process moves to completion also quite rapidly. Now it is time to put the fly-away pigeons in a bird launcher. You want to launch the bird without the dog pointing it and when the dog is totally unaware of the bird and its location. When the dog sees the bird lift up and take flight, the same rules apply: Any chasing will be halted by E-collar stimulation. Once the dog whoa's themselves on their own at a flushing bird, you have successfully taught the dog the basics of stop-to-flush.

I'm very cautious about E-collar use when training steadiness in the field. Since I have used the E-collar to drive my dog to a pile of dummies after force-retrieve training, I am very reserved to stimulate a dog when a bird is on the ground, either alive or dead. The E-collar could be telling the dog to retrieve when we want the dog to "whoa." My simple E-collar rule is no stimulation when the bird is on the ground and any necessary discipline needs to be the old-fashioned style such as a flushing whip or, in my case, a fly-swatter.

After stop-to-flush training, I like to begin full-on steadiness training. For this I like to take a goose decoy weight and tie a 40-foot length of parachute cord to the weight. At the other end of the cord I attach a live chukar by the foot. I rig up three set-ups like this and randomly place them in a 20-acre bird field. I also set out a couple of launchers with a pigeon inside for a stop-to-flush prompt.

The dog wears the whoa-training harness and is allowed to search and point the chukar. With the dog on point, I slip up to the dog and attach my 10-foot check cord. I flush the chukar and just as the bird hits the end of the parachute cord I blank a shot. It looks to the dog that I shot the bird as the bird comes to the ground as it reaches the end of the cord. The heavy goose decoy weight anchors the other end of the cord to the ground. I then walk to the dog and command "heel" and begin walking directly away from the bird as the dog walks with me at heel. The dog is then released to search, but not allowed to return to the bird. The same scenario is repeated on chukar #2 with the dog heeled off from the bird on the ground and released to search but not allowed to return to bird #2. After chukar #3 has been pointed, flushed and blanked, we go back to the #1 or #2 bird as they are still on the ground. You are probably wondering why I would train using this exercise when the actual test will be so different. I have found that by making the dog heel off what looked to be a shot bird and not being allowed to instantly return to that bird as soon as they have been released to search creates a dog that better understands how this new game is to be played and that they must always wait for a command at every step of the game.

During the search in a hunt test, your dog may come upon birds that are up walking about the bird field. Your dog will be expected to sight point these birds and you are to handle them just as you would, had they stayed hidden and were scent pointed. This drill is excellent in duplicating the sight-point dilemma often experienced in the Utility search. Once the dog has found all three birds in our training scenario and heeled off each bird the dog knows where all three birds are located in the training search field and enters those areas and will be looking for a bird that will be up walking. Your job as a handler is to handle these sight-pointed bird no differently than if they had stayed hidden and were scent-pointed. In an actual test you hope that you will see any birds up walking before your dog sees them and you'll then be on alert to "whoa" your dog should it be necessary or possibly bring our dog into that bird downwind to possibly establish a scent point.

Another advantage when using leg-strapped chukar anchored to the ground is a cost savings to the trainer. These birds can be used daily and put back in the bird pen at the end of the day.

It is now time to test your steadiness training and plant several chukar in the field to be pointed, flushed and then shot. I have the whoa-harness on the dog for the first several runs. Just a little insurance that the dog will hopefully respond as has been trained and the harness is along as a reminder.

When the dog establishes point, I like to move ahead of the dog, located the bird, and make the flush with a nudge of my foot. I don't look back at the dog and quickly shoot the bird. If the dog has not exploded past me, breaking to retrieve the shot bird,

George Decosta performing retrieving drill separate from pointing and steadiness sequence.

I fire a second shot at the bird while it is on the ground. Any discipline required due to lack of steadiness is handled by my training helper and not me. I want the dog to suspect any person in the field is capable of dishing out discipline for bad manners on birds. During the actual test, the dog should think that any one of the three judges may also, at any time, apply discipline.

Again, I retrieve the shot chukar and have the dog honor my retrieve. It's the retrieving that causes breaking issues and lack of steadiness. If my dog always expects to stand stationary and watch me do all the retrieving, their retrieving anticipation won't interfere with their steadiness as much. At times I will have my helper send a dog he has had walking along with him on lead during our search to make several retrieves while the steadiness training dog is required to honor. A dog willing to honor another dog performing the retrieving duties is the steadiest of all performers.

I do my retrieving drills separate from steadiness drills, but also in the same search field. Here I walk out in front of my dog that is standing from a whoa command, fire a blank, and throw the bird. Then I walk back to the dog and ask it to fetch. Eventually I graduate to walking out and shooting a live bird. I always walk completely back to the dog before sending to retrieve. I always stroke the dog's right side with my right hand and the give a tap on the back of the head and say "fetch" at the same time as the head tap. Here again I am attempting to bypass the dog's anticipation to retrieve by adding several cues before the fetch command. Probably the last 10 or so dogs I've run in a Utility test never made a retrieve from a complete steadiness sequence until during their actual test. During training I made all retrieves.

My only steadiness requirement when hunting wild birds is that I always flush the bird and never the dog. After the flush I don't want them chasing birds not shot at, such as a hen pheasant, but I do expect them to explode when they see a rooster fold up in the air following a shot. I never require dogs to be steady to wing, shot, and fall while hunting wild birds, just the flush, so all of the Utility steadiness training is for a one-day show to earn a title. Seems to be a waste of time and effort to some but I have found that if I want to let my grandsons shoot some planted birds the dog trained through steadiness training will quickly return to the roots of that training as they know when birds have been planted and when the birds are wild. Now we have a much safer setting in the field for both the boys and the dog. Also, once a dog has completed steadiness training there is a much better understanding as to the expectations we have for them as they encounter wild or planted birds in the future. If I hunted preserves, I would probably insist on steadiness completely to the fall merely for safety precautions and as a controlled exercise for the dog.

Maximizing Your Performance or Utility Search Score

There are some definite do's and don'ts handlers need to consider when running a dog in any of the advanced hunt tests. An assortment of circumstances will confront you during a test that were not in the plan for the days run and some of these situations will have components that you have not trained for. Your goal should always be to earn the maximum amount of points that day for the performance your dog has given you and without some previous consideration as to how will handle these unforeseen situations will help from losing unnecessary points.

Joe Masar accepts a shot bird from a perfect retrieve by his spinone during a utility field search.

When handling a dog in the field search the handler must be mindful of the scoring that takes place during both steadiness and also the retrieve of shot bird. If a dog breaks and flushes and chases the bird the score card will have a zero at the flush and a zero at wing. The handler would have scored much better to have given a stern "whoa" as he approached the dog and another stern "whoa" as he flushed the bird to help guarantee some successful scoring on the judge's card. If this were successful the scoring might have been a 1 or 2 at flush, possibly a 4 at wing, a 4 at shot, and a 4 at fall. That is a much better start than a complete zero on this first bird.

Handler positioning gunners before flush.

I would usually take this approach when running a dog in Utility as I wanted to set the stage at that first bird that my expectations were the same as in all the training sequences we had previously done. The second, third, and fourth birds were then handled without any warning commands prior to the flush.

During field retrieves the handler often sees retrieving from his dog that he has never witnessed before in training. Dogs love to parade in front of a crowd at every chance and during tests it is just one of those chances. The parade usually has the dog making a wide swing behind the handler leaving the expectation that the bird will not be delivered. This requires a "come" command from the handler to get a completed retrieve and also a lower score on that retrieve. Taking birds to one of the judges or a gunner is also another form of parading. If you kneel to encourage a proper retrieve or even pat your thigh you risk a lower score. I usually waited until my dogs had turned and headed back to me to take an opportunity to set the opened gun I was carrying on the ground in an effort to create movement for my dogs to notice. If things were looking like roses for the retrieve I would give a sharp "come" command and take my deduction. With five other people in the field with you that movement might be what helps your dog focus on you and not get lost among the crowd bringing back their shot bird. Asking your dog to heel and deliver birds earns no more points than snatching the bird from the dog's mouth as he runs past you, so there is no need for fancy deliveries unless it is necessary to set the stage for future retrieves. The same holds true for every retrieve your dog performs regardless if it is the drag bird, the duck search bird, or the long water retrieve bird. Take the bird from the dog at the first opportunity.

Judges and apprentice judges prepare to read scores. Photo courtesy Nancy Anisfield.

If a dog breaks before being sent at the duck search or at the long retrieve it is best to let them break and don't try to stop them. Stopping the dog takes their eye off the mark on the long retrieve and it diminishes some of their desire at the duck search. They have already been penalized for breaking so bringing them back to their original place and giving them a command to retrieve gains you nothing. If the attempt to stop a dog from breaking is unsuccessful you risk further deductions for ignoring a command.

I could probably write several more pages here about the various observations I've witnessed when judging Utility tests where handlers attempted to help control a dog without giving verbal commands. Posture signals usually come to mind. And possibly another page of the attempts I have personally made when running dogs in Utility. The best advice I can give someone preparing a dog for a Utility test is to show up with a trained dog as most judges have seen it all and very little gets past them.

Judges doing the physical examination after the dog has come from water and coat is wet.

Steadiness training for hunting wild birds should see the dog steady to flush at the very least.
Photo courtesy Nancy Anisfield.

Training for Hunting

STEADINESS TRAINING FOR HUNTING WILD BIRDS

One of Gene Hill's famous quotes is, "whoever said money cannot buy happiness forgot about puppies" and that phrase rings the same truth today as when originally coined. With pointing dog puppies, the staunchness they display on point when adults and hunting is usually the difference in the success one achieves in the field. Some instinctively remain staunch pointing naturally while others are like coiled up springs ready to attempt a pounce toward their find at any second. Trained steadiness overcomes these variables we observe from pup to pup within a litter.

Most training for steadiness on birds follows one of the many techniques traditionally used by dog trainers of all the various pointing breeds. Basic "whoa" training is the kingpin necessary for securing a finished pointing dog.

About ten years ago our kennel began searching for a better way to help clients that didn't have years of experience in the field handling their dogs find more success when hunting wild birds. Their timing when handling their dog was always after the fact and seldom did they see the same results as the trainer had previously demonstrated in the training field on planted birds. It became obvious to me that the dogs that charged pointed birds did so in an attempt to beat the handler to their finds were just as satisfied having a good chase following the flush as they were when they performed well and a bird was rewarded them as a retrieve when shot. It only made sense to me to break these young outlaws from chasing birds in the air and most of the steadiness issues would naturally resolve themselves. After all, our dogs love chasing everything of interest to them: birds, rabbits, deer, balls, etc. Hence, we began breaking our clients' hunting dogs from chasing by flighting homing pigeons in front of them during their search and using stimulation from the e-collar to halt the chase. Gradual increases in the intensity and soon the dog learns it's much safer to stop and stand and watch these birds fly off than to chase. One might suspect that a dog might lose interest in retrieving from this method. This will never happen if patience is used in training and the dog is verbally rewarded with a "good boy" when performing correctly and receiving no stimulation is their reward for avoiding a chase. Once the

Tempting the dog to break with a live harnessed pigeon. Photo courtesy Nancy Anisfield.

youngster refrains from chasing homers coming from the trainer's hand, it's time to expect the same with birds coming off the ground. Here, a homer is launched from a remote launcher when the dog approaches the area of the planted bird without smelling or knowing of its presence. It's critical that the dog is unaware of the bird and launcher as the bird surprisingly appears as a wild flush.

Again, the dog is stimulated for chasing and rewarded for not chasing by feeling no stimulation and a verbal "good boy." This is basically stop-to-flush training and once the chase has been taken away from the dog as they become reluctant to charge birds or race their owner to make a flush; they feel safe as long as the bird stays on the ground and doesn't take flight. They are also much more satisfied to stand their natural instinctive points much longer and allow the handler the flushing duties. The handler only has to discourage chasing birds in the air and a silent approach with a soft "whoa" reminder is all that's necessary when in the field during Fall hunts on wild birds.

Once the chase is forbidden, it is much more likely to observe favorable pointing manners. Most of us have witnessed our own or a friend's dog ruining a day in the field by chasing a bird during a hunt and ending up moving every bird in that field as they continued chasing bird after bird, with none of the owner's screaming commands able to halt the chasing and eruption of the entire field's birds.

There are only two rules that we insist our clients follow in the field. The first is to never stimulate their dog when the bird is on the ground. This could create blinking and discourage good instinctive pointing. The second is to never shout "whoa" when stimulating the dog during a chase. We want the dog to believe their chasing is what caused the stimulation; not that the stimulation is coming from the handler for not obeying a "whoa" command. They must associate the stimulation from their actions.

After our dogs are performing well at stop-to-flush training it's time to let them start pointing birds and discourage chasing following the flush. Here is where some insight as to which birds are going to primarily be hunted helps formulate which technique is necessary. Planted birds used at hunt clubs, preserves, and in the various hunt tests can easily be caught and are usually pointed at short distances, requiring complete steadiness until the flush. Our dogs just sense the ability to get close on these birds as they can smell and sense the difference here and with a wild bird. Especially if there is any human scent on the bird or in the planted area. Wild pheasants also require dogs pointing their birds up close as the birds will often run out from under the dog-requiring relocations. Most dogs learn in time to relocate on pheasants when the scent diminishes, indicating the pheasant is sneaking off. Hungarian and chukar partridge in the wild require long distance pointing, as often in late season hunts the birds become so skittish that 50 to 100 yard points become a minimum. Here the cover is short and the dogs sense they are visibly exposed to their quarry and instinctively learn to stand well off their birds to avoid flushing.

Wild birds will teach dogs, in time, how close they can get before they flush but if one is only going to hunt chukar the training should emphasize extreme caution and pointing established from long distances. For the chukar or hun apprentice we

Staunching three youngsters on the same planted bird lends increased merit, but checkcords are a must. Photo courtesy Nancy Anisfield.

launch our homers from the launcher as soon as we know the dog has acknowledged scent and don't let them rode in before establishing point. This training is done in short cover with birds planted downhill from the searching dog. Heat thermals will carry the scent uphill, giving the dog long distance locations, as is often the case on wild chukar hunts. Few flushes are required to convince the dog to establish a solid point the instant scent is located.

For the pheasant hunters (wild or preserve), thicker and taller cover is used for training and the dog is permitted to stand much closer to their birds as this is necessary to avoid birds attempting to slip off like a snake in the grass using their famous disappearing act.

Choosing the correct training format for the different individual dogs is to best move the dogs through their training program quickly, looking for results that will last from season to season, and be dependable; regardless of the expertise of the handler. Understanding the different game birds one chooses to hunt can significantly affect a dog's performance if their training has had the focus of that individual bird. There is no substitute for training on wild birds but with nesting seasons, limited availability of wild birds, alternate bird sources are to be expected, so liberated birds are often the only resource available.

Most of our game birds genetically have different survival techniques that they use to survive various predators, both from the air and the ground. These survival techniques are also the ones they use to avoid the hunting dog and the hunter in the fall. We are blessed here in Idaho to have such a diverse variety of upland birds, and each of these species seems to have their own unique survival strategy for avoiding predation. While not including the five species of grouse found in our state, it would be our belief that Hungarian partridge are the most difficult for a dog to become acutely proficient at establishing point on. They don't run as much as chukar or quail, so they don't leave a highway of scent as to their whereabouts. They are usually laying so flat to the ground that they cannot be spotted, even in a plowed field. They erupt

LEFT: Knee-high cover with pheasant likely less than 10 feet in front of the dog.
RIGHT: Standing chukar with little cover to hide the dog's approach often sees a dog standing over 100 yards off the covey.

as a single covey and there is seldom a straggler left behind following their flush. Late in the season, and especially after the first snow fall, a dog must establish point some 50-100 yards off the covey to find success. When advancing a covey, a big arcing circle is required by the handler to get into reasonable shooting range.

Chukar are close behind the huns as far as the difficulty the dogs have when trying to establish that rock hard productive point. The primary difference is that they often choose to run rather than flatten out and hide as huns do. They will especially run uphill if possible and I've never seen a hunter that could outrun a covey uphill. Because of the steep terrain, choosing to hunt above suspected covey locations gives the dog it's best performance advantage. The heat thermals moving the bird's scent uphill making a covey easy to locate at great distances by the experienced dogs. If I were a betting man, I'd suggest that the average pointed covey of chukar was 100 yards or more when the dog was at a higher elevation than the birds. Here, just like hunting Hungarians, the dog's training needs to ask for pointing at a great distance from the birds to see optimum success.

Pheasants ask for a much different scenario, as their predatory escape is to run and hide; or to fly if the predator gets too close. As long as a pheasant is on its feet it has the advantage. Once they tuck and hide it's the dog's duty to pin them in place by establishing point close enough to discourage any movement by the bird. Here the training is quite standard and dog relocations are often necessary if the bird is continually sneaking off. A good pheasant dog will usually be standing within several yards of its bird when pointing.

Pen-raised birds require the most steady pointing dogs. Dogs trained to never flush a bird on their own is a must. They need to understand "whoa" and obey as if it were coming from a Marine Corps sergeant. Dogs sense the lack of a wild nature from pen raised birds, and once they have pounced and caught just one of these birds it can be a lifelong battle to convince them to behave as they were trained.

I'm convinced that wild birds give off a much different detectable aroma, raising the prey drive bar considerably higher for our pointing dogs. The pointing intensity usually proves this theory when comparing that of a pen raised bird to that of a wild bird. The distance a dog stands off a bird when pointed also affects intensity. Long range points on Huns or chukar appear much

Chuck Johnson bearing down on a wild pheasant in Montana. Photo courtesy Blanche Johnson.

more relaxed than that of a wild rooster pointed from several yards in front of the dog's nose. Any way you slice it, however, it's a "red-letter day" when your training pays off on your first fall hunt with that dog fresh out of training; regardless if wild or pen raised birds are being hunted, as long as a good productive point is established.

The visions that are permanently placed within our dog's brain creates that undeniable sound of silence during the hunt that will continually echo affection in a form of cooperation only to the one that has fed, cared for, hunted along side, and especially trained as their special friend. There is always a green light telling the world how special this owner is.

CHUKAR HUNTING TACTICS

Chukar hunting can be a cruel master, as all perusing this sport can attest. It draws you in with the promise and excitement from your first solidly pointed covey, but then immediately crushes you with one of any number of insults. Shots with only one foot firmly placed on the ground, a covey exploding in all different directions, birds running until out of gun range before taking flight-they're all abusive, especially once you've been bitten by the chukar hunting bug. One must always remember, however, that things don't incessantly work out as planned, but the ride still goes on regardless. It takes many Decembers to put enough age and experience on a dog before they become a veteran performer on a chukar hill.

Shot making is a skill that all wing shooters would like to master, but the variations offered on a steep canyon chukar slope never seem to have the same presentation as the previous. Thus, finding that magic groove on a left to right downhill crossing shot may find an embarrassing conclusion when the birds escape unharmed leaving you with nothing more than several empty shells. After surveying many of the Northwest's avid chukar hunters, it seems as though most dread this left to right downhill shot more than any other situation experienced while chukar hunting. As Bill Dillon (one of Idaho's premier wing shooters) put it, "When a right handed shooter swings from left to right, you are pulling the gun away from the shoulder and head, causing your head to come away from the stock. It may feel easier, but keeping your cheek firmly planted on the comb of the gun is very important — hence the saying — wood-to-wood." There is a counter-argument on swing direction. When a right handed shooter swings from left to right, the gun barrel is pointed in front of the target. When this happens, it is easier to see the target with

The find!

The flush!

both eyes. When swinging from right to left, the barrel should be in front of (to the left of) the target. Your non-shooting eye is on the left side of the barrel, putting the barrel between the left eye and the target, which is on the right side of the barrel. Some people argue you shoot better when both eyes are on the same side of the barrel as the target. I don't put a lot of weight on this argument because your shooting (master) eye is the one really doing the work. A lot of shooters put a piece of scotch tape or a Vaseline spot over their non-shooting (off) eye to prevent it from causing problems. For me, being right handed and one that likes to start my swing from behind a single bird and swing through this bird when shooting, it is much easier to continue my swing and avoid stopping my swing at the instant the gun catches up with the bird when swinging to the left. Whereas when I'm swinging to my right there seems to be an inept tendency to stop my swing at that precise instant that I catch up with the bird, causing a shot that is behind rather than out in front of the bird to adjust for the necessary lead required.

Birds are also more easily taken when the rise comes from uphill, above you, rather than those coming up downhill from you. When the birds take flight from below you, they are usually flying down and around the slope and it is particularly difficult to avoid shooting above the bird. Uphill rises usually are mere right to left or left to right shots with often times a mixture of these situations. The birds seem to also rise singularly with each taking their own course of escape, whereas many down hill rises usually see the whole covey exploding together, tempting the gunner into a flock shot, which rarely finds success.

Similar to our modern day golf excursions, a day on the chukar slope has so many varying scenarios that mastering all these different shot encounters would take the weekend participant a lifetime to conquer. Ironically, I can post my best golf scores when only playing with six of the 12 clubs in my bag. These are my high percentage shot makers which seldom let me down. It's the other six clubs that play havoc with my game. The same approach helps with my percentage of success on a chukar hunt;

The shot!

getting my high percentage shots at a higher frequency puts more birds in my bag. I'm continually looking for that right to left crossing shot with the birds being flushed from above me.

Like most sportsmen of today, most of what I've learned concerning hunting, fishing, and of the outdoors, has been gifted from others that have previously conquered these passions. Just as there have been many to have increased my awareness of field training hunting dogs, there is but one man that I can credit my knowledge of success related to chukar hunting. Most everything I've learned concerning chukar hunting was learned in the 70s from Idaho's legendary chukar enthusiast, Joe Leonard. A limit of birds during this era was ten and seldom did Joe return from a hunt without his daily bag, and it was accomplished with a 28-gauge pump. Our post-hunt conversation was always of the day's dog work, unexpected experiences, and the number of shots it took Joe to acquire his limit, which was usually 12 or fewer shots. Joe would not take a bird that his dogs hadn't handled properly, allowing him to make the flush and he felt that light little pump gun he shot helped him dismount the gun between birds so that each bird taken was shot with the gun being remounted as each new shell was chambered.

Often, during my hunts, I find myself taking a break with my dogs on a picturesque rocky outcropping and catch myself reminiscing of Joe, his pointing dogs, and all the theories he applied toward the success he had enjoyed with this sport. Larry Mueller once wrote an article about his experiences with Joe on a chukar hunt in Eastern Oregon for Outdoor Life Magazine. The article also endorsed the homemade chukar belt Joe had created for carrying a limit of birds at your waist rather than in a game bag attached to a vest. Joe always felt the birds were too beautiful to crumple together in one's vest, plus the weight was much easier carried from your waist. I still have the belt Joe had made me in 1975 and still use it on some hunts today. The chukar hunting theories that Joe was so passionate of were always discussed on the prehunt trip in the vehicle and once again rehearsed during the trip home.

The retrieve!

One of the rules one had to abide by when hunting with Joe was to avoid hunting birds at their watering hole. He would bark out, "if all you're interested in is killing birds, then be on top of them at first light and again at noon when they're most vulnerable, and be at those watering spots." Then with that special twinkle in his eyes, that only Joe could display, he'd remind me in a soft sincere voice, "for me it's all about dog work, and the dog work I'm talking about can only be seen at midmorning when they've taken to their roost." His personality seemed be that of a crusty old salt water fisherman, but was actually quite serene once you got to know him. It was for this reason we never left for a hunt before 8 a.m. It was an hour drive to most of our hunts, and this would put us on the ridgelines by 10 a.m. If you started too early, the birds would be moving from their watering area to their roosting or feeding area and they would usually run up hill as you approached, avoiding any good hunting opportunities and especially good dog work.

What I've retained from those special days afield with Joe pertaining to shot making comes, ironically, from the use of solidly trained dogs; those trained to hold their finds and never flush birds themselves. You see, it's the dog that allows you to get those valued shots with the flush coming from above you and increasing the frequency of left to right shots. It's quite simple in theory, but the playmaker is a dog that is staunch following his original point and reliable until the flush. As the midmorning heat thermals are carrying the bird's scent up the canyon walls the best scenting for the dog is from the ridge tops. The dog is usually above the birds and those with superior noses are able to locate birds at amazingly great distances. Rather than advancing past the dogs in pursuit of their find, one must refrain as this will only result in the dreaded down and across shot, with the birds dropping out of sight instantaneously. When approaching his dogs, Joe would say "just envision rolling a beach ball down the hill and if it would roll off to the right or the left of the dogs, that is where you go." The basic idea is to leave the dogs on point, retreat quietly down the hill on the right or left of the dogs while trying not to disturb the birds. Once you feel you're below the birds, side hill until you're directly below your dog. Now as you advance back up the hill you should have the birds between you and the dog and the flush should offer a crossing shot with a more likelihood of seeing some single flushes as opposed to the entire covey exploding at the same instant. More than likely the birds will take the course that the rolling beach ball would take, so experiencing more right to left shots can be more predictable when one creates a flush that will give this shot. It requires a very reliable and well trained dog to complete this scenario and also pull it off. You usually need to slip down some 100 yards or more below your dog and off to the side some considerable distance, which is most advantageous when you're out of sight of the birds. Basically, you're circling your dog's point to get below the birds. But first an educated guess using the canyon's fall-line to get a feel for which direction the birds are most likely to escape, and also positioning yourself for your highest percentage shot must be formulized.

The common denominator necessary for success is a dog trained to hold birds at long distances from the covey and one that is comfortable when left standing alone while you slip out of their sight to set-up your ambush. Often times on slopes or flats, I will circle several hundred yards before advancing back toward my dogs. I have on occasion retreated nearly back only to find their faces with "deer in the headlights" eyes, indicating the birds have been walking ahead of my approach and the dogs are now the blockers while now sight pointing a covey of birds directly to their front. December and January will find chukar feeding on sage covered flats during mid-day. Here they find new cheat grass sprouts as a protein food source and aerial protection or shade from the low sage plants. When on the flats and both of your feet are planted firmly on the ground, it's a red letter day when the circling technique works, the dogs remain staunch and you get your left to right shot on a covey of birds that don't all rise together.

Joe and I hunted together for nearly 20 years and he was more than 30 years my senior, but still a hard one to keep up with during a chukar hunt during those years. He hunted every Tuesday, Thursday, and Saturday from the season opener in September until the closure on January 31. I must now be coming full circle in the phase of one's experiences when continuing a hunting passion for more than five decades. I am now past the age that Joe was when I first met him and began our hunts and find myself not needing near as many kills to satisfy my ego. Just as Joe had done during the final ten or so years I hunted with him, I now find myself unloading my gun after four birds are on my belt and just enjoying the rest of the day watching my dogs work and taking pictures. I've taken hundreds of pictures of some of the most beautiful high desert scenery one could ever ask to see with my dogs standing pointed coveys of chukar. LaFaye teases me that if we could dine on all the pictures I've taken of my dogs on point or the deer, elk, or sheep I've experienced, our freezer would be stocked for a lifetime.

After Joe retired from hunting, I would always take him a mess of chukar late each year up until he was 90 and passed. Always after the birds were mature and with a good offering of yellow fat covering their breasts. On my last visit; when Joe was 90 years old, nearly blind, and struggling daily with worn out knees, he was still as sharp as a tack and could reiterate nearly every memory of what his dogs gave him on all of his hunts. He had to quit hunting after turning 80, but seeing him cry at each of my annual offerings of several plump, and perfectly cleaned birds is what I understood and admired of this man. His sincerity toward his passion was what he passed on to me, and it is a true treasure that few are ever given.

DUCK SEARCH TRAINING WHILE WATERFOWLING

Many times when waterfowl hunting, a duck is dropped that isn't seen by our hunting companion. Possibly they are making a different retrieve of a previously shot bird or perhaps their sight is obscured due to their location within a blind. A blind retrieve is usually executed giving hand signals to put the dog in the area of the downed bird. There are many times, however, that a wounded bird has escaped to a place unknown to any of the hunters in the party and only random hand signals can be used in an effort to locate the downed bird. All of our versatile breeds have a natural willingness to search and scenting capabilities far beyond our imaginations, so why not exploit these instincts and put them to work helping to avoid lost birds. These birds can be best located from a duck search, with a far better success rate, than from a dog that has learned to retrieve solely with the help of their owner/handler giving retrieving cast from hand signals. Also, many times the owner/handler has no idea of the exact location of this crippled bird and it most likely has swam to a distant hiding place. Most of our versatile dogs, once taught by this most effective game, show a tenacious delight while performing these searches. Much like a youngster at his third Easter egg hunt, there is no holding them back. Here they search much as they did in the field for upland birds, mostly on their own with a high spirit of adventure. The retriever searches under the pressure of its owner/handler, performs a mechanical blind retrieve, operates only from directions given by whistle stops/hand signals, and usually never gears up their search as the dog searching on its own.

A good percentage of waterfowl taken are retrieved by performing a duck search on a crippled bird.

The Formula for Training Duck Searches

1. After Force Retrieve Training, send the student dog to a pile of five plastic dummies or paint rollers at several locations. Perform this exercise daily until the dog responds favorably and will retrieve all five independently, showing the enthusiasm seen prior to force retrieve training when a dummy was thrown. All the dummies can easily be seen in this exercise and about 20-30 yards away. Put the dog up immediately following the exercise to help him absorb his success. The dog is told "dead bird" prior to sending to help them understand this is a new game and new expectations will soon surface. Send the dog on a consistent command such as "fetch" or his name. It is important to understand what you are attempting to accomplish and why sending your dog to a pile in the beginning is so important. First of all, when as a youngster your dog chased objects thrown and then retrieved them. The game of chase is what created the retrieving in those early years. To teach a dog to search a marsh, we need to replace the "chase" with "a search." Also our youngster retrieved primarily only from vision and it was the eyes that usually found the prize. Now we are going to eventually ask the dog to use its nose to locate their quarry and their eyes and brain to help them remember where they have searched. Also, and this is the most important thing to consider, is the water retrieves have always previously had the excitement of a splash and a retrieving dummy thrown in sight to retrieve. We are now going to train our dog to do a blind retrieve primarily with their nose with no chase or splash as enticement. This is why the force retrieve is so valuable in our training. Some will argue that the force retrieve isn't necessary, and it's not with some dogs, but as a waterfowler I want my dogs to retrieve for me when asked or told and not merely retrieve for themselves only.

Sending the dog to a pile of dummies with a "fetch command."

2. Repeat the Force Retrieve exercise across small bodies of water as was previously done on land. Start with ten yards and move up to 20-30 yard swims. Find various different water locations to make sure the dog understands the task expected of him. We are building confidence so that when the dog is told "dead bird," they will expect success to only be found on the opposite bank, across a body of water, not on the side they are sent from. All dummies can be seen by the dog. Again, signal the expectations by saying "dead bird" prior to sending for each retrieve. The dogs that fail duck searches usually only try searching on the side of the pond they are sent from, refusing to cross the water. They basically spend their time looking for a bridge while acting as though they are truly searching in earnest for you. We now have the beginning of a memory blind established and the dog should be confident there is a prize on the other bank every time asked to cross for a retrieve. Instead of hand signals as done in retriever field trails, we are going to ask the dog to search with their nose and not rely on our directional commands.

3. Once the dog will successfully cross water five times in a row to retrieve dummies that are in plain sight, it is now time to raise the bar and begin placing the dummies in the grass on the opposite bank requiring scenting as the only way for success. At times our student becomes bored and shows a sluggish attitude telling us the former "chase" game was a much more fun retrieving game. I like to begin placing either dead birds or sometimes live flightless birds in the grass on the opposite bank when I see things beginning to deteriorate and this usually happens when there is nothing in sight to entice a reliable retrieve. The birds should instill the enthusiasm we are looking for. It was the force retrieve that insured the dog knew what the job in hand was about; and the use of birds to create that happy attitude necessary to accomplish this most difficult task.

Without any dummies thrown creating a chase, the drill becomes a job and reliability comes from repetition.

4. Using remote launchers is the easiest way to establish the next step. Dogtra makes a launcher with a built in duck call that can help create the correct purpose we are looking for in our student. Here a cropped winged pigeon is put in the launcher and when the dog is 1/2 to 3/4 across the pond released in front of the dog, splashing down in plain sight, and frantically trying to swim using its wings only. Care must be taken to have the launcher positioned so the bird is pitched out over the water in the beginning. Later on the bird can be pitched on land to create a search using their nose. The duck call from the launcher can be used to add excitement for the dog also, and I usually like to have several quacks come from the launcher prior to sending the dog. Again, this creates more excitement in the dog's mind and the fervor improves. I often times move the launcher down the bank some 15 to 20 yards from the dog's expected retrieving location and once they have reached the opposite bank will ask for a quack from the launcher. The dog should begin its search in the direction the sound had come from once at that location the cropped wing pigeon is launched out in from of the dog. You must be aware, however, that this procedure using the verbal quacking sound of a duck will create a certain amount of searching while using their ears and creates a false interpretation of what we are attempting to develop. It must be advisable to avoid over training using launchers and their audio features too much.

5. Once our pupil will cross random water with enthusiasm with expectations of a live bird appearing in front of them at some location on the opposite bank, it is time to raise our training bar and ask for a search. Here a live duck has been drug along the bank some 50 yards or so from where the dog is expecting to find a bird from our established pattern blind. When no bird appears the dog should begin using their nose and start searching. Tracking a duck along the edge of the water is quite easily performed and the duck will be the same reward as our

Next will be to run the same drill across water.

cropped winged pigeon from our launcher, except a much enhanced prize. In the beginning the duck can be shackled to make for an easy catch for the dog. But, by allowing the duck to swim freely and be only rendered flightless due to one wing being clipped, we up the ante to the level to create the excitement necessary to see our dog finding success on even the most difficult searches.

6. Once the dog is into the new game of tracking to find the prize, it's time to give the ultimate reward and seal the deal between handler and retriever. Here a live duck is left with seven wing feathers removed from one wing, rendering the bird flightless. The bird should be left in slight cover but in the water. Once the dog gets into the area of the bird, the duck chase is on. It is rare that a dog can catch a wing-clipped duck in the water as they usually dive and surface some distance away. Here is where the dog learns to love performing duck searches. The duck chase creates the passion within the versatile breeds and every time the duck dives and disappears, the search becomes stronger and more invigorating from within our student. If there is one thing I have learned over the years from training dogs to perform admirable duck searches, it is that it is the duck chase and the duck getting away four or five times before being caught that creates this enthusiasm that we are wanting to instill.

One of the advantages of duck search retrieving as opposed to the blind retrieve using hand signals is that you really never quit hunting yourself while the dog is performing his own hunting for that previously downed bird. Sitting in the blind following several downed mallards and sipping on warm coffee, or calling other possible ducks, while my dog is searching for vanished birds possibly not seen shot is much more my style of hunting; rather than standing in front of my blind shouting directions for retrieves. The versatile performer that can perform duck searches voluntarily will surely help put a good bounty of waterfowl in your freezer at the season's end.

A Gentle Force Retrieve Method

This was the last chapter I wrote for this book for several reasons. Mainly due to the uncomfortable nature of the topic and also my own personal dislike for performing this training. I must admit right up front that I have never personally force retrieved a dog from beginning to end using the traditional ear pinch or toe hitch method. I have tried, but discovered years ago this training is not well received by my nature. So at this point I must come clean that I have paid other trainers in some fashion to do the force retrieve training on over 50 dogs of my own to date. It was easy when I had a trainer working for me as I merely passed the task off to them.

Owning a hunting dog that doesn't retrieve properly and will not finish the job by delivering shot birds to hand is somewhat like throwing a shadow at the wall in the dark; there is no completed effect just like the dog unwilling to finish a retrieve properly and with class. The enjoyment experienced following a well-placed shot that is followed by a retrieve completed to hand is like crossing the finish line in first place every time you race.

Possibly the most important factor following successful force retrieve training is the relationship the dog will have with their owner. There is a bond that develops where the dog will willingly allow their owner to now become the alpha representative of the relationship. Most all the obedience previously taught will now be expressed in a form of cooperation where the dog's anticipation of commands will see them willingly performing tasks prior to the command. Or at least much more willingly to obey commands with a happy tail and good eye contact.

Understanding the genetics favoring retrieving that an individual versatile dog either has or does not have helps in the decision process as to which method of force retrieve best matches that individual dog. There are three genetic markers that control the effectiveness a dog retrieves by. First is having the instinct to chase, which is by far the most important. Second is the instinct to pick-up, own with their mouth, and parade. Third is the instinct to return and share with the person that feeds and cares for them, which is the cooperative dog. The dog displaying all three genetic traits will be the easier dog to take through this gentle force retrieve method.

Whether you choose to call this training procedure force retrieve, force breaking, force fetch, the trained retrieve, or controlled retrieve the method of training and final result is all the same. The dog is first taught to hold an object which is often times a wooden dumbbell or retrieving dummy. Next, discomfort is applied from either an ear pinch or toe hitch and when the dog yields to the discomfort (pain) and opens their mouth to vocalize the object is placed in their mouth and instructed to hold.

There are many forms of the force fetch procedure, but the end result is a reliable retriever or a finished retriever. I cannot imagine owning a dog that didn't have the training that at least requested retrieves to hand once a bird or object had been picked up. The hunters that hunt chukar where downed birds often end up several hundred yards downhill from the gun or the waterfowl hunter jump shooting small bodies of water and fallen birds end up on the other side of the water both know of this importance. Dogs leaving downed ducks on the opposite side of a body of water, dogs leaving found upland birds in heavy cover, and dogs unwilling to pack downed birds back up a steep hillside following a sailed chukar or Hungarian partridge are far from the finished retriever we all want to hunt behind.

There are gentler approaches that can achieve very favorable results that the novice trainer can use. The professionals know how to breeze through the force retrieve steps and are capable of reading the dog's progress, but there is usually a point in the formal force retrieve using the ear pinch or toe hitch where the dog will balk and decide they are unwilling to advance. Here is where the professional earns their money. I confessed to myself years ago that I am not capable of finishing this procedure without some kind of mental scars left on the dog. I designed my own gentle method to accomplish this training from many readings of what the Labrador field trial community was doing with very young pups. They are starting their training with eight-week-old retrievers. At this young age there is no urgency to reach completion as there is with a dog that is a year or two years old.

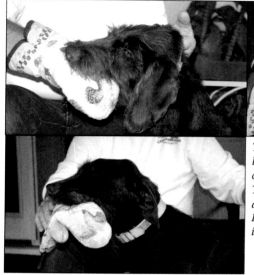

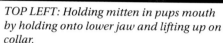

TOP LEFT: Holding mitten in pups mouth by holding onto lower jaw and lifting up on collar.
TOP RIGHT: Holding the mitten with no assistance from the handler.
LEFT: Sliding the hand out of mitten but insisting that the dog remains holding.

I begin with a 10- to 12-week old pup and use a paint roller as my retrieving dummy. Paint rollers are soft and fluffy enticing playfulness from the pup. Also, there is no cord attached for the pup to attempt to retrieve and end up dragging their prize back to you as is the case with retrieving dummies. I rub some pheasant scent purchased from the local sporting goods store into the fluff of the paint roller to help stimulate more interest from the pup. This becomes the pups retrieving toy for the next month. Lots of daily retrieves in the house and around the yard where the pup is most familiar to encourage a playful chase from the pup. Also, remember to always be trotting away from the pup to encourage a retrieve back to you. Once the pup is willing to chase and pick-up the thrown paint roller multiple times I switch to an oven mitten or ski mitten. Again the mitten has pheasant scent rubbed over it for an enticing scent for the pup.

Somewhere at about four months old and the pup is willingly chasing and returning retrieves back to me I begin the first step of the gentle force retrieve procedure. I like to start in the house and time my sessions during a television program using the commercials as my stopwatch. Each session lasts only the length of the commercial period. I put the oven mitten on my right hand and place the fingered portion in the dog's mouth and clamp my thumb under the dogs lower jaw and hang on. There is a wrestling match of sorts in the beginning as the pup insists on spitting out the mitten, but with persistence I always win and calm the pup with gentle "hold" commands. By lifting straight up on the pup's collar with my left hand I am able to control the wrestling match much better and soon the pup gives in and calmly holds the mitten with my hand inside. I am actually holding on the pup's lower jaw. At the end of the commercial it is time for both the pup and myself to relax and discontinue the training until the next commercial.

Once the pup will reliably hold the mitten with my hand inside it is time to begin sliding my hand out of the mitten while the mitten is still in the dog's mouth and I continue insisting on "hold." It will amaze you as to how fast pups at this young age will give in to your "hold" request and before long will hold the mitten through a complete commercial break.

Now comes the hard part, however. We need to have the pup come and carry the mitten. If someone holds the pup as you back up 10 feet and ask the pup to "come" I will guarantee the pup will spit out the mitten before advancing to "come." Continued requests to "hold" along with your "come" command will eventually register with the pup that they must obey both requests at the same time. For the rest of this dog's life you should insist on holding any object retrieved complete to hand and the "hold" command is all that should be necessary. At times it is important to revisit the "hold" step to help solidify your expectations. Once the pup will carry the mitten to you without dropping it, I switch back to their scented paint roller and continue my drills. You will again need to open the dogs mouth to accept the roller.

As this pup grows up it is a good idea once they will walk on lead at heel to put any object from a mitten, to a retrieving dummy, to a dead bird in their mouth and have them carry the object for extended walks. Now they are getting used to holding for continuous periods as a routine but most importantly from the command "hold".

It is important that you can now return to throwing the oven mitten or paint roller for the pup to retrieve. They will chase the thrown object and as they reach to pick it up you give an encouraging "fetch" command. Now you are introducing "fetch" which is basically saying "pick it up." They must also return and "hold" until you ask for a release.

Tossing the mitten for a retrieve.

We have now completed the most important phase of the force retrieve and with some dogs this is all that is needed to end up with a reliable retriever. The full-monte comes, however, from teaching the "fetch" command without a chase where the retrieving object is merely laying on the ground in front of the dog. Every dog is different and sometimes (but rarely) a dog has high enough genetic retrieving instinct to pick up the object without a chase and not require further training. In some fashion, however, the dog must understand that if you request a "fetch" of an object on the ground, with no chase involved, that their job is to pick it up and "hold."

I start the next phase by having the dog on a 15-foot-long check cord and place the paint roller on the ground about one foot in front of the dog. I give the paint roller a kick with my foot launching it at least 5-10 feet away and say "fetch" at the same time. I am merely throwing the roller with my foot instead of my hand from the dog's perspective. As I advance, I boot the roller shorter and shorter distances and in the end I intentionally miss the roller with my foot, but the response from the dog is usually to pounce on it as they have previously done when I commanded "fetch." From here you can lay several rollers on the grass and as you walk past each one with the dog on a leash request, "fetch." This procedure must be fun and an encouraging happy voice from you is a must.

Once I get the dog to this stage of the gentle force retrieve training, I always support the process in the end with my e-collar. The e-collar is set on a very low intensity and I only use a nick. A nick is given just before the "fetch" command. The nick is not a correction, but a conditioning letting the dog know of the seriousness of the command "fetch" and my authority.

Expecting the perfect delivery.

Dead birds should now be used just as in the previous steps to guarantee the dog understands the same work ethic is required when retrieving birds as was expected with the roller or retrieving dummy. Begin with the "hold" and "come" drills and advance to throwing dead birds for retrieves just as previously done.

This method reduces undue stress to your dog that can come from the traditional force retrieve procedure for both you and your dog. This process takes much longer, but if you are training your own dog and not paying a trainer, the timeline shouldn't be as important as the end result.

An honest evaluation of your dog following the hold and carry phases of this gentle force retrieve method should tell you if your dog can learn to pick up objects without a chase while avoiding the agony of the ear pinch method. I must admit that the majority of my personal dogs had the ear pinch method for force retrieving. It is much faster and helps get me on to other formal retrieving drills much faster and at a younger age. Hopefully your patience is much better than mine and you can find success in either all or part of this technique.

Tracking Live Gamebirds While Hunting

Quite often an upland bird is shot and our hunting companion is unaware of the downed location. Especially when hunting heavy cover such as a cattail slough or the dense cottonwood and briar tangles of a river bottom. Many times the bird was wounded and escapes the usual retrieve by slithering off to an unknown location or hiding spot. Often several hundred yards away, the bird makes the easy retrieve a nightmare, potentially provoking disappointment as our bag ends up bird-less.

The dogs trained to track live birds becomes the "ace" when called on to find these birds, whether it is for yourself or a bird your hunting buddy has lost. Very simply pull a small handful of feathers from your game bag and place them on the ground where the bird was last seen. Call the dog to this location. Grasp the dogs collar and show him the feather pile and merely command "dead bird, fetch." From here you merely stand back and watch what mother nature has instilled in your hunting companion.

It's not actually as easy as was just described, but once trained so the dog understands the task, it really is that straightforward. The versatile dog's genetic background and makeup makes this a task they revere and often times they make retrieves for you that seem impossible to accomplish. These accomplishments come from dogs with excellent noses, great concentration, and a strong retrieving instinct powered by prey drive.

TRAINING FOR THE LIVE TRACK

1. First the dog needs to realize that he can track just as easily as he can search to find downed birds. This is very natural for retrievers, but what we are teaching here is to track rather than search. Pull some feathers from a dead bird and place the on the ground in green grass. Pull the bird into the wind about 30-50 yards. Pull the bird by the feet so you are pulling against the grain of how the feathers normally lie on the bird. This will leave more scent and pulling into the wind makes the task much easier for the initial work. While keeping the dog on a lead, show the feather pile and fluff them up in the dogs face to create an

interest. All this time be saying "dead bird." Let the dog advance down the track and use the lead as required to keep them on the track and not allowing them to search randomly. Only several exercises are required and the dog will soon be able to track their way straight to the bird.

2. Advance the tracking by pulling down wind and cross wind drags. These are much more difficult. Also begin to put some bends in the drag to also raise the bar. It won't be long before you will be asking the dog to perform 200-500 yard drags and the excitement to perform will be a focused accomplishment that your dog will deliberately execute with pleasure.

3. Now it's time to play hardball and go to the live bird. Any gamebird can be used, but either a chukar or pheasant seem to yield the best results. Here we only want the birds scent on the ground to follow, where previously when dragging a dead bird, we were also leaving our scent for the dog to follow. There are many ways to leave a live birds track, but we have found the most effective and most cost effective is to draw the bird across a field using a fishing pole and reel. Here a bird is attached to the fishing line by both wings so it cannot fly. Good strong monofilament line on a bate casting bass setup is ideal. Place the bird on a fresh feather pile and have a friend hold the bird in place. Do cross wind tracks or into the wind tracks in the beginning to create confidence for your dog as this track is going to be much harder than the drags used to create the tracking scheme when dragging a dead bird. Walk out in an arc some 50 yards and reel the bird slowly to you with the reel of the fishing pole/reel setup. It is important to walk out in a huge arc so your sent will not be near the actual track of the bird. Make sure there is no scent on the ground where the track is going to be laid, such as previously walked by either humans, livestock, or other dogs for several hours.

4. At the end of the track a dead bird can be left as the reward for the dog. A live bird will create more desire for the dog not showing enough purpose. Once the dog has performed several tracks successfully this developed process will be forever imbedded in the dog's memory bank and nearly no training will be required to pull off that impressive track on what once would have been a non recovered bird.

Clyde Vetter with a North Dakota winter rooster. Photo courtesy Clyde Vetter.

Training for Antler Shed Hunting

When all upland bird hunting and waterfowling come to an end each year, I find myself dealing with cabin fever within several weeks of these closures. My hunting season ends January 31 each year and by March 1 I'm finding myself looking for some dog training or spring steelhead fishing to wrap my time around. For most all areas of North America there's another type of hunting you can enjoy during the hunting off-season: shed antler hunting. As the snow begins to melt in the northern regions, most deer and elk begin shedding their antlers. With snow still on the ground the antlers are harder to find as they are usually covered with snow making antler locations nearly impossible. In the southern regions the timing begins usually in February. Collecting sheds before they become weathered to a white shine or squirrels and porcupines chew off the points of the antlers finds the most sought after antlers.

The training is much easier and complete if your dog has been through a complete force retrieve training program. With the force retrieve in place you can require much more obedience from your dog on the retrieves and also a better understanding of your expectations. Shed hunting is similar to a duck search, except the search is on land for sheds and water for the duck. Both require confidence that there is a prize to be found. Success in the duck search comes from scenting and primarily use of nose where shed hunting is primarily accomplished from sight hunting (occasional sheds are recovered from scent, however).

I like to begin with a small piece of elk antler that has been sawed down to about 6 to 10 inches, making it more natural for the dog to hold and retrieve. Just as was done previously with a plastic retrieving dummy, I have the dog hold the antler piece and walk at heel carrying the object. Next, comes short retrieves where the dog enjoys a chase but is required to return and deliver under the obedience of the force retrieve.

To create a search and antler find that has a great deal of enjoyment for the dog I like to go to a simulated drag using a dead bird, but leave the antler instead of the bird at the end of the drag. It needs to be fun and enjoyable for the dog from here on for the dog to experience the success you wish to see later in the field. Tom Dokken has a product called Dokken's Rack Wax that can be purchased and applied to the horn to help restore the original scent a horn had when first dropped. This will help bring the dogs natural instinct to retrieve and parade when they find the antler piece in the field.

LEFT: Force retrieved dog holding a small piece of antler. RIGHT: Force retrieved dog holding a complete antler.

Next, an antler needs to replace the small piece of elk horn that I've originally started with. A small whitetail shed or a small deer rack from a harvested deer will be your best bet. Artificial sheds can also be purchased but the actual deer sheds are best if you can acquire one. Repeating the drag method of searching for the antler moves through its paces quite rapidly and your success will be revealed from the enthusiasm your dog displays when returning with their prize.

Eliminating the drag and requiring the dog to search randomly for the antler can seem clumsy at first as some dogs will tend to revert back to searching for upland birds and abandon a shed search. For this reason, I always return to the areas that I have pulled drags previously in to help overcome this concern. Familiar areas to search helps instill a memory process that dogs at times fall back on. You will find that after weeks or even months your dog will return to locations where the horn was previously found from drags expecting to find the horn in the same place. The geographic memory of the versatile dogs is exceptionally high and very effective in training when applied.

Often times when out for a walk on the river bottom along the Boise River or when at our cabin and taking a walk through the woods, I will take an antler along and drop it on the ground in plain sight for my dog to easily see. I will then swing back through that area making sure my dog picks up the antler and I insist on them carrying the antler back to my truck or cabin. Possibly a few short fun retrieves along the way helps recreate the fun they need to find from shed hunting and shed retrieving.

It's now usually a long wait for spring to arrive and to try out your new shed antler training, but a new hunting skill placed in your dog's memory bank should ascertain a new sport for this team to enjoy. Your dog has previously earned his stripes from training and when cabin fever sets in now you have a new diversion to enjoy with your dog. Both will receive the rewards of fresh air and exercise which is at times hard to come by in the spring. When your dog returns with that first found antler shed and its location completely unknown to you, there will be a truth in your eyes that says, "we are truly a shed hunting team."

Training for Blood Tracking

There is nothing like renewal than the opening day of deer or elk season for most sportsmen across North America. One serious stumbling block that all sportsmen face is the search for a wounded big game animal which is one of the primary risks of this sport. Archery season has its own needs to track animals after the shot as most require a reasonable blood track to locate the animal. We have all watched how easy this is on the outdoor channel when watching various whitetail or elk televised shows, but reality certainly tells us that many of these animals are never recovered and don't make the show's highlights. Here all the blood tracking, which is done by only humans, is only visual tracking of lost blood from the animal.

In Europe, versatile dogs are expected to track wounded big game, such as deer and wild boar. A stalking and tracking sequence is part of the Bush Test. It is comparable to the NAVHDA Utility Test in difficulty. The purpose of this test is to simulate a deer hunt. It is performed just before the blood track. Before attempting to teach this procedure, the dog needs to know heel, sit, down and stay as verbal commands and hand signals. In this test, the hunter carries a gun and pretends he is hunting a deer. At the beginning, the hunter commands his dog to heel and proceeds to walk slowly in the woods. Once the stalk begins, the hunter is not allowed to speak to the dog or to turn around and look at the dog. The dog must heel closely behind the hunter. The hunter, with a gun, walks about 50 steps, as if stalking a deer. The dog must stop and start with the hunter. The hunter commands the dog to stop, using the palm of his hand. The hunter walks another 15 steps and then commands the dog to come, by waving his hand. The hunter and dog stalk another 50 steps at which point the hunter commands the dog to lie down and stay. The dog remains lying down, while the hunter continues to stalk slowly for another 35 steps and out of sight of the dog. At this point, the hunter fires a shot and waits two and a half minutes before going back and leashing the dog. During this latter sequence, the dog must remain quiet and lying down.

In the blood track, the versatile dog has to locate a deer and inform the hunter of its location. The dog must not mutilate the quarry. A good obedience foundation is critical in executing the stalking sequence, and, in particular, the blood track.

Dogs must be proficient at performing drags similar to the drag of the NAVHDA drag in the Utility test. In Europe, a bringsel (usually a small 6- to 8-inch deer leg and hoof) is attached to the dog's collar. The job of their dogs is to track and locate a small piece of deer hide too large to retrieve and flip the bringsel up and catch it in their mouth to signal the found carcass. They retrieve only the bringsel back to the handler and then lead the handler back to the discovered carcass.

Although the bringsel sequence seems difficult to teach, they say that it is not. Before training in the field, make the dog carry the bringsel around, keeping the exercise very happy and repeatedly saying "where's the deer." Next, set the bringsel on a deer hide and stand close to the hide and say to the dog "where's the deer." Praise the dog when it picks up the bringsel, making a big fuss about it. Repeat this exercise

The checkcord and half-hitch around the flank.

over and over again. After a while, start putting the bringsel a short distance from the hide. As the dog progresses in this exercise, move farther and farther away from the hide, before giving the command "where's the deer." The automatic connection you try to build is once the dog sees the hide, it tries to find and pick up the bringsel. This has to be automatic. The final step is to attach the bringsel to the dog's collar. Give the command "where's the deer" and most dogs will quickly learn to grab the hanging bringsel and come back to you.

I have never trained a dog to blood track as described here, but owned one that had been trained for blood tracking. The dog was Hery Ze Strazistskych Lesu which I purchased from Jiri Hrbek in the Czech Republic. I loved to demonstrate this task with an old rolled up piece of elk hide when people came to visit our kennel. Jiri came to Idaho about eight years after I had purchased Hery and their reunion was spectacular. All the commands Jiri used were in Czech and Hery responded as if they had been reunited from only a day or so being apart. I told Jiri I was unable to get blood for tracking so I was using maple syrup as a replacement. He just shook his head and muttered "silly American."

Starting the dog on a track two hours later.

The dogs I have trained for blood tracking have all been from a revised method I created after seeing the values from Hery's performances. I primarily perform a modification of the NAVHDA Utility drag where I leave that old piece of rolled up elk hide and use maple syrup for the dog to follow. Instead of waiting for the dog to return after locating the hide, I follow behind the dog and at times use a long lead so I can keep up.

I'm not convinced the dog is following the scent from the squeeze bottle of maple syrup or my footprints adding my scent. I usually wait an hour or two in hopes my scent has dissipated and the dog is only following the scent of the syrup. Acquiring sufficient volumes of blood for training purposes is quite difficult whereas syrup is in every grocery store.

I know my method has merit as I have located two arrowed bull elk that an archer lost and one whitetail. One of the bulls had been arrowed close to daylight by a hunter hunting elk here in Idaho from Minnesota. I had finished blue grouse hunt for the day and decided to take a back road the long way back to our cabin when I came across the archer and his friend walking back to their camp. I offered them both a ride to their camp and asked if the had had any luck. With a sorrow filled face one explained that he had an arrow in a large bull but they were unable to recover the animal.

This seemed like a perfect chance to experiment with my blood tracking method of training in a realistic situation instead of the scenarios only I had experienced. It felt like moving from the playground to a stadium with an audience of two out-of-state archers.

We went to the last place they had seen the elk on its feet and I unloaded my dog, grabbed my shotgun, and put on my bird vest. Both archers in unison informed me that it would be illegal to shoot the bull if we located him with my gun. I smiled and let them know that it would also be against the law for me to be using a dog in any fashion for deer or elk hunting in Idaho. I was just out with my dog grouse hunting and the shotgun and vest helped disguise what we were really up to. In this case recovering game seemed to trump any laws concerning hunting big game with dogs. After all, I was merely out on a casual grouse hunt and my dog and I just happened to come across this arrowed elk.

It wasn't 15 minutes after I told Dusty to track at the location the elk had last been seen that we found her chewing on the ass end of the bull. This was a trophy 340-inch trophy 6 x 6 that I'm sure is hanging on the wall of someone from Minnesota.

The other elk recover was a bull my son-in-law had lost when archery hunting near our cabin. We have had our cabin near McCall, Idaho for 16 years now and Rick has taken a nice bull 15 of those 16 years during the September archery season.

I was returning home from the NAVHDA Invitational that was held in Minnesota and decided to stop and spend the night at our cabin rather than drive the extra 100 miles to our home. After dark Rick showed up with that success grin pasted all over his face and I knew he had just arrowed and elk. I was puzzled, however, as there was no blood on his hands or clothes and he informed me that the bull had laid down in a closed logging road but wasn't dead when darkness came. He couldn't get close enough for another arrow for fear of the elk spooking and so he felt returning at daylight was his best option for recovery.

I went back the next morning to help him get the bull out and was going to hunt ruff grouse while he did all the dirty work. He insisted on keeping me away from his favorite elk haunts as my grouse hunting and shotgun were going to ruin his chances. I had always honored this request, but on this day I was going to have my way with his forbidden grouse.

To our surprise when we got to his elk all that remained was a pool of blood on the ground. Without thinking or creating a plan for recovery, I rubbed some of the blood across Jessie's nose and commanded track. Neither Rick or I could hardly keep up with the dog as she raced down the grass covered logging road and Rick kept blurting out "is she tracking the elk or just running down the road?" Then it became obvious as she lost the track as if it had just vanished from the road. As we caught up to her she darted off into the brush on the downhill side of the road, sounding like a bulldozer breaking brush on her way down the slope.

All of a sudden there was complete silence from the brush below us. I told Rick to knock an arrow as I was sure Jessie was on point and this was his elk. When Rick reached the dog he rejoiced in complete laughter and when I arrived it was clear the dog had tracked the elk. There lay a trophy bull that was dead and Jessie at work as hard as she could work trying to bury the animal. She had the entire head and neck submerged under pine needles, leaves, and dirt. For a short period it was funny as we were watching some prehistoric instinct coming out in the dog. The humor was short lived, however, as we could not get her to quit. She was in a zone I had never experienced before and the only way to control her was to snub her by her dog collar to a small tree with my belt.

As everyone knows that owns a versatile dog of any or the breeds represented the tracking can be some of the most favorable and enjoyable asset these dogs lend to us. The most amazing experiences I have witnessed dogs performing have always involved tracking and I am continually amazed by these accomplishments.

The Best Don't Always Reproduce Themselves

I try to start each of my days with Alan Jackson's song, "Drive;" It brings back those memories of my youth and sharing time with my father as he prepared me for my years to come. My dad's last bird was shot over Cedarwoods Dusty Rose, when he was 75, on a pheasant hunt one late December day in Idaho. I'll always remember them both for what they gave to me. The only thing more painful than losing Dusty was losing my father. Both were gone in their "golden years," but still at the peak of their game. Both, also, gave me my most memorable days in the field and I will be forever grateful for those memories. Inscribed on my father's tombstone is this quote: "Once in a while the footsteps of someone special cross your path and your life is never the same again." This too is at Dusty's grave. It's been 14 years since I found her lying in her bed with gastric dilation-volvulus (bloat), which is more commonly known as a twisted intestine. Surgery was unsuccessful on this ten-year-old, and due to the circumstances, there was not even time for a brokenhearted "goodbye."

Dusty was a cousin to Cedarwoods Calendar Girl, but never reproduced herself in her progeny as Cally had. Examination of Dusty's pedigree shows her lineage to be lacking the motherlines of Haverhill's Aletta and I'm sure this was the difference in their progeny production. Both Cally and Dusty were the products of my beginning years as a breeder breeding Pudelpointers.

Dusty may not have been a top producer, but she was "The Real Deal" when it came to producing game. Allow me to reminisce about the life of the best hunting dog I ever had the privilege to walk behind. I've had and seen a lot of great ones, but Dusty had a special spark that created memories no other dog has given me.

It all began when I picked this exceptionally curious young female from a litter of pups out of my bitch Haverhill's Axcell from an exceptional young Prize I NA and UT male named Birchwood's Homer. I have to thank Bodo Winterheldt for his help as he artificially bred the uncooperative young lovers in John Gordon's garage. John owned the sire, Homer, but he never saw what his dog produced in Dusty Rose.

I decided to give this special young lady to a good friend, Mike Smith who lived in Grangeville, Idaho. Mike was a teacher/coach in this small community and a dear friend. He was an avid bird hunter, hunting ducks and pheasant on the nearby Joseph Plains and chukar on the breaks of the Salmon River. It was the perfect home for a pup showing exceptional promise.

Mike phoned me one evening to say he would be coming to Boise and returning Dusty to me. "You see," he said, "at five months old, this little high-roller can find every chukar in the Salmon River, but if you want to bring any home, you'd better give her the gun." After Mike had returned the dog, I found out later from his wife that when he learned of my losing Dusty's mother to antifreeze ingestion, he felt compelled to return to me what he felt was the best bird finder he had ever seen. He recognized her specialty, but did not have the experience necessary to control her, as he had been able to do with his Labradors, which work near the gun. Since Mike had housebroken Dusty when she had lived with him, I allowed her complete house privileges with a bed in our family room and also a bed in our bedroom next to me. This was her home until her untimely death at ten years old.

I steadied the dog as soon as she returned from Mike and from that time on she held whatever she found for me to flush. She pointed everything she could or couldn't see that was alive, regardless of their covering; feathers or fur. I hunted her on chukar until the end of January and she was six months old while applying some extensive steadiness demands on her with these wild birds. At the end of the hunting season, I found I had a dog nearly ready to pass a Utility test as her natural abilities were so cooperatively in place that the training would be minimal.

Cedarwood's Dusty Rose.

Cedarwood's Dusty Rose UT Prize I at 11 months old.

Dusty breezed to a perfect score in her NAVHDA Natural Ability test at nine months old and immediately earned a Utility score of 180 points and a Prize II at eleven months of age. A year later she was re-tested in Utility and earned the coveted Prize I with 195 points.

I will always remember the senior judge at the reading of Dusty's Utility score, explaining to the gallery the unfortunate consequences that can come from testing a dog in Utility at eleven months of age. The next time I tested under him, I was running Dusty's littermate (a female pup I had originally picked for myself), Cedarwoods Delta Dawn. I ran "DD" in her Utility test on Saturday and then her Natural Ability test on Sunday. She received a Utility prize before her Natural Ability prize. On Sunday, when the judge realized I was running the same dog they had judged in Utility the previous day, he conceded that these two dogs developed at extremely young ages and the two youngsters had not received any extreme training for their Utility preparation.

It was during Dusty's second hunting season that I learned how profound this little lady's hunting success actually could be. Idaho's best pheasant hunting takes place in the sugar beet fields in October before the beets are harvested. The birds seek shade and overhead protection from the 18-inch high flowering beet leaves. These birds can be extremely hard to locate as the heavy beet leaves block the scent cone from extending around the bird and the birds can slip away completely undetected while hiding under the foliage and running down the corrugate rows. It was the opening day and my son Bryce, my daughter Brooke, her husband Rick, and I were on our annual crusade in search of these wily roosters. A good friend, Dick Herz, from Oregon, also joined us with his two sons-in-law. In several hours of hunting behind six finished Pudelpointers the group had limited with our 21 roosters. While I was primarily handling the dogs and watching family and friends enjoy this remarkable day, I observed that Dusty had found 18 of the 21 roosters taken. All birds were taken off-point as the birds found in beet fields hold extremely well, feeling completely secure under the umbrella of beet leaves. The other five dogs were also NAVHDA Utility prized dogs, but Dusty's somewhat independent searching method just kept putting her on the birds first. Her technique was completely different in that she found where a bird had been previously roosting and then tracked the bird to its new location. She would search cross-row as much as possible hoping to find a bird on the move and, once on it, would put together a track that only a bloodhound could equal. Once the scent became warm, she would snap into a point that would rival any veteran pointer.

She never false pointed and rarely crowded her game to the point of creating a flush. Brooke was a quick study that day and learned early on to stay focused on Dusty and let the others follow the other five dogs.

I would have to take my shoes and socks off to count the number of roosters I caught (not shot) off Dusty's points in sugar beet fields by locating a rooster's tail feathers laying uncamouflaged between the leaves and grabbing the bird.

As years went by and days in the field with Dusty accumulated, there were many experiences that I knew would never happen again with any of my future dogs, regardless of their exceptional abilities. She seemed to take every experience and put it in her memory bank, only to find use for it on a future hunt. With Dusty, you never

A Hell's Canyon ram pointed by Cedarwood's Dusty Rose.

knew what to expect when finding her pointing. Many porcupines were shot off-point with her; how happy I was to see her steady-to-shot on these prickly enemies of our hunting dogs.

Once when duck hunting with flooded timber along the Boise River, I shot a pointed beaver over Dusty. The beaver had been flooded from its home and was hiding in a clump of brush like a pheasant would. Dusty had gone on a duck retrieve and ended up on point instead of bringing back my duck. A complete surprise to both of us and from then on she thought it her duty to search and point any bird or mammal on our hunts. Over the years she stacked up quite an assorted inventory.

I took several foxes off-point while pheasant hunting and once made a double on coyotes from one of the islands of the Snake River while jump-shooting ducks. I would have taken a triple but I was shooting an over/under and couldn't reload fast enough for the third coyote. Dusty also pointed several skunks during her career, but I never had the nerve to shoot one; just a quick "heel" and we got the hell out of there!

It wasn't a complete chukar hunt without Dusty sight-pointing several groups of mule deer, but the most amazing accomplishment came on a chukar hunt in Hell's Canyon. Dick Nachbar and I were hunting on the Oregon side in January and the winter snows had pushed the birds and big game to the lower elevations. We were hunting an extremely steep area with magnificent cliffs above us having unparalleled views. While admiring the view above me I spotted Dusty on a pinnacle rock outcropping some 100 yards above. She was standing on point. All I could see was her back and tail, but the intensity was equal to that of her previous beaver point some years previous.

Rather than climb to her, I chose to slip around the slope underneath her and below the rock outcrop she was perched on, in hopes of finding a covey of birds more at my level. To my total surprise, I was slipping up on two bighorn rams lying in their beds. I got to within 30 yards of the regal pair before they exploded across the canyon walls. When I looked up, I realized Dusty had a view that a sheep hunter would have died for. My hunting partner, Dick Nachbar, is an experienced sheep hunter and both of us had previously taken four different rams, each from a different sub-species, so this was an experience we could truly appreciate.

The rams were Dusty's best find, in my book, but that certainly wasn't the end of the list accomplished points for this dog. When she was eight years old, I began grouse hunting more than in previous years, as we had built a second home in the mountainous region of McCall, Idaho. There were ruffs, blues, and spruce grouse in abundance with the season opening on September 1. On these hunts, several whitetails exploded from Dusty's points along the creek bottom while on ruff grouse hunts. Blue grouse hunts found several elk pointed at the heads of dark timber north slopes instead of a flushed grouse. But her pointing a black bear cub was the real hair-raiser! It all seemed somewhat cute, until Momma started bouncing in the brush right next to us as though she were trying out a trampoline. To say the least, I grabbed my dog and vanished!

Her last point came at our hunting/training property along the Boise River south of Boise. This river bottom is covered with cottonwoods, dense brush and willows, as are most river bottoms. We call this property "the Swamp" for good reason — the 40 acres require hunting in hip boots to negotiate around the cattail sloughs and ponds. Dusty and I were looking for a late December rooster and she had just disappeared into a dense group of cattails at the far end of a pond. She was now silent, as I could not hear the normal rustling that dogs make in hot pursuit through dense cattails. When I found her, I was also looking straight at the butt end of an elk some ten yards to her front. At that exact moment, the elk exploded, drenching me with swamp mud from head to toe as it burst quickly from sight. When I later hooked up with my son-in-law Rick, I told him, "You'd never believe what Dusty just pointed at the head of the redhead pond." Draining my enthusiasm, he replied, "Probably the elk I've been seeing the tracks of all over the place, was it a bull?" There aren't supposed to be elk in the agricultural river bottom of this area.

So goes the saga of Cedarwoods Dusty Rose. She spent her life going every place I could take her, including the golf course. She rode in the front seat of my truck as should all special dogs and slept every night in her bed next to ours. Her only misbehavior was the night she ate five rib-eye steaks Dick Herz had brought to our home to celebrate a successful pheasant opener. Dusty had eaten all five steaks that were out thawing. She had snatched them off the kitchen counter and ate them, wrapping paper and all. There can't be much flavor in wrapping paper, but this most likely, was an attempt to hide all evidence; but she was still able to put on her usual stellar performance in the field the next day.

A Versatile Day with a Versatile Dog

A typical January sunrise was obscure and mostly denied as the dense fog allowed limited visibility across Idaho's Snake River. The wings of the early rising waterfowl filled the airway with constant feeding chatter and whistling wing beats of the restless birds. Mallards and widgeon maintained their individual flocks as they glided in their familiar wing cupped acrobatic maneuvers over the waterway. The fog this morning was dense with the 200 yard far bank of the river nearly obscured from our sight. Only the faint outline of the far bank's tree line gave a hint of its distant backdrop. The actual hunt lasted for several hours and when we had taken our bounty of 21 birds

Cedarwood's Mtn Huckleberry perched down river from the mallard decoy spread and guarding the string of goldeneye decoys.

(mallards and widgeon) the temperature had risen from a very frigid 12 degrees to a seemingly pleasant 23 degrees. With these low temperatures the dew point hadn't given the fog a chance to burn off and the floating slush on the river's surface never surrendered.

As with all sincere "dog men," the highlights of the hunt weren't the exceptional shots or the best calling of that day's hunt; it was centered on the dog work we had witnessed on this morning's hunt. My male Pudelpointer, Cedarwoods Mountain Huckleberry (aka Huck) had made two retrieves on winged birds that took him to the opposite bank of the Snake River. The floating slush and ice made the dog's visibility very obscure, but he "went the distance," as he always does. Who would believe a pointing breed could do the work required on this frigid winter day, and especially on a river this big. The passion the

The 12-degree morning put ice on everything including the dogs.

Pudelpointer has toward waterfowl and their inherent love of water, makes them one of the premier water dogs among the pointing dog breeds; especially during harsh winter conditions. A young female Pudelpointer and her mother were also along for the hunt, and the youngster's playfulness in the water while retrieving in these frigid conditions, was also a testament to her future value as a true "water dog."

As our three dozen decoy spread was being picked up, the conversations continued as to the wealth a good water dog brings to a hunt, and how special some of the work seen on this day truly was. But with still three quarters of the day left, the conversation quickly changed; our next dilemma was deciding which of the upland game birds to peruse for the duration of our day's hunt. From our duck blind we usually could see the chukar slopes of the Oregon Owyhees, but with today's fog it was a mystery as to the visibility we would find on these chukar hills. Fog and chukar hunting can be an adventure all in its own. Most chukar hunts find the hunter miles from the vehicle and getting lost in the fog is something one doesn't want to experience in this vast landscape. With the GPS world we live in today, there is much better security on hunts when fog hides familiar landscapes and all terrain begins to look the same. Possibly, a few more hours would find the sun making its way through this thick fog. We chose to hunt a pheasant/quail covert on the way to those chukar slopes in hopes of seeing the fog lift prior to our arrival.

This proved later in the day to have been a good choice, as the fog gave the pheasant hunt some advantages as the late season birds were not as aware of our approach as they would have been on a clear sunny day. The chukar hunt never saw sunshine until we crested the top slopes in the late afternoon making beeper collars and GPS readings a prerequisite to maintain an organized hunt. We finally arrived at the top of one of my favorite chukar slopes, with the fog quite dense and keeping track of the dogs a constant concern. As we gained elevation in our climb in search of chukar coveys we eventually rose above the fog finding a blue-bird day with perfect visibility to hunt in.

As with all hunts starting out on waterfowl and ending pursuing upland birds this day's hunt was one with its own unique memories. All in all, a successful day for the diary. A young/rookie Pudelpointer along for the day's hunt had pointed her first rooster pheasant, had numerous quail finds, and some classic backing of the older dog's points later on the chukar slope. This was a full day's work for the youngster, starting with her first experience in a duck blind as an "opener" and ending after an introduction to 3 upland gamebird species. This, the youngster's first versatile day in the field, and her memory bank was starting to fill from this day's positive bird exposures. By the end of our day we had experienced a typical versatile hunting excursion, often seen by North America wing shooters when the sun finally set that evening. It is days such as this that help explain the increasing popularity by North American sportsmen and sportswomen with the versatile breeds available today.

More than 40 years ago and on a day very similar to the hunting adventure described here, sent me searching for a Pudelpointer. I owned a brace of Setters and several Chesapeakes which I was competing in AKC retriever Field Trials at the time, and also training gundogs for clients throughout the Northwest. But after training a young Pudelpointer for a client and hunting this dog for him during a fall hunting season, I could see the obvious values offered by the versatile breeds; now able to leave home to hunt a variety of birds with only one dog for the day's workload. One dog to hunt both waterfowl and upland birds; no more compromising performance in the absence of the specialty dog. The Pudelpointer appeared to have the winter waterfowling abilities I required, and if I was ever going to leave my Chesapeake at home on a serious duck hunt, this could possibly be the substitute breed to take.

The late John Kegel from Ontario, Canada helped me find my first Pudelpointer. Kegel was one of the men that originally helped create the North American Versatile Hunting Dog Association (NAVHDA). He also introduced me to Jim Steven's Haverhill Kennel in Alberta,

Chukar hunting in dense fog.

Canada where I later acquired my initial breeding stock for Cedarwood Kennels. Since that time, I have hunted behind and actively bred Pudelpointers, adhering to the mission statement that initially drew me to this breed; which has always been tested and proven dogs used for breeding only.

Hunt tests are the common denominator for all of the versatile breeds' success. With chapters in nearly every corner of North America, the dogs can easily reach the testing grounds necessary to maintain the testing requirements for these breeds. With an encouraging future ahead, the stewards of all versatile breeds can hopefully observe a favorable future for their chosen breed of versatile dog, as decades of hard work and consistent hunt testing have certainly paid off for all of the versatile breeds seen today.

Versatility is what makes each of the versatile breeds standout amongst sporting dogs. Over the past 40 years while testing and judging versatile dogs in the NAVHDA's testing system, I have seen many of the other versatile breeds demonstrate what originally drew me to the Pudelpointer; dogs that can retrieve waterfowl in winter conditions and hunt all of the upland bird species admirably. During my training career and while operating Cedarwood Kennel taking in client dogs for training, I trained more than 600 versatile dogs from all the versatile breeds. Pudelpointers, GSPs, GWPs, Griffons, Large and Small Munsterlanders, Vizsla's, Weimaraners, Brittany, Pointers, and Setters (both English and Red). From this experience I have acquired a sincere admiration for all of the versatile breeds of hunting dogs.

Many versatile days of hunting lie ahead for the sportsmen and sportswomen that will start off their day afield with one of the versatile breeds of sporting dog at their side.

My first versatile dog Axcell came to me with the help of John Kegal in Canada.

Bryan's Song

When someone mentions the 1950s or '60s, most are reminded of the introduction of Elvis, The Beatles, or possibly a specific automobile body style that has retained popularity to our present year such as the '57 Chevy. Each decade seems to have its specific special significance that is personal and individualized within our memory. One of the decades of time in my life, the '90s, will always bring to mind the loss of two of the best friends I have ever known. First I said "goodbye" to my father after a firewood cutting accident and then to my dearest hunting companion, Cedarwoods Dusty Rose. Dusty died of gastric dilation-volvulus (bloat), which is more commonly known as a twisted intestine; she was only eight years old. As mentioned before, on Dusty and my father's tombstones is the quote: "Once in a while the footsteps of someone special cross your path and your life is never the same again." My dad's last

Pat Saunders' Cedarwood's Lasting Impression.

bird was shot over Dusty when he was 75 and on a pheasant hunt one late December day in Idaho with me. I'll always remember them both for what they gave to me and hope they are again joined together at one of heaven's special coverts chasing birds as each so loved to do.

There's a genetic likeness to my dad that I often see at a glance in a mirror or shaded window when passing by. That image would always remind me of the frequency that others have expressed in a comparative likeness that I had to my father; both in looks, our smile, and the way we walked. With Dusty, however, I had never seen one of her pups showing a genetic phenotype to her appearance or her genotype expressed in her intensity when on game birds. Her concentration was intense as she snapped into her frozen statue like profile when establishing a point as no other dog I'd ever witnessed or produced at my Cedarwood Kennel. I never retained any of her progeny so I had no memories of her to see in a pup performing this classic pointing pose. Often I am reminded of a pup's sire or dam when in the field just as I am my father when that quick glance in a mirror takes me back to my dad's past.

Dusty's genetic likeness did surface, however, one March day on a NAVHDA judging assignment I was on in Florida. It was in a seven-year-old male Pudelpointer that was unmistakably the mirror image of my Dusty Rose. Even more amazing was that the dog's call name was also "Dusty," obviously proudly given to this male as a pup after his mother. Cedarwoods Dusty Rose had a founded reputation back in her day, as she was both a NAVHDA natural ability and also a NAVHDA Utility Prize I performer and had passed her utility test prior to her first birthday at eleven months old. A friend and fellow judge, Pat Saunders from Jacksonville, Florida was handling this male that looked so much like my Dusty Rose and named Cedarwoods Lasting Impression in Utility at the Florida chapters test. I knew from my first glance that I didn't need to examine the dog's pedigree to learn of this dog's lineage; the genetic portrait was as vivid as past momentary glimpse in that mirror and seeing my father's face looking back at me.

I had previously sold Pat two different Pudelpointers. One a male that was now 13 and the other was currently a three-year-old female. So where did this seven-year-old male come from I wondered? Later I would discover that Pat had purchased the male, Dusty, from an internet ad placed by Scott Winebrenner from Wisconsin. My memory was reminding me of selling Scott a pup some years back and I could vividly remember some of the "dog talk" conversations I had with Scott some seven years prior. He wanted a top upland and waterfowl performer and had thoroughly studied my breeding stock's pedigrees and NAVHDA test scores. He was also involved in the VDD testing system with several drathaars that he owned. He had settled on a pup from Dusty Rose as no dog of her breed had the performance record she had established in tests and he felt his odds demonstrated the best success with a pup from my Dusty Rose.

My curiosity was overwhelming as to why Scott had sold this dog. It couldn't have been for profit as he had only asked for the dog's original puppy price. I later found he had too many dogs at home and was forced to reduce his inventory.

Pat Saunders' litter. Cedarwood's Your Bryans Song is one of these pups.

At the conclusion of the NAVHDA test, and after watching Pat and Dusty complete their utility test with a convincing 182 points, I was compelled to learn more of Pat's acquisition of this dog. Pat assured me that the dog was a natural and had required little training to give the performance I'd witnessed and judged. Pat then filled me in on the details of the dog's purchase and shared his disappointment after he had discovered several notes hidden under the rug in the shipping crate Dusty had arrived in. The notes were from Scott's nine-year-old son Bryan and written as only a young boy would express when saying "goodbye" to the friend he had spent the past seven years growing up with. Dusty had come into Bryan's life when he was two years old and the history of their bond was evident in the notes asking the new owner of Dusty to "take special care of the dog he loved so much." Initially, Pat was infuriated when finding he had purchased a dog that had been sold without the emotional approval of a young boy who had been sharing his bed with this dog. Pat's guilt was elevated as time elapsed and it became obvious to Pat that his new hunting companion had a special personality and display of affection that a young boy would only naturally have bonded to. First on Pat's agenda was a phone conversation with Bryan's father to express his disappointment in learning he had purchased this dog without the approval of Scott's nine-year-old son.

Understanding the special bond a young boy and a hunting dog develop, Pat suggested that maybe a mandatory reading list for parents such as Scott while raising young children with a hunting dog should include *Where The Red Fern Grows* and *Old Yeller*. This hopefully would give a parent the understanding of how deep-rooted this bond can exist in adolescent boys, especially with regards to a hunting dog.

The guilt of Pat's purchase created Christmas, birthday, and special occasion cards to Bryan, complete with pictures of Dusty's hunting excursions. Also included was how well Dusty was doing and all the locations their adventures had taken them to. Pat was Florida's State DU Chairman and an avid waterfowler and this passion had found his waterfowl excursions as far from Florida as Alberta, Saskatchewan, Alberta, and Alaska along with his regular trips to Louisiana and Arkansas. The life of Cedarwoods Lasting Impression is one that all versatile dogs long for, specially planned hunting trips and daily lounging in the home with two other companions to share time with on their own couch for comfort.

After observing the likeness of this male to my mother Dusty Rose, my passion to bring those genetics back into my kennel's gene pool started the theme for what this chapter is based on. Pat owned a young female Pudelpointer named Cedarwoods Waterwing who had been both NAVHDA natural ability and utility tested with good hip radiographs. A breeding formula between her and his male Dusty looked to produce the result of what I was hoping to create. When I proposed my interests in this breeding, to my delight, Pat was completely agreeable. His only request was that I market and find appropriate homes for each of his pups and he offered to split this litter's profits with me if I was willing to take over all the duties of registration, sales and awarding all guarantees necessary to future owners. With that I could get the pup I wanted for my breeding program from my half of the litter.

Pat's next request solidified what I already knew of Pat Saunders's generosity and the kindness within the heart of this crusty, burly waterfowler from Florida. His request was to give his share of the litter's profits to young Bryan Winebrenner in the form of a college education fund. It was this sincere gesture that choked me up for several minutes with the need to turn away and catch my breath. You see, compounding Bryan's loss of his childhood friend Dusty, he had also since lost his 44-year-old mother Kristin to medical complications from primary pulmonary hypertension. At this point I suggested we have the entire litter's profits go toward Bryan's education fund. Nothing could ever replace Bryan's loss of his mother, but Pat's kindness and sincere pre-arranged generosity would hopefully make a difference in his life, letting a young boy know he has a special friend down south in Florida sharing the love of a Pudelpointer name Dusty with him. In our language of "human speech" mere words cannot express the loss a young boy deals with when life hands him a journey such as Bryan was given. But hopefully, the humanity and kindness Pat displayed made a difference in this youngster's future.

Pat followed through and raised a wonderful litter of pups from his two dogs. He and his seven pups flew from Jacksonville, Florida to Boise, Idaho when the pups were six weeks old. He stayed with me for a week mothering his pups and required near perfect resumes for each of the pup's new homes. I also found a special little female that reminded me of her grandmother, Cedarwoods Dusty Rose, and appropriately named her Cedarwoods Your Bryan's Song. The name came from the story of Bryan Piccolo and Gayle Sayers movie Bryan's Song, but more essentially Pat's new friend, Bryan Winebrenner.

My recollection of a young boy losing his mother and a salty old waterfowler's generous heart will always be remembered in this pups registered name, Cedarwoods Your Bryans Song. In our sometimes selfish world of puppy mills, pets sold in malls, and so many exploiting their dogs merely for monetary gains, it does my heart proud to know there are still those that take opportunity when available to make the unselfish decisions and do something special for both their own hearts and especially one of our youth's. This chapter celebrates that generosity and will hopefully help readers know just a little about my friend and your NAVHDA judge from Florida, Pat Saunders.

Winter Chukar Hunting

The blizzard finally comes to an end. The south-facing slopes of the canyons accept the majority of the daily sun now and have been mostly swept clean by the frequent strong winds that have driven the snow into drifts at every low spot on this rugged landscape. In the wake, the bitter cold has taken over. But yet, here on these ridgelines and colder north-facing slopes a covey of 12 chukar are buried beneath the snow, waiting out the wrath of this winter storm.

It's the insulation of the snow that helps them survive these conditions as they tunnel under its surface to create individual warmer burrows. They have survived the brief periods of the annual hunting season and constant threat of coyotes and hawks, but the biggest enemy is yet to come: Winter blizzards, sub-zero temperatures, and the scarcity of food.

For now the odds are stacked against these small red-legged partridge and hopefully the warmer spring weather will arrive soon. These are the conditions most all of our game birds face in most geographic locations across North America. These are also the reasons the upland hunter finds so much favor in his favorite game bird. Their winter survival is usually beyond our imagination.

For the chukar, the south facing slopes near the sun warmed rock ledges may provide the only food source for these bird's survival. These massive rock

January chukar hunting is a magical adventure all its own.

outcroppings will absorb the sun's light and convert it into heat energy, yielding the first sprouts of annual cheat grass. This will be the chukar's only food source and the primary diet until spring and its moisture provides insects for a higher yield of protein for both the adults and their broods.

December and January chukar hunting is of special interest to the avid Northwest upland hunters, as it is during this period that the most exceptional dog work can be observed. The cooler air temperatures allow the heat thermals created in the warming canyon walls from the various rock formations to transport the bird's scent up to the top of the ridgelines. Experienced dogs often find standing birds at startling distances in these conditions, several hundred yards from their covey finds.

It is also during these cold days that the cooler temperatures allows for six to eight hour hunts without risking canine heatstroke or rattlesnake encounters. These are the dangers of early season hunting and dogs are lost annually to these hazards.

Most chukar hunters experience seasons that begin in September or October and extend to February 1. The early season requires considerable amounts of water to maintain hydration for both the hunter and their dog. Water must be packed as the warm creeks or pond water can have poisonous blue-algae blooming or Giardia present. Winter conditions usually have snow for the dogs to hydrate with or from fresh water that is found throughout most hunts, sparing the hunter the need to carry large volumes of water.

For the chukar hunter the winter season sees a variation of weather conditions rarely experienced with other game bird hunting, making each hunt a new experience with fog, snow, rain, high winds, or possibly a blue-bird sky to hunt in. These deep canyons can fill with ground fog or a winter snow blizzard can diminish visibility to fewer than 50 feet. The experienced chukar hunter keeps his dog's location with a GPS tracking collar or a beeper collar and often has to rely on his own GPS device to find his way back to his vehicle during these unexpected weather conditions.

But when it's a cool crisp winter day with a blue-bird sky and solid footing from the frozen ground, it is for sure a "red-letter day" to be out on one of those extended hunts, to one of your special coverts that only you frequent.

One of those "red letter days" on a winter chukar hunt.

The Czech Connection

One of my all-time favorite movies is *The French Connection* starring Gene Hackman. So when I was searching for a title to this chapter highlighting an import from the Czech Republic, the title of this favorite movie came to mind, and hence, the name "The Czech Connection."

As all good articles about dogs should have a favorable and memorable beginning and finish with a happy ending or a life lesson to be learned, this chapter is no different. The substance of this piece has a very special place in my heart which always kindles a smile of memories past.

The saga began in 2004 with a phone call from Bill Athens in Ohio letting me know of a four-year-old Pudelpointer male that had been offered for sale by Jiri Hrbek in the Czech Republic. I was familiar with Jiri's dogs and their bloodlines and the possibility of acquiring one of his dogs drew an instant interest. The dog had earned six different Prize I classifications in Europe including blood tracking. Jiri was offering the male to a North American breeder in hopes of creating more genetic diversity for the breed and he felt there was more opportunity in America for this accomplishment. Many in Germany still remembering WWII were not willing to breed to the Czech or Austrian Pudelpointer breeders yet leaving North America as the best possibility.

The dog was a 70-pound male named Hery Ze Strazistskych Lesu and his phenotype matched his call name (Hery) appropriately as he wore a long, soft coat requiring a field cut for my hunting conditions with the amount of burrs experienced in the West. I was in need of new genetics for my Cedarwood Kennel so I overlooked the unfavorable coat on the dog as my needs were such that I felt the coat could be controlled with suitable breedings. With Hery not having the coat I was looking for in a proposed stud dog, I was confident his coat would transfer to the desired medium-harsh coat in his pups when bred to my Cedarwood females. His size was also not ideal for my own hunting conditions as the environment favors chukar hunting, requiring a dog with good stamina capable of extended trips from the truck while facing very rigorous climbing and steep slopes. Again, I felt that I could mask any deficiencies from Hery's stamina and size with breedings with my Cedarwood females. After all, Hery was sporting six different Prize I qualifications included their coveted Memorial title, which is comparable to our VC in NAVHDA, and I wouldn't be required to test him here in North America; I would only need to certify his hips with Penn Hip x-rays.

I arranged to meet Jiri at Mike Pallota's Pine Ridge Kennel in Ontario, Canada to see the dog and watch him work. I first flew to Cleveland, Ohio and rode to Ontario with Bill Athens, who was purchasing Hery's littermate Heidi Ze Strazistskych Lesu as a breeding female for his Killbucks Kennel. What I didn't know at the time was that I was off on an adventure of a lifetime that would help cement my breeding needs for years to come. Hery was from a breeding with Jiri's Czech female but his father was a German sire so his genetics were very diverse and exactly what I needed to expand my own gene pool. The needs for hereditary traits from another line of Pudelpointer pushed the decision forward and if I was going to continue breeding Pudelpointers, I needed to roll the dice on this dog and purchase Hery.

After Hery arrived at our Idaho home, he found his new home to have a swimming pool in the backyard and a heated and air-conditioned kennel facility as his new residence. During Hery's first hunting season in North America I took him to Saskatchewan for snow goose hunting, North Dakota for pheasant hunting, and Oregon and Idaho to hunt waterfowl, quail, chukar, and pheasants. This was quite an upgrade from the Czech Republic, where he had been a master at hunting wild boar and pheasant tower shoots with his previous owner. What I discovered on my hunts with Hery was the highest IQ that I'd ever seen before in hunting as a team performer. He was also a very affectionate, clownish dog that everyone visiting our kennel fell immediately in love with. Especially the women, he was a true "ladies man." He was a very unique dog that maintained his near perfect obedience training received in the Czech Republic throughout his life.

It was during Hery's second hunting season with me that I decided to let a friend, Hal Bleyhl house Hery for me as he was borrowing the dog nearly

Jiri Hrbek.

weekly for his pheasant hunts. I could still use Hery for any breedings I wished for my kennel and Hery could experience constant indoor living with Hal and his wife Flo; so Hery went to his buddy Hal's and lived there until the ripe old age of 15.

The heart of this chapter actually begins when 83-year-old Hal took Hery in and made him his house companion. Hal had never owned a dog personally, but had been a Purina salesman many years prior and had a sincere understanding of the care required in owning or housing a dog. I gave Hal a plastic dog crate to put

Jiri making a statement with his Czech Pudelpointers.

in the back of his pickup for safe travelling, but that was promptly returned as Hery was now a front seat companion always riding shotgun. Hery also had his place in the front seat of Hal's Lincoln Continental and usually along to help run errands. I'll never forget my first visit to check up on the two of them and found a padded dog bed in every room of Hal's home. Coming to America with a home having a swimming pool in the backyard was no longer such a luxury; Hery had now moved up to a more extravagant world and lifestyle at Hal's.

After several years Hal's wife Flo had a stroke requiring nursing home care to rehabilitate. Hal went every day to visit Flo and Hery went along also. Flo once told me that she and Hery enjoyed breakfast together but Hery didn't like his toast with grape jelly as she did; Hery only wanted butter on his toast. He had obviously won over her heart just as he had Hal's. It wasn't long before Hery had become the therapy dog for the entire nursing home and all 150 patients knew Hery by name. When it was time for Hal to head back home he would blast a loud whistle and Hery would appear from any one of the patient's room at the facility.

As time passed, so did Flo and much to the surprise of Hal's family and friends (including me), Hal remarried some six months after Flo's passing. As plans were made for the newly married couples living quarters, Hal's new wife Pat wanted to remain in her home; but didn't want a dog inside as she had white carpet and white furniture, feeling a dog just wouldn't fit. Hal solved this problem by buying the adjacent three-bedroom home for Hery to live in. This is the first dog I've personally known to have their own three-bedroom home. A gate was installed between the two backyards for quick access to Hery's home and a big-screen TV and a recliner for Hal to watch the morning news and football games with Hery. All those dog beds were also placed in every room of the home. Hal could now still enjoy Hery daily but it would now have to be at "Hery's place." Hal claimed he even got Hery to accept grape jelly on his morning toast.

My latest import from Jiri's Czech Republic line.

Again, as time passed so did Hery. He died at 15 years old and had created three of my stud dogs during his breeding years, along with many excellent hunting companions for my Cedarwood clients. With Hery passing at 15 and Hal now 90 I didn't expect another dog to be in Hal's dreams, but I misjudged his passion to have a dog at his side and after all he still hunted. What was I thinking, he had just killed a six-point bull elk and wanted to go pheasant hunting but needed a dog to hunt with.

When Hal phoned me expressing the need for another dog, I was taken aback to find he didn't just want another Pudelpointer, but wanted one from the Czech Republic. It needed to be an adult dog as a puppy would just be too much for a man who had reached this 90-year milestone. Hal was looking much past 90 with a goal to reach 100, but needed a dog as his companion to make this happen. The man had just taken another six-point bull elk, travelled all over Europe with his wife Pat, and been on the Pacific Ocean salmon fishing with several old Navy friends. Aging is something that hadn't altered his activities as it does to so many. Hal is a WWII veteran who has more patriotism for our country than any American I had personally met and helping fulfill his dreams was a reward I definitely wanted to be part of. This is a man that has made every annual Navy reunion regardless of the state hosting to revisit the life endeavors of his Naval buddies that he stood next to during those WWII years.

I guess timing truly is everything in our lives as it wasn't that long after Hery's passing that I received a phone call from the man that had been housing one of my stud dogs for me: Cedarwoods Sharp Shooter (aka Eli), expressing the need return Eli to me as his recent retirement had brought on various travel plans and housing a dog would be too difficult. Eli was the dog I had used to retrieve the kicking tee following kickoffs at Boise State football games. There wasn't a Boise State football fan that didn't know this dog as thousands had posed with him before games or at halftime for a personal photo.

More importantly, Eli was sired by Hery. With this I instantly phoned Hal and asked him if he would like to keep one of Hery's sons for me as I was again looking to house one of my stud dogs. As soon as Hal learned this was the dog I had used to retrieve the kicking tee at Boise State games and was sired by Hery, his immediate reply was: "I'll be there in 15 minutes," and 15 minutes later I was watching Eli leaving while riding in the front seat of Hal's Lincoln Continental.

Hal lived to see 93 and Eli maintained Hery's three bedroom home adjacent to Hal's during those special years while with Hal. While pulling Hal's bike throughout the neighborhood (Eli in his harness) the dog would pull Hal's bike every day just as Hery had previously done. Eli and Hal would entertain the neighborhood daily and both were grinning from ear to ear. Such a wonderful man, this friend of mine Hal Bleyhl has been to these two dogs. A man that was always sincere, never boisterous, and always acted as though he had been "in the end zone" before.

After Hal's passing, Eli went to live with Hal's daughter and son-in-law and continues to enjoy a wonderful indoor life with dog beds in every room of the house. I have since imported another male Pudelpointer from Jiri Hrbek in the Czech Republic named Lord Ze Strazistskych (aka Czar). Czar has found his place today as one of my top stud dogs just like Hery had done so many years prior.

Young hunters are much more likely to appreciate their dog's performances if they have been involved in the training of their hunting companion. Photo courtesy Sherman Bilbo.

Giving Back to Our Youth

We are continually reminded that as sportsmen and sportswomen that we need to give back. Usually wildlife or the environment is the subject of this request. I find that in our hunting dog world, we have a different priority when giving back is discussed, and our focus should be to give back to our youth the wonderful partnership a good dog brings to the hunt. The love of upland hunting and waterfowling is usually passed on within individual families following years of hunting experiences the family has encountered together. The passion and quest to pursue upland birds comes quite naturally to our novice youngsters and so does waterfowling. But the bond one obtains from owning and hunting over a trained dog is often overlooked within our giving back movement. Young hunters are much more likely to appreciate their dog's

A NAVHDA youth day.

performances and rejoice in the memories of positive performances from their own dogs if they have been involved in the training of their hunting companion. A stronger bond develops if they have run their dog in a NAVHDA test as here they worked and performed as a team.

Waterfowling and turkey hunting both offer the best results to help young hunters catch this "hunting bug" as neither require extended walking and shooting opportunities that are only offered with little warning. Turkey hunts rarely see a dog along to make the retrieve and many families don't have access to waterfowling opportunities. Becoming a skilled wingshooter on the fast flying ruff grouse or quail can become quite discouraging leaving a youngster questioning the fun they were supposed to experience on this hunt. The extended walking required to hunt sharptail, huns, or chukar can also discourage a young hunter leaving very little inspiration to make another day in the field pursuing these birds. The pheasant hunt creates the best odds of finding success for the novice hunter and the pen raised birds offered at hunting preserves is often the best bet. We start our young baseball players on a t-ball team where the ball is stationary to help build confidence and graduate on to Little League so why not begin the young wingshooter with hunts that offer the best possibilities for success.

Various national organizations are making great strides today to help our youth

Mindy Bilbo following a pheasant hunt with her two Pudelpointers.
Photo courtesy Sherman Bilbo.

find themselves having positive experiences in upland bird hunting and waterfowling. Pheasants Forever and Ducks Unlimited, along with The National Turkey Federation are paving the way with many other organizations following this lead. I am personally extremely proud of the efforts that NAVHDA has taken to introduce youngsters to the training opportunities needed to own and hunt with a trained dog. One of NAVHDA's annual publications is dedicated to our youth and you can just imagine how one must feel when they find their picture in a national magazine. Clyde Vetter has done a wonderful job in inspiring NAVHDA to take a focus on youth. NAVHDA's Youth Development Program along with their Facebook postings keep chapters busy giving back to our youth in the form of dog training. Many chapters such as Florida's Palmetto Chapter offer scholarship funding to their local youth, while the Yankee and Sebasticook Chapters offer considerable youth opportunities on their schedules. This youth exposure is usually focused on the youngster working with their own dog and training experiences are the result.

I did several breedings in New Mexico with a dog I had previously sold to Mindy Bilbo. Mindy had trained and tested her dog in NAVHDA's natural ability test after the pup's first year and followed up in utility the second year. She was 12 years old when she handled the dog in Utility and earned a 201 Prize I. When we selected a stud dog for Mindy's breeding, we selected my grandson Hunter's dog. Hunter had trained and handled his pup Romo in natural ability and as a team trained and handled Romo to

Grandpas Idaho duck guys.

A youth day at Southern Adirondack Chapter. Photo courtesy Adirondack Chapter.

a 204 Prize I in utility with me. Hunter was 8 when he handled Romo in natural ability. Everyone learning of Mindy's litter wanted one of the pups as they were convinced the parents had to be extremely trainable dogs if two kids had trained and handled the pair to a utility Prize I each.

As a grandparent I have watched many a football, baseball, basketball, lacrosse, and hockey games with a total sense of pride to be able to say "that was my grandson that just scored." But I must confess that watching the joy on a grandson's face when that decoying mallard folds or a pheasant or quail collapses takes top prize for my ego knowing one of my grandson's made the shot. Listening to the two of the boys rib each other that their dog made more retrieves or at least the hardest ones following a hunt is priceless. They both own their own dogs and my accomplishment of giving back is on track from the relationship each has acquired from personal training opportunities. I refer to them as "The Idaho Duck Boys" and am blessed to have been able to enjoy duck camp most Fall weekends and all of their Christmas school break with the two. They have both graduated from entertaining themselves while playing with puppies at grandpa's house to expecting to go ducking at my swamp property and watch their own dogs perform. We end most hunts with a stop at the Garage Cafe for plate sized pancakes and hot chocolate. Not sure a fall or winter day can get much better than this.

When the two boys were six and eight I was running a dog at all Boise State home football games retrieving the kicking tee following kickoffs. I would rotate the two boys and take one with me to each game as an assistant. Their job was to manage the dog on the sideline so grandpa could watch the game. Not sure if the dog was babysitting the boys or the boys were babysitting the dog, but we ended three years without incident.

Having grown up with a relationship with their own dogs, I would expect both boys to always want a dog in their lives. Girls may someday become a priority but I'd bet a Franklin that they will always own and have a hunting dog at their sides.

Index

Made in the USA
Middletown, DE
26 October 2024

63057223R00119